EMPOWERING DIALOGUES WITHIN

1.9.17

516.944.4414

D1453653

Author's Note

The mandala on the cover has an even number of sections suggesting crystallization and accomplishment. There is a hint of personality parts poised around an unseen Central Self. The mandala slips off the cover, inviting the reader to open the book and start an inward journey.

KATE COHEN-POSEY

EMPOWERING DIALOGUES WITHIN

A Workbook
for Helping Professionals
and Their Clients

WILEY

John Wiley & Sons, Inc.

This book is printed on acid-free paper. ⊗

Copyright © 2008 by Kate Cohen-Posey. All rights reserved.

Published by John Wiley & Sons, Inc., Hoboken, New Jersey.
Published simultaneously in Canada.

No part of this publication may be reproduced, stored in a retrieval system, or transmitted in any form or by any means, electronic, mechanical, photocopying, recording, scanning, or otherwise, except as permitted under Section 107 or 108 of the 1976 United States Copyright Act, without either the prior written permission of the Publisher, or authorization through payment of the appropriate per-copy fee to the Copyright Clearance Center, Inc., 222 Rosewood Drive, Danvers, MA 01923, (978) 750-8400, fax (978) 646-8600, or on the web at www.copyright.com. Requests to the Publisher for permission should be addressed to the Permissions Department, John Wiley & Sons, Inc., 111 River Street, Hoboken, NJ 07030, (201) 748-6011, fax (201) 748-6008, or online at http://www.wiley.com/go/permissions.

Limit of Liability/Disclaimer of Warranty: While the publisher and author have used their best efforts in preparing this book, they make no representations or warranties with respect to the accuracy or completeness of the contents of this book and specifically disclaim any implied warranties of merchantability or fitness for a particular purpose. No warranty may be created or extended by sales representatives or written sales materials. The advice and strategies contained herein may not be suitable for your situation. You should consult with a professional where appropriate. Neither the publisher nor author shall be liable for any loss of profit or any other commercial damages, including but not limited to special, incidental, consequential, or other damages.

This publication is designed to provide accurate and authoritative information in regard to the subject matter covered. It is sold with the understanding that the publisher is not engaged in rendering professional services. If legal, accounting, medical, psychological or any other expert assistance is required, the services of a competent professional person should be sought.

Designations used by companies to distinguish their products are often claimed as trademarks. In all instances where John Wiley & Sons, Inc. is aware of a claim, the product names appear in initial capital or all capital letters. Readers, however, should contact the appropriate companies for more complete information regarding trademarks and registration.

For general information on our other products and services please contact our Customer Care Department within the United States at (800) 762-2974, outside the United States at (317) 572-3993 or fax (317) 572-4002.

Wiley also publishes its books in a variety of electronic formats. Some content that appears in print may not be available in electronic books. For more information about Wiley products, visit our web site at www.wiley.com.

Library of Congress Cataloging-in-Publication Data:
Cohen-Posey, Kate.
  Empowering dialogues within : a workbook for helping professionals and
their clients / by Kate Cohen-Posey.
    p. ; cm.
  Includes bibliographical references and index.
  ISBN 978-0-470-28193-2 (pbk. : alk. paper)
 1. Psychotherapy.   2. Introversion.   3. Self-perception.   4. Self
psychology.   I. Title.
  [DNLM: 1. Psychotherapy–methods. 2. Introversion (Psychology) 3. Personality.
4. Professional-Patient Relations. 5. Self Concept. WM 420
C6787e 2008]
RC480.5C575 2008
616.89′14–dc22   2007047637

Printed in the United States of America.

10 9 8 7 6 5 4 3 2 1

To my parents,
Ann and Hy Cohen,
who started me in this amazing new career
by checking, rechecking, and editing all my school papers;
beginning the dialogue with the question—
"What are you trying to say, dear?"
You are always close by, helping from the other side.

CONTENTS

VIGNETTES, FIGURES, AND EXERCISES

The names of clients, friends, and family members whose stories appear in this book have been changed even though people (especially clients) have most generously given written permission to use their case stories. To further protect anonymity, details of lives have been altered and, in some cases, literary gender changes were performed.

VIGNETTES

Chapter 1

Vignette 1: Dulci, 1.4
Vignette 2: Betty, 1.7
Vignette 3: Mary, 1.9
Vignette 4: Fred, 1.9
Vignette 5: Dulci, 1.10
Vignette 6: Karen, 1.10
Vignette 7: Amiee, 1.14

Chapter 2

Vignette 1: Robert, 2.2
Vignette 2: Jaleigh's Angel, 2.2
Vignette 3: Odette, 2.5
Vignette 4: Layla, 2.6
Vignette 5: Rita, 2.7
Vignette 6: Jaleigh/Mountain Spirit, 2.11

Chapter 3

Vignette 1: Sasha, 3.5
Vignette 2: Alice, 3.7
Vignette 3: Donna, 3.8
Vignette 4: Jaleigh, 3.10
Vignette 5: Julie, 3.11
Vignette 6: Jenny, 3.12
Vignette 7: Betty, 3.13
Vignette 8: Tony, 3.13
Vignette 9: Karen, 3.14

Vignette 10: Eli, 3.15
Vignette 11: Sasha, 3.16

Chapter 4

Vignette 1: Louise, 4.4
Vignette 2: Melanie, 4.5
Vignette 3: Alex, 4.6
Vignette 4: Celia, 4.12
Vignette 5: Rebecca, 4.13
Vignette 6: Dulci, 4.16
Vignette 7: Joyce, 4.17
Vignette 8: Odette, 4.19
Vignette 9: Rita, 4.20
Vignette 10: James, 4.21

Chapter 5

Vignette 1: Tony, 5.4
Vignette 2: Rita, 5.8
Vignette 3: Melanie, 5.10
Vignette 4: Tara, 5.11
Vignette 5: Angie, 5.13
Vignette 6: Hanna, 5.14
Vignette 7: Odette, 5.15
Vignette 8: Emily, 5.16
Vignette 9: Penny, 5.16
Vignette 10: Joyce, 5.18
Vignette 11: Theresa, 5.18
Vignette 12: Jeff, 5.20

FIGURES

EXERCISES

PREFACE

In 1923, Martin Buber published *I and Thou,* which contained his **Philosophy of Dialogue**. *Empowering Dialogues Within* invokes the spirit of Buber by using his dialogical method to delve into the core of the psychological realm. Although his theory was concerned with a social reality, he recognized a contact seeking "inborn Thou" and purpose-driven personality parts that cause "I-it" monologues. Unknowingly, Buber had begun to define the multifaceted mind where interaction happens between inner entities through subvocal messages. He believed that the inborn Thou may have to recede within due to bashings from people striving for control and power (Kramer, 2003).

This unfortunate state of affairs is a product of the survival instinct. Out of necessity, people must use and manage their environment by taking an *I-it stand* in which they interrogate, convince, and judge others for personal gain. However, people can also spontaneously open themselves to their fellow beings without any agenda. In these I-Thou moments of *meeting,* a dialogue emerges that conveys more than words. Two people confirm each other as they are while acknowledging and contending with their differences. Through asking questions, showing understanding, and evoking potentials, both parties become more fully human (Kramer, 2003).

The inborn Thou's longing for real relationship is supported by an "Eternal Thou" (God force) that is always present, pulling people toward genuine meeting. A third catalyst for dialogue is the "central Thou"—a dynamic group leader through which vital fellowships form and renew themselves. In the psychological landscape, this hidden leader is the central Self that relates to and radiates outward to all personality parts of the internal community. With coaching, this innermost Self can sally forth and make genuine contact with internal adversaries. In this manner, compassion, calmness, and self-respect are born.

This text rests solidly on the ideas of many great minds that fleshed out the terrain of the intrapsychic domain. Generations of theorists defined subpersonalities, higher Selves, ego states, and personality parts. Developmental psychology offered clues about how major subpersonalities and the Self are formed. Vivid models of the multifaceted mind abound, and treatment approaches that encourage communication with and between inner entities are beginning to flourish. But none convey the mysterious elegance of Buber's dialogue in which opposites unite without lessening their opposition. While Buber's philosophy of interpersonal relations makes a strange bedfellow with those who probed the psyche, this text turns to him again and again for guidance on encounter,

---

Uroboros or the snake swallowing its tail encircles a void—a beginning before a beginning. It also suggests a tube entering a tube, adding an inner layer to the previous. The tension between layers creates dynamic interaction, which is the subtext of the philosophy *and psychology* of dialogue. Drawing by Pelecanos Theodoros in a Greek manuscript of an alchemical tract titled *Synosius* (1478). Adapted from "Ouroboros," n.d., *Wikipedia,* retrieved September 2007, from http://en.wikipedia.org/wiki/Uroboros.

engagement, and contact. When the Self is restored to its full glory through dialogue, there is little need to integrate subpersonalities; instead connections are made.

Empowering Dialogues Within thoroughly identifies the parties involved before exploring how to engage inner troublemakers:

- *Chapters 1 and 2* present the true Self and provide exercises for becoming reacquainted with core being.
- *Chapters 3 and 4* describe directing, distracting, and emotional entities and offer exercises for identifying these parts to dis-identify with them.
- *Chapter 5* teaches techniques that *turn* monologues and debates into dialogues. The Self is coached to engage tyrannical or distracting personality parts so that they will loosen their hold on vulnerable energies.
- *Chapters 6 and 7* detail the steps of *Empowering Dialogues,* give a history and philosophical context of treating people as a plurality of parts, and offer psychoneurological evidence of the existence of Selves and subpersonalities.

THE ORDER OF THE READING

The order of the chapters suggests making the acquaintance of confident curious inner Selves (in Chapters 1 and 2) before approaching divisive personality parts. However, if you are plagued by tyrannical voices that demand rigid restraint, perpetual preparation, or absolute acceptance from all people, you may want to dive right into Chapter 3 to gain a better understanding of these dictators and then read Chapter 4 where you can meet them in a more intimate way that will allow you to hold them at bay compassionately.

Use Chapter 5 to master the *internal art* of dialogue, which empowers the knowing Self and softens personality parts' extreme messages. But, as soon as you can catch your breath, return to the beginning of the book to learn about the spiritual *instincts* that are as innate as your drives for pleasure and aggression. These forces of observation, intuition, reason, and centering will fine-tune your encounters with inner adversaries.

Chapter 6 reviews the previous material from a clinical perspective. Techniques from EMDR and comparisons with emerging ego state therapies are used to illuminate fine points. Chapter 7 is for the academically inclined and shows how *Empowering Dialogues Within* takes its place in the evolution of psychology and history at large.

Like the author of *Martin Buber's I and Thou: A Guide* (Kramer, 2003, p. 7), I invite you to enter into a dialogue with this text. My wish is that you study the forthcoming ideas as though hearing a living voice, explore how they are different and similar to your own assumptions, reflect on their meaning, and share them with a larger community of readers.

ACKNOWLEDGMENTS

There are so many people to thank and so little space. Memory prevents me from recalling the name of the workshop leaders who introduced me to ego-state therapy when I was ready to make a quantum shift in the way I worked with people.

Much appreciation goes to Cara Chamberlain who read my manuscript when it was wordy and information-dense. Yet she was always gentle, positive, and full of unexpected esoteric wisdom. While I was dabbling in character development of tiny scenarios that illustrate the theory in my work, Cara was living a double life, putting muscle and flesh on the denizens of her novels. Any publisher of fiction should not miss an opportunity to have Cara Chamberlain's titles on their front list. She can be easily found in Billings, Montana, by Googling her husband's wonderfully unique name: Bernard Quetchenbach.

Joan Carr also had the perseverance to read this manuscript before I could part with a single word or idea. I have visions of her sitting bleary-eyed in front of her computer because she did not ask for a hard copy, and I doubt she printed the plethora of pages. Similar thanks goes to my niece Deborah Neal who always encourages me.

Virginia Culbert, who read *I and Thou* in the original German, was my Buber expert and confirmed that my preface was philosophically correct.

Sharon Kirkland deserves credit for the wonderful insight in Chapter 3, linking the location of the third chakra (home of personality parts carrying parental demands) to a person's navel through which family values travel. Sharon shares my love of esoterica, and together we have traveled the frontiers of inner space where few people have gone before.

I owe a debt to Trudy Cory Rankin whose Center for Creative Studies is an oasis in a remote region of Florida where people gather to flesh out thorny issues of life and meaning while consuming delicious food. Here my material had its first debut, and I discovered that *Empowering Dialogues Within* warranted a separate presentation from its more extraverted sibling—*Making Hostile Words Harmless*.

I am always grateful to my friend Paula Douglas do da who keeps my spirits high with her greetings and salutations (vintage 1950s) and who has the most impressive resume of spiritual adventures and misadventures of anyone I know.

My reverence for my husband Harry grows exponentially over the years. He creates the space and foundation for me to do this work, never complaining when I've abandoned him for my muse, but beckoning me away from the computer when I'm neglecting the bare necessities of life.

I want to thank the folks at John Wiley & Sons, who plucked me from obscurity and solicited me to write *Brief Therapy Client Handouts* and then were willing to support me in birthing an "emergent therapy." Their interest in combining Buber's philosophy with psychology was a welcome surprise and showed me that they trust their reader's thirst for new integrations of ideas and deeper truths. It has been pure joy to work with my editor, Lisa Gebo, who rediscovered me and kept coming after me when a computer gremlin started hiding my e-mails behind + signs. She has been an amazing real-live muse.

Most of all I am blessed by my clients who are always willing to travel this road with me, helping me refine my therapeutic arts, putting up with the strange *props* I use in therapy now, and simply smiling at my stocking feet, which compliment my otherwise professional attire.

INTRODUCTION

I present to you the drama that has been unfolding between my clients and myself over the past several months. I have gone beyond choosing from my bag of tricks acquired over 30 years and have fallen into a treatment orientation that is mysterious.

I wonder if the cubist painter Pablo Picasso (1881–1973) knew his benefactor when he began to fragment objects and show multiple facets simultaneously. I reflect on my own training to discover which of the masterful predecessors whom I have studied might have planted the seeds that have been prodding me to say to clients: "What part of you thinks you have to take care of everything?" "What is your special (inner) friend saying about this situation?" "Go inside and tell the controlling part of yourself that you know it is afraid to let go. . . . " "Tell me what happens."

I want to know if the stuff that happens in my office has the makings of a method to lead people out of the labyrinth in which they often feel trapped, or whether it is a hodgepodge of questions ending in blind alleys. I am on a mission to discover if other clinicians and researchers believe, like Picasso, that exposing multiple facets of a person (or object) can lead to a higher unity. Even more than wanting to authenticate a treatment method, I seek clarification of *what* is happening between my clients and myself and ways to embellish and enhance the power of the process.

Happily, as I begin my research, I find that my work is well-rooted in the past but different enough to be considered a new leaf on the psychotherapy tree. The surprise has been that this approach's closest cousins are treatment orientations I have only been introduced to secondhand and some that I have never known existed. Therapy schools and their originators' brilliant minds will be given proper acknowledgment with parenthetical notation. The jargon that permeates the study of mind and spirit is bypassed, and descriptive, practical language is substituted whenever possible. Words like *personality* and *Self* and technological terms are listed in a Glossary to clarify definitions.

I sense that a mighty force is pushing me to write this book; that my clients are contributing authors as they help me discover their inner identities; that I will be meeting many great minds who have laid the foundation for this work; and that you, my readers, will always be with me, challenging me to make more understandable the mystery of how people become truer to themselves and freer in spirit.

The Mandala is a labyrinth, suggesting the beginning of a journey and active searching (Fincher, 2000). *Source*: "Labyrinth," n.d., *Wikipedia*, retrieved September 2007, from http://en.wikipedia.org/wiki/Labyrinth.

Chapter 1

Discovering the True Self

Elijah stood atop Mount Carmel clad in his skimpy loincloth and hairy cloak taunting King Ahab and 450 priests his wife Jezebel had imported from the neighboring kingdom of Tyre (I Kings 18:20).

Why does your god Baal do nothing to end this 3-year drought? As the mighty god of fertility, is it not his job to send rain? Why have you allowed your foreign-born wife to slay Israel's prophets simply for demanding loyalty to YHWH, the true God!? He glared at the hoard of Israelites gathered for the spectacle.

The hour has come to choose! Build two altars. Place a bull on each. Have Baal's priests send fire down from heaven to consume the sacrifice.

The priests cried out to Baal all morning, shouted his name, hobbled and danced, gashed themselves with lance and sword until blood gushed out, but neither fire nor rain came. Then Elijah did a strange thing. He dug a trench around his altar, filled it with precious water, and doused the bull offering as if to shield the sacrifice from heavenly fires. But when he called on the God of Israel "the fire of the Lord fell and burned up the sacrifice, the wood, the stone, the soil, and licked up the water in the trench" (18:38).

The Mandala on this page combines the thousand-petaled lotus: symbol for the 7th (crown) chakra, with the upward/downward pointing triangles, symbol for the 4th (heart) chakra that integrates earthbound and spirit-bound energies. Interpreted graphically by Gavin Posey.

The Lord he is God! cried the people, and on Elijah's order, the priests of Baal were massacred in a nearby valley. But Elijah's victory was short-lived. Jezebel, on learning of the slaughter of her priests, threatened his life.

The mighty Elijah fled to Mount Sinai in the wilderness of the southern Kingdom and hid in a crevice between two rocks. God understood Elijah's fear and instructed him to stand on the mountain so that the presence of the Lord might pass by. He witnessed a great and powerful wind that tore the mountain apart, but the Lord was not in the wind. Then came an earthquake, but the Lord was not in that, and even the fire that followed had no sign of the Lord.

Finally, came a gentle whisper asking, *What are you doing here Elijah?* When he heard this soft murmur, Elijah pulled his cloak over his face and stood at the mouth of the cave. (I Kings 19:11–13)

With this theological breakthrough or masterpiece of literary irony (whatever your point of view), Elijah, who had just brought down a fiery rain of the Almighty's power, discovered God in the still small voice. The deity was no longer some force of nature out there to be worshipped, but a focal point of quiet calm that could always be found by true seeking. This *innermost Self* may simultaneously be the center of our Being and a gateway to the infinite. Connecting to our *core Self* is an essential alliance to have when befriending the bullies, the Jezebels, and the Ahabs that also occupy our inner domain so they can be divested of their power and put to good use.

Terms like *the still small voice* and *true Self* may sound foreign to the well-tuned psychological ear. How would a quest for this inner spirit help in subduing the parts of us that demand rigid conformity, perfection, never-ending accomplishment, and universal acceptance? Even if a core Self exists, its unveiling would seem to come at the end of a psychological journey, not at the beginning. The history of psychology supplies some interesting answers.

PSYCHOLOGICAL PIONEERS

The word *psychology* warrants deeper defining. The first meaning of *psyche* in the *American Heritage Dictionary* is "The soul or spirit, as distinguished from the body." The second definition states, "The mind functioning as the center of thought, feeling, and behavior. . . ." It comes from the Greek *psukhe* meaning breath, life, or soul. In the sixteenth century, *psyche* was wed to *logos* to produce *psychology* or the study of mental (and spiritual) processes and behavior.

In the late 1800s, the new science of psychology still dipped into the well of ancient wisdom that would not dare to separate body, mind, and spirit. As science took precedence over simply studying the psyche, more emphasis was placed on behavior that could be observed. Subjective experiences that could barely be spoken and heard became eclipsed (Wilber, 2000). Today, we have had to coin a new term, *holistic health* to rejoin body, mind, and spirit.

SCHISM OF MIND AND SPIRIT

If psychology was originally the study of mind, spirit, and behavior, then psychotherapy would be the treatment of the same. Sigmund Freud (1856–1939), the first practitioner of this science that was still more art than fact, dove deep into the unconscious to uncover repressed instincts through free association and dreams. His theory evolved over a period of 36 years, and he repeatedly asserted that his *psychoanalysis* was a new science with its capacity to explain every possible form of human behavior. Using the mindset of modern science in which reason rules spirit, Freud explained religion as a response to the experience of utter helplessness and God as an idealized father. Freud had his supporters and detractors, but in embellishing or refuting his theories, most followed suit and ignored spirit.

Roberto Assagioli (1888–1974) was one of the lesser-known original psychoanalytical pioneers. He was fascinated by Freud's unconscious process, but in 1927, he developed his own theory of *psychosynthesis* that posited that there is a superconscious that houses spiritual instincts, which are just as real as the sexual drives that live in the subconscious. At the apex of the superconscious, there is a *Higher Self*. It is unaffected by the flow of everyday mind chatter, or bodily aches and pains, and is capable of mastering and directing the mind and body.

Some might want to credit Carl Jung (1875–1961) as the pioneer who kept the soul in psychology with his concept of a *collective unconscious*—a reservoir of all our human experience. It can never be made conscious and contains imprints or *archetypes* of our potentials and needs. These include the archetypal mother, spiritual force, shadowy unspeakable desires, opposite gender qualities (anima/animus), hero, maiden, wise old man, God (need for meaning), and Self (need for unity). However, like Freud, Jung insisted that he was an empirical scientist and that everything he talked about was within the psychological realm. By his own logic, Jung implied that the spiritual is nothing more than the psychological. Assagioli wanted to make a distinction between primitive shadowy archetypes and potentials like the wise old man that came from the superconscious. He stated that there is not only a difference but also an actual antagonism between these two kinds of archetypes (Rowan, 1990).

Rejoining Mind and Spirit

While other analysts treated neuroses and disorders of the mind caused by repressed emotions, Assagioli addressed disorders of the mind *and spirit* caused by lack of access to the subconscious and energies inflowing from the Higher Self. Rather than starting by investigating repressed conflicts and complexes, Assagioli thought it best to establish a source of strength that could widen the channel of communication with the superconscious and create safety. He said treatment of emotional disorders could be blocked when higher psychological levels have not been activated (Assagioli, 1965/2000).

Using Dante's *Divine Comedy* as a model for an inner journey, a person who finds him or herself lost in a forest of despair but sees illumination on a far-off hill needs a guide. Dante's initial guide was the Latin poet Virgil, representing human reason, who told him he must first make a pilgrimage through hell (the lower unconscious) and the mount of purgatory (the middle unconscious) before he could find the light he sought. When Dante reached the summit of the mount, Virgil vanished, and Dante was now guided by Beatrice who represented divine wisdom and could lead him through paradise—the superconscious (Assagioli, 1965/2000).

STARTING AT THE END—DEFINING AND DESCRIBING HIGHER SELVES

Like Dante, we may be impatient to tackle the tyrants who create despair in our lives by insisting on rigid control, perfection, continuous accomplishment, and universal acceptance. However, it would first be wise to connect with an inner guide whose wisdom and understanding can recognize and transform the forces that torment us. For many people, this simply requires remembering the name they use for a higher part of themselves—*my common sense, special friend, professional Self, deeper Being, inner mind, stoic Self, free spirit, intuition, inner peace, guardian angel, calm center, brother*, or, of course, Elijah's *still small voice*, as the first vignette shows.

Vignette 1: Dulci

Dulci could find little light in her shadowy existence over the past 3 years of psychiatric hospitalizations for severe depression, heavy medication, unending grief over her father's death, memories of a torturous divorce, and conflicts with her relentless, manipulative mother. Not expecting much, her therapist asked, "Have you ever heard anything like a still small voice within you?"

"Of course," she replied. "I hear it all the time."

"Tell me more."

"I had an appointment and was planning to drop my children off at the babysitter's but I kept hearing a voice in my head saying, 'Do not do this.' I called my mother and asked her to watch my children while I kept my appointment. In her usual contrary way, she made an excuse. I pleaded with her for a while, but then out of frustration told her to forget it. The next day I was on my way to the babysitter's trailer, and the voice was louder—'You Cannot Do This!' I called my mother again, and said she was going to have to watch my kids, and I just took them to her house and dropped them off."

"That night, after returning home with the children and settling down for dinner, my husband asked me if I had heard the news about the babysitter. Recognizing my puzzled expression, he proceeded to tell me that her trailer had burned to the ground. If my children had been there, it is doubtful that they would have escaped with their lives."

Some people would say Dulci has psychic abilities, but in her mind she just has an inner voice that seems to know things. Did it come from Assagioli's Higher Self? Was it her intuition?

There are psychologists and religious practitioners who have their own names and descriptions for such higher parts of the Self. Taoism talks about reason beyond cleverness and knowing beyond knowledge. Some Native Americans teach young people how to find spirit guides and power animals that provide amazing insights and connection to inner sources of strength and wisdom. Mystics from all religions talk about a core or essential Self that we used to be before the world impinged on us and that we may become again as we remove our outer layers. It is the center of our being and the point at which we connect to the infinite (Moody & Carrol, 1997). Saint Teresa (1515–1582), a

Spanish mystic, was even loftier and more precise in identifying the inner voice. She said these *locutions* were divine words that enter the mind spontaneously and are translated into readily understood language that provides heavenly consolation (Gilbert, 2006).

The American William James preceded Freud and Jung in the field of psychology. Less bent on squeezing mind and behavior into the confines of science, he acknowledged spirit. In his 1200-page masterwork, *The Principles of Psychology* (1890), he said that the hidden *spiritual Self* is the most felt and at the same time the most incomprehensible (Rowan, 1990). Carl Jung said the *Self* is the main organizing principle of the mind. It provides the energy to fulfill potentials and possibilities. Like Tibetan Buddhists, Jung used mandalas or circles with complex designs (found at the beginning of each chapter) to access the Self symbolically and to meditate on the pattern of wholeness within (Fincher, 2000). Abraham Maslow (1908–1970), founder of humanistic psychology, describes the *core Self* as that which actualizes a person's latent capacities.

Perhaps Assagioli gives the best description of a *Higher Self* as a center of pure awareness and pure will capable of mastering, directing, and using the mind and body. People have a personal or small self that is experienced as distinct, separate, and individual. The Higher Self feels both individual and universal and has a sense of freedom, expansion, and communion with others. Although the Higher Self is not revealed directly, it becomes known in different degrees through imagination, intuition, aspiration, and heroism, which the personal self gradually comes to acknowledge. Unlike Freud's superego, that internalizes rigid codes of conduct and parental commands, the Higher Self draws its conscience from spiritual principles, such as loving thy neighbor as thyself and compassion. It may point out but never admonishes (Assagioli, 1965/2000).

In 1968, when the humanistic psychologists Abraham Maslow and Victor Frankl started using the term *transpersonal psychology*, Assagioli adopted it at once, thinking *transpersonal* was precise and descriptive (Rowan, 1993). A *transpersonal Self* suggests a universal, unconditioned Self that uses the personality as an instrument to witness our mental, emotional, and physical experiences while not becoming identified with them (Wilber, 2000).

CORPORATE SELF

Some have speculated that we must have more than one Higher Self or, if there is just one that it comes to us in various forms and with many names (Rowan, 1993). In support of this position, the metaphor of "The Corporate Self" (Figure1.1) is offered. Although the upper echelon is represented as a foursome, the names of many inner guides, internalized literary characters, and mythological or theological figures may at times occupy a particular position. The corporate officers are emphasized in this chapter while the *division directors, workforce*, and *inside agitators* (of the triune personality) are explained in Chapter 3.

TRANSCENDENT SELF—THE CEO

The chief executive officer (CEO) is the Higher Self, transpersonal Self, or real Self (discussed previously). This is the expansive Self that witnesses the ordinary "I" and moves from realms of *physical* sensations, to *emotional* tensions, to fleeting *thoughts*; all the while, remaining light and free of pleasure and pain. But then the expansive Self falls into an opening where it becomes what it observes—all is in it, and it is in all. This witness remains a sleepless giant within "that moves from waking to dreaming or deep dreamless sleep and can report your dreams back to you in the morning when you wake up" (Gilbert, 2006).

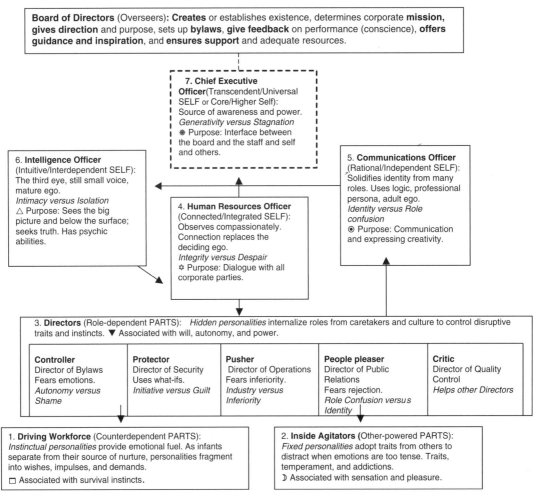

Figure 1.1 The Corporate Self: Organization of *Selves* and *Parts. Note:* Analogy to corporate structure from Carter McNamara (2003). The *Board of Directors* is totally spiritual and beyond the scope of this work. Numbers 7–1 correspond to the *chakras* (energy centers) found in Yoga—✳ △ ◉ ✿ ▼ ☽ ☐.

Limitless Being can also take an earthy route to transcendence by melting boundaries between Self and others and cherishing differences. Each time such genuine encounters happen, more of the world is embraced (persons, nature, art, and all that is eternal) creating a cosmos of pure spirit in the midst.[1] In the Yoga tradition, the CEO sits in the 7th chakra (energy center) that crowns the top of the head and is pictured as a thousand-petaled lotus, symbolic of connecting the corporal body to spirit.

Although pure awareness and conscious decisiveness may be separate tasks, out of respect for Assagioli, they are both considered functions of the CEO in this metaphor. He stated the Higher Self "not only has a static self-awareness but is also a dynamic power . . . capable of . . . mastering, directing, and integrating all psychological processes and the physical body. . . . I am a center of awareness and of power" (Assagoli, 1965/2000, p. 105).

INTERDEPENDENT/INTUITIVE SELF—THE INTELLIGENCE OFFICER

The intelligence officer sits at the right hand of the CEO. We have met her previously as Beatrice who led Dante through paradise (the superconscious); the still small voice that offers intuition; Jung's archetypes of the hero and wise old man (or woman); and the nine muses of Greek mythology who presided over the arts and sciences offering inspiration to poets, mathematicians, and other artists. This interdependent Self is the dream master, synthesizing images from diverse sensory impressions and decoding myths, symbols, and the very dreams it creates. It presides over states of imagination, reverie, daydreams, visions, and trance experiences.

Yogin would find the intelligence officer in the 6th chakra located just above and between the eyes. Legend has it that when an early race of humans was evolving, their brains developed enormously and their inner Being was impressed with a *third eye* to give them direct vision of divine realities. As they grew physically and became less innocent, the third eye atrophied but remained located near the pineal gland and can be accessed through the 6th chakra. The challenge of this energy center is to look beyond what is on the surface of a situation, to see the big picture, and to seek truth. It opens our psychic abilities that, at one time, were natural.

The intelligence officer may speak in the voice of a host of inner guides and take the form of spiritual masters from Jesus to the Bodhisattva—a human who has achieved liberation from the world of illusion and voluntarily returns to help others reach enlightenment. It may be a mythological unicorn or a literary character like Ulysses who comes to tell us that life is a journey to be lived, not a series of problems to be solved (Stone & Stone, 1989).

Vignette 2: Betty

Betty was worried about her mother's health and *Brother*, her inner guide, told her that everything happens for a reason. Thinking this was too much of a cliché to be wisdom from an inner guide; her therapist asked if this wasn't rather ordinary advice. Betty immediately reported that Brother was showing her a multitude of boxes each with moving screens depicting the lives of various people who were foreign to her. She said in each scene there was a Brother or a guardian who appeared in different garb. Her therapist asked her if the people in the moving pictures knew about the guardians, and she replied that some did and some did not. She said Brother was reminding her that she was not alone and that there was a pattern to life that she might not understand.

---

[1] Two routes to transcendence are described here: (1) Eastern mysticism that seeks union with the "All" described by Ken Wilber; and (2) earthy, social mysticism in which opposites yield to dialogue without losing their uniqueness described by Martin Buber.

INDEPENDENT/RATIONAL SELF—THE COMMUNICATIONS OFFICER

The communications officer takes the CEO's left flank. He is well-known for logic, reason, and common sense. Mentioned previously as the Latin poet Virgil, he kept Dante on a steady course through the emotional torments of hell and the penance of purgatory. Reason can be energizing and exciting as the mind focuses on a problem to be solved, reviews stored information, and analyzes and resolves riddles. Or, it can be the cool, professional, impersonal Self that evaluates situations objectively, does not instantly react, and stays above the fray. It takes command when a waitress deals with a rude customer or a teacher talks to an irate parent. When the situation requires, the communications officer's voice may be firm and powerful, but never shrill. Not surprisingly, it emanates from the 5th chakra in the throat that yogin attribute to communication. It expresses the divine within, rather than attempting to gain approval.

During the climate of feminism, reason and *left-brain thinking* were devalued compared to *right-brained* intuition and inspiration. But reason and logic often precede intuition and can create their own altered, heightened states. The muses favored the scientist and mathematician as much as much as the artist, as the story of Arthur Koestler (1904–1983) will attest.

Koestler was a novelist, journalist, and critic who happened to be imprisoned during the Spanish Civil War. While awaiting a death sentence, he began writing mathematical notations on the walls of his cell and found himself in an intellectual ecstasy over one of Euclid's mathematical proofs involving concepts of infinity using finite numbers. For some moments, he stood in awe at the mathematical perfection of the moment until a nagging thought reminded him that he was in prison and might be shot. This was immediately answered by a strange idea: "*So what! Is that all? Have you nothing more serious to worry about?*" (Moody & Carrol, 1997, p. 279).

INTEGRATED SELF—THE *HUMAN* RELATIONS OFFICER

The human relations (HR) officer is often thought of as an inner nurturer or calm center. A counterpart to the CEO that dissolves boundaries that separate the Self from the world beyond, the HR officer finds missing personality parts and embraces them. Because of its central position, it might be considered the heart of the company—"the point that Earth grounded Heaven and Heaven exalted the Earth . . . where Spirit is found" (Wilber, 2004, p. 47).

In the Yogi tradition it is the 4th or heart chakra that is related to love and meeting of opposites without diminishing differences. The HR officer is a juggler with an incredible knack for balancing the needs of the mind and body, masculine and feminine energies, and observable (persona) and hidden (shadow) traits to create the experience of what people call *being centered*. The conventional wisdom "to do what your heart tells you to do" means to be lead by your center, not by emotions.

Inner guidance may first come from the *intuitive* intelligence officer until *reason* is sufficiently developed for the independent communications officer to gather various roles into a single identity. Once the HR officer makes connections between seemingly opposing facets of the personality, *integration* brings moments of directions from the transcendent, knowing CEO. Whether the Self is present from birth or develops over time, each person must make his or her own personal, fascinating journey of discovery.

DEVELOPMENT OF HIGHER SELVES

The brain *evolves* outward from the **reptilian**, old brainstem; to the **mammalian**, emotional brain; to the **neocortex**, thinking human brain. But the Self must *involute* by having its outer edges rolled away to expose the inner core. As each layer of self is revealed, a new perspective and manner of identifying with the world emerges in the journey to one's most authentic being.[2] Appendix B compares the *evolution* of reason with the *involution* of the Self and the *elevation* of the spirit.

SYMBIOTIC, SURVIVAL SELF

The boundary between the needs and wishes of the young and the needs and wishes of caretakers are blurred. Life is about attachment and developing a trust bond with a source of nurture (*trust versus mistrust*). Viewpoints are based on instinct. People who have lost touch with reality, terminally ill patients in the clutches of their reptilian brains, and starving masses revert to their survival, physical Selves.

Vignette 3: Mary

In her late 30s, Mary could not understand the overpowering love for another man that consumed her after 7 years of marriage to her kind, gentle husband. Her fears of the havoc "she" would wreak on him and heartbreak "she would cause" her ever-doting parents entrapped her.

When her parallel lives became intolerable, she finally fled. Her sweet husband, who had deferred every decision of their married life to her, became a stalker and trespasser, and her parents filed a missing persons report in a vain attempt to bring her back into their enmeshed (symbiotic) cocoon. Now out of her chrysalis, Mary is fluttering on gossamer wings, unsure of her direction and of her new bold friend who does not fit into the conventional mold that allowed her little independence.

A butterfly cannot return to its chrysalis. If Mary decides to rejoin her husband, there will be yet another metamorphosis that will infuse a new level of independence into their relationship.

COUNTERDEPENDENT, EMOTIONAL PARTS

As infants separate from their source of nurture, their personalities fragment into parts. Impulses, wishes, and demands are acted out. The task of learning autonomous control of bodily functions and taking initiative to exercise willpower can result in painful shame, doubt, and guilt (*autonomy versus shame and doubt; initiative versus guilt*). These toddlers and preschoolers are self-centered. They have a magical, first-person viewpoint in which the ego is all-powerful and wishes are fulfilled. Gang violence, team spirit, ethnic vengeance, and corporate groupthink are born of the counterdependent Self.

Vignette 4: Fred

Fred sought help because his union had rescued him from the jaws of joblessness by convincing his employer that he should have counseling instead of a pink slip. The counterforce of his bullheaded supervisor had ignited Fred's counterdependent Self and he impulsively lashed out at her when she misused company policy to coerce him into tasks that were not his responsibility.

---

[2] Stages of the involution of the Self are a combination of ideas from Wilber (2000), pp. 47–53; pp. 102–108, *Erikson's psychosocial crises (shown in italics);* object-relation theorists; and the author's interpretation and nomenclature. Note that Erikson's last two crises are reversed because the author believes people must be integrated before they can be generative.

OTHER-POWERED, DISTRACTING PARTS[3]

Tendencies to be dependent, demanding, oppositional, and withdrawn are adopted from valued persons and society. They can solidify into personality traits. School-age children are *other-centered* and only see through the eyes of family and peers on whom they depend for a sense of security, worth, and power—giving them a second-person perspective. A primitive ego defends against painful emotions by seeking pleasure and using blame to **distract** attention away from anxiety. Conflicts are *inter*personal. Depression is experienced as detachment, uneasiness, or physical concerns. The industry of this stage, used to gain skills, can easily turn to feelings of inferiority in moments of frustration (*industry versus inferiority*). Images of self and others flip-flop from heroic to hideous. A mythic worldview transfers the power of the ego to deified others. Epic heroes or villains, adventurers, and wild rock stars may be seeking vitality powered by others.

Vignette 5: Dulci

Dulci (Vignette 1) whose intuition told her not to leave her children in a babysitter's trailer that, indeed, incinerated that very day, usually fears she has no value because her new independent, responsible husband does not *need* her and the children will soon leave home. Her past performance of providing security for stores by apprehending shoplifters has earned her a reputation that could blossom into a career designed for someone with *inner knowing*. But a life that is not lived to fix, control, and "make her family happy" seems meaningless to Dulci who is currently dominated by her other-powered parts.

ROLE-DEPENDENT, DIRECTING PARTS

Instead of *imitating* characteristics from valued people, teens can *internalize* perceived strengths and weakness from caretakers to **direct** disruptive traits and impulses. A protective father, maternal caretaker, ruler, or preacher are the building blocks of identity formation and provide internalized roles that the ego (decision maker) uses to control or *act-in* emotions (*identity versus role confusion*). Rather than needing others for security or power, an inner parent can offer comfort or demand self-sacrifice and perfection. Adolescents become witness to internal arguments between an independent Self that wants to meet new people and a clinging part that hangs on to the friends it knows. This makes conflicts *intra*personal and triggers anxiety and depression. A third-person, sociocentric worldview demythologizes others and transfers power to social units (cliques, relationships, family, country, etc.). Philanthropists, patriots, and romantics may be operating from parts ruled by these roles.

Vignette 6: Karen

Karen is on uneasy terms with an internalized "Reverend Oscar Charles Dawson (OCD)"—who visits her occasionally to preach at her—that she is responsible for all the evil in the world and that she might bash her precious dog's head in with an andiron or drive her car into an oncoming semitruck. When the Reverend is around, Karen is on red alert, her mind racing to prevent any catastrophes her unworthy Self might be inclined to commit.

---

[3] "Other-powered parts" have earned a reputation in psychiatric literature as *personality disorders*. The title "Other-powered" is used to describe the Self's journey toward independence and beyond.

INDEPENDENT, RATIONAL SELF

Gradually, the herd mentality is escaped, truth is sought, and individual identity solidifies from the myriad of roles that have been played (*identity versus role confusion*). Felt needs and cultural values are balanced by a newly formed entity ready to be knighted into selfhood. Worldcentric viewpoints transfer power from the group to the rule of scientific, universal beliefs. Issues of self-esteem can be fueled by the lure of competition. Self-made women, successful entrepreneurs, university students, and medical researchers might not have gained their status without an adult ego and independent Self.

INTERDEPENDENT, INTUITIVE SELF

The rational, independent Self starts to soften, becomes less judgmental, more sensitive, and welcoming of differences. Imagination, reverie, creativity, visions, and meditative trances are valued alongside reason. Rather than making decisions, intuition finds consensus between various values and diverse desires. Fidelity to causes and persons become second nature, as is openness and intimacy in relationships (*intimacy versus isolation*). A pluralistic worldview[4] sees interdependent parts working in harmony. If problems arise, they may stem from concerns about the nature of existence—the demands of freedom, the anxiety of isolation, the quest for meaning, the use of death to define life (Yalom, 1980). The idealist, humanist, political activist, missionary, feminist, and animal rights enthusiast—all embrace the interdependent Self.

When Karen (Vignette 6) is not being visited by the "Reverend Dawson," her independent Self is busy writing poems, books, and teaching at a university. You might find her interdependent Self at a demonstration for peace or keenly following political debates. There have been moments when Karen has been so transfixed by the beauty of nature or its raw cruelty, that her personal Self dissolves and she finds her Self in the uncarved territory of integration and transcendence.

---

[4] The preceding worldviews are power based. The magical ego transfers power to deify others who become demystified when the social unit is the locus of control until even it falls under the rule of universal principles. In the last two stages, Selves simply observe interrelated parts and underlying unity.

1.11

POSTCONVENTIONAL INTEGRATION
AND TRANSCENDENCE

The journey toward individuality and independence is horizontal, with the Self gaining new perspectives of reality. During this phase people believe that whatever level of selfhood they have achieved is *the* way to be (Wilber, 2000). Independents with their rational worldview think interdependent sensitivity creates slackers and ideologues. Role-dependent conformists worry about the impulsiveness of counterdependents and the individualism of independents. Sensitive interdependents can be the most judgmental of all in their prejudice against prejudice.

In the next stage of involution, a yeasty rising takes the Self to new heights (Figure 1.2). Instead of having beliefs, however calming or empowering they may be, the believer dies and becomes a transformer, one of the movers and shakers that walks with effortless effort to become his or her own most impossible dream.

The postconventional Self can see that each of the previous levels has value in its own right. The counterdependent might need to take over when confronted by an assailant. Other-powered parts can help people fit in when first joining an organization. The role-dependent directors can bring stability during chaos. The last few miles of a marathon race may require the symbiotic, survival Self to step in. During a job interview the independent Self should be front and center. Finally, the interdependent, sensitive Self can strengthen the bonds of marriage.

INTEGRATED SELF[5]

The body and mind that previously worked as a well-trained horse and rider now become a centaur or man-horse (Wilbur, 2000). This connection makes the decision-making ego unnecessary.

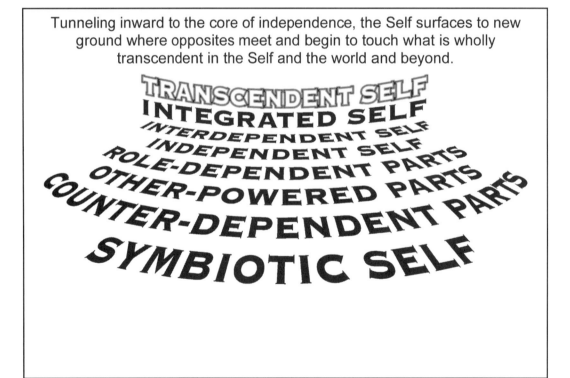

Figure 1.2 Involution of the Self

---

[5] Traditionally, *integration* suggests making compromises, reducing differences, and so on. This text views integration as the Self making contact with personality parts to understand and honor differences.

1.12

Counterforces meet without losing their opposition—activity/passivity, reason/emotion, masculinity/feminity, and so on. This increases self-awareness and versatility (Rowan, 1993). The danger of this stage is that people who have attained mastery might resist their *call* in what has been aptly named the "Jonah complex." They may hang on to their illuminations or doubt their insights, doing nothing with them (*integrity versus despair*). A holistic worldview sees the underlying process and interconnectivity of everything. Opposing positions arise from each other and resolve themselves with answers to unsolvable problems. Every age has people on the cutting edge of humanity—Eleanor Roosevelt, Jimmy Carter, Nelson Mandela—who emerge in the face of resistance from independent scientists or interdependent leaders. Not all are so well-known.

In spite of his work problems, Fred (Vignette 4) was a *tai chi* master. He befriended the orneriest of dogs on his postal route by getting down on all fours and panting at them. When his therapist gave him a nonverbal demonstration of how to defuse verbal potshots he, in turn, showed her a thing or two about movement, by giving her the Ginger Rogers' moment of her life with a country waltz step. In very little time, Fred was not only deflecting his supervisor's efforts to intimidate him, but began redirecting her attempts to bully coworkers as well. He was back to his agile, spontaneous Self, whose animal and human natures were so well connected that he easily crossed boundaries between species.

TRANSCENDENT SELF

The transition from the connected to the transcendent Self is gradual. Because all facets of the personality are enfolded in a compassionate embrace, the Self becomes more limitless and real. It can meet others as equals who have similar and contrasting qualities. Individual differences are overlooked, yet unique qualities are valued. A cosmic viewpoint recognizes the relatedness of all things, the ties between people, and the union with the creative process. Much like a Bodhisattva who accepts rebirth to help others see through illusion, this generative Self cultivates and cares for the next generation (*generativity versus stagnation*). But the desire for transcendence can be the final obstacle to self-release.

The barefooted, bald-headed mystic who has forgotten how to live *in* the world while not being *of* the world can have a blankness that is neither detachment nor union. Only 1% of the population rises above the need to be rational and inclusive to begin to integrate opposing forces and see underlying processes. Of those, only 0.1% transcend the Self (Wilber, 2000, p. 52). Although some may think of Gandhi as a martyr, he overcame his opponents by refusing to see himself as separate from them. In 1948, Mother Theresa felt called to leave her convent in Calcutta to live among the poor and dying. For her, giving *was* receiving and her efforts became a worldwide endeavor.

Journey to the Center of the Self

The pace inward may be two steps forward and one step back. A peak experience of self-transcendence may offer a temporary spiritual high to a woman performing rote religious rituals; or a man who has embraced the wise-father role may find himself suddenly regressed into a counterdependence, magically expecting his children to know his wishes. But generally, the Self hovers around one level until it becomes too constricting. Each move inward offers a wider view, greater freedom, new fears, and different goals. Often, the problems of one level can only be solved by taking a step inward and looking backward at troubling personality parts. Always there is a glimmer of light from the radiant Self beckoning within.

RECOGNITION OF HIGHER SELVES

Elijah heard the faint whisperings of *the still small voice*. But this is not the privilege of prophets and saints. For some it is the voice of reason, a thought on wakening, or a knowingness that is beyond definition, as the following story will show.

Vignette 7: Amiee

Amiee came to therapy tormented by fears that she would contaminate her parents and daughter with germs and lose the only people on whom she believed she could still depend. She had finally left the man who was supposed to be the perfect husband. The bride who was bright and self-assured became a wife with confidence who was mauled to shreds by complaints that she was not neat enough, clean enough, or strong enough to stop morning sickness when she was pregnant. Sex was conducted at warp speed with a bare minimum of nudity. At the culmination of a therapy session in which she targeted images of her husband's physical rejection, she announced, "I'm fine. It was him. My brain knew it all along!"

In a later session, Amiee came in depressed because her hope of finding an old boyfriend had been dashed. When asked what part of her was depressed, she said it was like a "little gnome sitting on her left shoulder, telling her no one would ever love her." Her fear of germs felt like a niggling lion that clawed at her from the right. Her therapist suggested that she go inside and ask the gnome when it had become a part of her. The ready response was that it had come with her husband. Then, after a long pause, she said, "No, it had tried to come in high school, but her *stoic Self* that held her head high and her back straight would not let the gnome come." Her therapist's interest in this stoic Self was piqued. She suggested it might want to say something to the gnome. Amiee turned her head to the left and said:

> Before I formed you in the womb I knew you,
> Before you were born, I set you apart,
> For I know the plans I have for you,
> Plans to prosper you and not to harm you,
> Plans to give you hope and a future

Amiee and her therapist sat stunned and awed by the moment. There was nothing more to be said and, of course, the gnome had shrunk to nothing. Amiee had been raised with a strong religious background, and her church had done much to lift her spirit, make her impervious to the petty insults of adolescence, and give her high goals in college.

Undoubtedly Amiee had memorized much scripture like the verses of Jeremiah 1:5 and 29:11 that poured from her mouth. But what she voiced in that session was not a rote recitation. It was something else that Amiee (later) dared not name. When she said, "My brain knew it all along!" it was clearly her independent, logical Self talking. The ancient verses of Jeremiah came from her deep Self or beyond. The exercises in Chapter 2 offer numerous portholes for all people to venture endlessly inward and find their own unlimited supply of guidance from Beings that dwell within.

Chapter 2

Exercises for Empowering the Self

"Now then, Piglet, let's go home."
"But Pooh," cried Piglet, all excited, "Do you know the way?"
"No," said Pooh. "But there are twelve pots of honey in my cupboard, and they've been calling to me for hours. I couldn't hear them properly before, because Rabbit would talk, but if nobody says anything except those twelve pots, I think, Piglet, I shall know where they're calling from. Come on." (Hoff, 1982, p. 14)

Pooh, who is described by his best friend Piglet as "a bear of little brain," has no difficulty bypassing all the mental chatter in which clever-rabbit types are trapped, unable to hear the call of their essential Selves. Although most people are not honey magnets, they can use the nectar and light of life to find their way home—back to their inner Selves. What is most surprising is that all life, when understood and utilized for what it is, can be sweet, even when it seems to taste of vinegar.

The mandala illustration on this page was designed by the author and interpreted graphically by Gavin Posey to represent the innermost Self—a "Web of Life" that forms a gateway to the infinite.

FINDING THE SELF THROUGH MEMORIES

If searching for Self sounds too difficult, you need only recall times when you have surprised yourself with courage you did not know you had, calm that you felt in the face of chaos, or steely strength that turned away temptation pulling at you with the force of a siren. Just as nature pushes an island above the ocean, the Self rises to assist people in times of need as illustrated by the first vignette:

Vignette 1: Robert

A middle-aged man named Robert overcame 3 years of anger-filled grief after the death of his father. His dependent personality parts had not been able to let go of the person who had mentored him and validated all his decisions for years. Robert recalled helping a friend whose wife had deserted him and taken all his assets. The reality of Robert's own *life-cycle* loss compared to the vicious betrayal of his friend could not be ignored. A voice from within said, "Okay, it's time to move on," and Robert's grief vaporized.

Higher Selves are not above using whatever language is necessary to make their point. Robert and his wife had sought counseling after she had moved to her own apartment. Those same dependent personality parts needed his wife's presence for security. He was tormented by his total lack of control and fear that she might be with another man. In the midst of his anguish, a voice came to him saying, "Look dumb a**, if she was going to be with another man, she would have left you by now!" Robert's jealous subpersonality was no longer a dominant force and continued to lose power with the memory of the poignant words of the *still small voice* from on high.

Just by taking a walk down memory lane, like Robert, you can begin to connect with the voices of reason, intuition, and transcendence within you. Strengthen your bond with inner Being by writing what you recall. You may want to name these Selves, draw them, or find an image on your favorite Internet search engine to provide a visual anchor.

Exercise 1

Memorable Moments

Think of times when you were surprised by your courage, calm, willpower, creativity, or intuition. If you have been tormented by grief, guilt, resentment, or some other distressing emotion, pinpoint any particular thought that helped it pass. You may be the survivor of a horrendous ordeal. Identify what was within you that kept you from being sucked down by the undertow, even if it seems *otherworldly*. Like the intuitive voice that saved the lives of Dulci's children in Chapter 1 (Vignette 1), what incidents have you experienced in which you discerned an approaching outcome with a knowingness that was more than a hunch. Write from its position, and talk about yourself in the third person. Include any drawings, graphics, or names that seem appropriate. You may want to start a journal filled with exercises from this book. The vignettes offer illuminating examples for each exercise.

Vignette 2: Jaleigh's Angel

I suppose I am one of Jaleigh's Angels. When Jaleigh was giving birth to her son, she was in labor for a long, long time. There was a problem and the doctor was telling her it was going to have to be either her or the baby. She was heartbroken. She wanted that baby so badly but she wasn't dilating and nothing was moving. They put her in a room by herself, and I could hear her crying, praying, and pleading with God to let both her and the baby live, so I put my two powerful hands around her womb and began to push. When the nurse finally came back, she saw that Jaleigh was fully dilated and told her to stop pushing until she got to the delivery room. Jaleigh said, "I'm not pushing, there's something in me doing it!"

Caduceus

Source: "Caduceus," n.d., *Wikipedia,* retrieved September 2007, from http://en.wikipedia.org/wiki/Image: Caduceus.svg.

EMPOWERING THE WILL

The very core of the Self is pure awareness and pure Will—the dynamic power capable of directing and mastering mind and body (Assagioli, 1965/2000). One Japanese proverb states, "To know and not to act is not to know at all." Children instinctively know when parental commands carry weight and when they are empty threats. Like Eliza Doolittle, we become sick of words and the mindless chatter that clutters our heads and crave the *show-me* Self that can act.

DEVELOPMENT OF THE WILL

Will is born from the power struggles when the young are learning to be self-governing. Initially, it opposes the Will of caretakers trying to teach social order, especially when obstacles to the **will to pleasure** are imposed. School-aged children use the Will to control those who can provide security, worth, or safety with their **will to power**. As teens internalize rules, they gain a **will to duty** and learn to control instinctual impulses and drives. Maturation continues and the Will is freed from its shackles as the independent Self embraces the **will to become** and accomplishes one unfolding goal after another. These very successes cause a ripened interdependent Self to ponder, *What does life want from me?* instead of *What do I want from life?* in its search for the **will to meaning** (Frankl, 1963). Finally, the integrated and transcendent Selves practice **will without willing** using the Taoist principle of *effortless effort* that works in harmony with the nature "to flow like water, reflect like a mirror, and respond like an echo instead of running around in circles" (Hoff, 1982, p. 85).

THREE PHASES OF WILLING—WISHING, CHOOSING, AND ACTING

The starting point for all self-change is the *will to become*. It occurs in three stages. **Wishing** is the appetizer of action and requires people to reach deep inside to discover their longings, passions, and forgotten dreams (May, 1977). Such harmful thoughts—*My needs aren't important; If I want something, I'll only be disappointed when I don't get it; Others should know what I want;* and *My desires might be a burden to others*—are enemies of wishing. Likewise, the *will to pleasure* or acting impulsively on any urge of the moment will thwart true accomplishment.

The independent Self exercises freedom in the second stage of will by **choosing** what it wants. True choosing must be accompanied by a personal bill of rights to make mistakes, have mixed emotions, break some rules, and to change one's mind. There are endless ways to rationalize or minimize options—*My parents couldn't handle it if I left my wife; By not studying hard, I won't look stupid if I make a bad grade; I might lose control if I say what I feel.* When people decide not to decide, they delegate decisions to others or to life itself and allow a situation to worsen until some external factor intervenes. Or, choices can be relegated to "the rules" or cultural values—"The Bible says you cannot. . . . " "Where I come from, children are supposed to live with their parents until marriage." Guilt over past choices can create a paralysis, but guilt over choosing not to follow your dream is the ultimate despair.

The chasm between Walter Mitty dreams and **acting** in the third stage of Willing can appear formidable. There is a time for baby steps and a time for ultimatums. By considering *what am I willing and not willing to do*, options can be examined and actions identified. A woman named Alice told her mother, "I will no longer do favors for you until you can show me you understand how I felt when your husband molested me many years ago." This simple strategy finally erased her mother's haunting words from her mind—"You know you enjoyed what he did."

Taking Steps toward Change

Baby steps seduce people into healthy habits. Start an exercise program by requiring yourself to walk down your driveway everyday, and then to the next driveway, and so on. Just defining behavior as a decision often initiates change.

Vignette 3: Odette

Odette had grieved her adult son's death for several years. She was asked if she ever wanted to stop mourning (implying that she had a choice). When she agreed it would be good to go on with her life, she was asked to imagine how she would act differently if she did let go and what that change would mean. Her tearful response was that if she enjoyed herself, it suggested that she no longer loved her son. Odette was then given an M&M to eat and asked if she could enjoy it and love her son at the same time, and that was a first step toward change.

EXERCISING THE WILL

Strengthen resolve by exercising the Will, much like one would work a muscle. Little things can be done every day just for their challenge—get out of bed five minutes earlier, suck on a lifesaver without taking a bite, use being stuck in traffic as an opportunity to practice patience, and always state your preference when a group is making a decision instead of saying the proverbial, "I don't care." Conversely, practice making movements using the fewest number of muscles possible when you rise to a standing position after sitting on the floor to make *effortless efforts*. Sometimes the Will operates covertly and you realize a desired change has occurred after you have transformed in some small way. Many mornings you may wonder how you will ever make yourself leave the bed only to find yourself up five minutes later brushing your teeth.

Never stop believing in yourself. Trust that you will eventually make a desired change—you have your whole lifetime. Events worsening can inspire change. It may take your child having 50 more temper tantrums before you remove all her toys from her room and let her redeem one back for every day that she holds her fire. If you have panic attacks, you may remain imprisoned in your comfort zone until you are driven to take risks to feel the onset of anxiety.

Exercise 2

Past Will and Current Testament

People write a "Last Will and Testament" or "Living Wills," but rarely do they establish intimate terms with their own Will. Use the following questions to recall how your Will has directed you in the past and how it is currently operating in your life.

1. What wish did you have as a child that came true because of your efforts?
2. What was the hardest decision you ever made or thing you ever did? Was it a one-time event, or did you have to decide/act over and over?
3. Have you ever found that you made a significant (desired) change in yourself and not even realized you wanted the change until you noticed you were different?
4. Did you ever wait for things to become intolerable before making a decision or willing yourself to take action?
5. Were you ever able to take a small step that resulted in a significant (desired) change?
6. Have you accomplished something that you thought would be hard by finding a shortcut or a way to work with the *powers that be* that made your efforts easier?
7. Was (is) the process of working toward your goal rewarding enough to make the outcome unimportant?

(Continued)

8. Did (does) anyone oppose your past accomplishment or current wishes?
9. What dreams and desires do you have now? Are they influenced by family, friends, culture, rebellion, greed, lust, or needs for attention *or* are your wish(es) a way to express and stretch some part of yourself?
10. Do your current goals and desires involve meeting biological needs for food, rest, novelty, security, or sex? Do they necessitate changing or controlling others? Do they involve acquiring a skill, personal growth, or service to others that requires focus, self-control, concentration, and/or total involvement?
11. Do you have more regrets about the things you have done or the things you have not attempted?

Directions: Take time to reflect on these questions. When you are ready, write a "Past Will and Current Testament" in your journal. Use the third-person voice of your Will to give an historical account of how it has grown, changed, and directed you.

Vignette 4: Layla

I am Layla's Will. When she was little, I helped her oppose people who had strange ideas about how to tie shoes or print the number nine. I taught her how to go along with others quickly to avoid such adult trickery as time-out, so that she did not get into trouble often. In turn, her mother yielded when I insisted she be able to wear five dresses at a time to preschool to achieve the southern-bell look, a juvenile goal that now appalls me.

But sometime in her youth, I turned my powers inward. Instead of resisting others, I wanted to help Layla develop abilities that I knew she had. Academics, dramatic flair, and social skill came easily to her. Those arenas required little assistance from me. But at the studio, dance demanded discipline. Natural grace, rhythm, and limberness can do little without a Will to insist that postures, attitudes, and positions be perfected. Once-a-week classes became several-times-a-day events. For Layla, the goal was never to be a professional dancer; instead, it was the feel of getting it right and the fun of performances.

In high school, the call to put her well-trained body to use came from the draw of the dance team. At her small-town high school, Layla was the only dancer with significant studio training, which catapulted her into a position of leadership. But with this advance came one of the most difficult decisions I have yet had to make for Layla—to stay with the team (which was often more of a sideshow of humiliation) and attempt to turn it into a praiseworthy performance, or to return to the ivory tower of the studio.

I chose the greater challenge. I held Layla to task, making her choose quality over quantity at team auditions even though it meant wounding egos, doing push-ups with girls who did not practice, and giving prima donnas corrective criticism that yielded Layla a crop of malevolent nicknames. But, by her senior year, there were dazzling performances, awards, and appreciative teammates.

Now, Layla is in her first year of college. When she did not make the university competition dance team, I would not let the pain of defeat crush her, reminding Layla that maybe she had been too picky in choosing just one team to audition for and directing her to a studio that delighted her with the level of training it offered. But dancing has given her much more than audience's accolades. She has acquired a kinesthetic understanding of her body, knowledge of its physical limits, and a keen interest in anatomy— all leading to the pursuit of orthopedic medicine.

I am very much with Layla now, strategizing ways to study molecular biology, college calculus, and other classes that will be far beyond any academic challenge she has ever faced. I look forward to helping her through the years of medical school to deliver her into a profession that will offer new goals and vistas.

SYNTHESIZING THE SELF

Memories of courage and calm and empowering the Will are all sure routes to the Self. The following imagery exercise dives deep to the very center of Self. It begins in a meadow like many of the tasks developed by Hanscarl Leuner in his *Initiated Symbol Projection Test* (1969), which was a treatment protocol designed to induce a series of waking dreams.

Exercise 3

Tunneling Inward

Imagine yourself in a meadow. As you walk through it, notice what you see around you; how the ground feels beneath you; and if there are fragrances, animal life, and trees. Notice how the sky looks, the time of day, and the temperature. In your walk, you will be very surprised to come to a tunnel. It can be in the side of a hill or mountain, or it may be a magical, invisible tunnel that only you can see, capable of transporting you to the center of an unknown destination. Begin your journey inward. You may walk, or there may be some form of conveyance within the tunnel. Some people feel their way in the dark, while others discover a mysterious source of light. Take your time to reach the center of whatever you are traveling through; you will know when you get there. The core of this mysterious place has a presence about it. You can meet it in the form of a human, an effect of light, an animal, or some old forgotten artifact. While waiting in this calm center for the presence to arrive, hours can pass in moments. You need not be too delighted as you discover who or what the presence is and the message it has for you.

Image or journal your own tunnel and presence before reading the vignette.

Vignette 5: Rita

Rita's slight frame was dwindling. Doctors had diagnosed her with a lazy stomach, and she literally became afraid to eat because food would lie in her stomach, causing nausea and indigestion. Yet, she was an attractive, bubbly woman who was constantly busy with friends, dancing partners, and an abundance of men coming in and out of her life until she met Roy. Roy romanced her as no other man had and then ripped her heart out, claiming he had to pursue a chance encounter with his childhood sweetheart. Roy's vanishing act paralyzed Rita's already sluggish stomach. The night she did the "Tunneling Inward Exercise," she was an emotional wreck, weighing less than 70 pounds.

Following her therapist's instructions, she began describing her meadow: "This meadow has bright green grass with little flowers popping up everywhere (Rita teaches preschool). The air is crisp, but there is enough sun to warm me, and I don't see any signs of fall. I'm following a path that leads to a beautiful mountain in the distance. Although it is far away, time collapses, and suddenly, I'm there."

Her therapist asked her to notice that there is a path going up the mountain (see Exercise 5) or a hidden opening that leads to a tunnel that cuts through to the heart of the mountain. Both routes hold promise, and she would know which one to take.

Rita continued, "I see some bushes and notice an opening behind them. I'm intrigued because from somewhere far away, deep inside, a glow lights the way. I follow the path, and the air becomes moist and thick, but pleasant. I know I'm traveling closer to the glowing light, but the tunnel remains dark and mysterious. It is a great distance to the inner chamber I seek.

Again time collapses, and I'm there. The air is warm and comforting but not too hot. I wonder if I am deep enough (in the earth) for some radiant form of heat and light. I do feel a presence, but nothing seems to be happening. I gaze at the smooth earthen surfaces of domelike walls. Something is changing but I cannot tell what. . . . I realize two huge hands have formed from the dome above and are reaching down. I am awed but not frightened as eight great fingers press me, touch me, move muscle against

(Continued)

> muscle, and play me like a piano, while giant thumbs support my back. It is not sexual or sensual . . . it's magical. I do not know how long it goes on. Time is collapsing again, and the hands have retreated. I walk out of the tunnel, back the way I came, until I'm in the crisp open air of the meadow again."

Rita had come to her therapist ruminating and rambling about her loss of Roy, yet in her inward journey she encountered a healing Self that knew her greatest need was to waken peristalsis, the wavelike contracting and dilating that her stomach so desperately needed. Ever ready to take Roy back should the flame of his rekindled *first love* flicker, Rita began to eat more, gain weight, and enjoy time alone without a constant parade of people marching through her life. The battle between personality parts acting the playgirl or the clinging vine had reached an impasse right in the middle of Rita's alimentary canal. It took a *kinesthetic Self* to unblock dammed up energies and lower the decibel level between dueling parts so Rita could begin to understand the quiet murmurings that knew her true needs.

MANDALAS

Tunneling inward is one way to find a route to the center of your Self. But, what if it were possible to draw a (symbolic) map to locate or define your core? Carl Jung (1875–1961) was one of the early explorers in charting the psyche. At 37 years of age, he quit his university post to devote himself to his and his patients' inner lives. Each morning, he sketched circular designs that he believed helped him develop more of his Self. These *mandalas* took their name from the Sanskrit word *manda*, which means essence. The suffix *la* stands for container, making a mandala the container of one's essence (Cunningham, 2002).

The Self was one of Jung's archetypes or ideal forms that gives people an image of their own unique, individual existence. Every organism is driven to assume a form characteristic of its nature. The Self is the driving force that compels people to find their own identity or to individuate. It does this by producing (thought) patterns, direction, and meaning. It is constantly digesting and unifying everyday experiences. Mandalas symbolize this with circular designs that organize perception, ideas, and physical sensations (Fincher, 2000).

Jung made it clear that the Self is at a person's core, not the ego. Unlike Freud, who defined the ego as the personality part that mediates between id impulses and superego rules, Jung thought of ego as the part that is consciously known, can be wounded or hurt, and needs protection. This *ego* is similar to Assagioli's *personal self* that is acutely aware of itself as distinct and separate. The Self stands behind the ego or *small self* as a safety net when it is challenged and not functioning well (Fincher, 2000).

Interpretations of Mandalas

Mandalas communicate information between the Self and the ego; and, conversely, they translate information from the personal self into symbols that speak to the Self. These designs reveal stages of a person's development in cyclic phases that repeat as a person evolves.

The uroboros or snake swallowing its tail, the illustration that tops the Preface of this book, encircles a void or a **beginning** before a beginning. Searching and starting a journey is suggested in the labyrinth illustration above the Introduction. The "Spiral" mandala (Chapter 7) may suggest the longing for growth toward wholeness or the need to translate knowledge into useful forms.

Mandalas may contain conflicting parts of a person's nature, but the very expression of tension within the safe boundary of the circle shows **reconciliation of opposites**. This can be seen in the

2.8

center circle of the mandala in Chapter 1. The upward/downward pointing triangles are an ancient, universal sign representing integration, union, and wholeness. The "Landscape" mandala (Chapter 6) shows the division of polar opposites (earth mother/sky father) with a new sense of Self (the tree) superimposed on split halves. It was designed by a 13-year-old female expressing a desire to interact with others suggested by a tree with its expansive canopy of branches that emerges in the foreground.

As the ego or "I" expands, mandalas start to show **alignment with the Self**. Circles with a dot in the center show a dawning sense of Self. The "Web of Life" mandala that heads this chapter reaches out to fill the fertile void creating a gateway to the infinite. When squares or four-petaled flowers fill a circle, the clash of opposites has been resolved, and the Self is ready to initiate action. Stars, flowers, or a human figure reaching out (with five points) show a sense of mission. Even a swastika with four bent arms radiating out from the center, add up to the five facets needed for movement and power. The profiles that were uneven in the Chapter 4 mandala have turned inward, become balanced, and integrated in the "Crystal" mandala that heads Chapter 5. In the center, is the suggestion of a vessel or container in which transformation can take place. Designs with even numbers greater than four (six-pointed stars, eight-petaled flowers) signify crystallization, accomplishment, or meaning. The thousand-petaled lotus in the "Crown Chakra" mandala (Chapter 1) is the traditional yogi symbol of the ultimate achievement of connecting the corporal body to transcendent Spirit.

During the height of achievement, seeds are sown for destructive processes. Shapes emerge that imply **fragmentation of the ego** when it is not fully allied with the Self. The mandala that heads Chapter 4 shows pie-shaped wedges of different sizes, which suggest unbalanced personality parts. The downward pointing triangle in the mandala for Chapter 3 is the standard Yogi symbol for bringing Spirit into matter in an act of personal power. Similarly, the spokes of a wheel can suggest collapse and the relentless turning of life. Prominent X-designs symbolize facing a crossroad. There may be tiny, scattered, fluid figures lacking shape. Designs can be disorderly or disjointed when defenses are weak. Concentric circles or *target* mandalas can suggest obsessive thinking, struggling to maintain control (rather than fragment), or the projection of anger onto others (Fincher, 1991).

Ultimately, fragmentation is overcome in new alignments. The **ecstasy of unity** is seen in mandalas with infusions of light from above, birds in flight, and focal points near the top of the circle (Fincher, 2000). It seems unusual that the "Landscape" mandala (Chapter 6) would have an eye peering into infinity at the apex of the mandala. However, it is not uncommon for mandalas to have mixed themes as they help us spiral inward again and again to find the transcendent Self.

Mandala Making

Making mandalas creates a sacred space into which the Self can be invited. This is an especially soothing exercise when experiencing a crisis, illness, or emotional wounds. Let everything you have read earlier float to the back of your mind so that the organizing capacity of your very own Self can resolve any impasses in your current mental state by following the simple instructions below.

Exercise 4

Creating Mandalas

Have a full range of colors at your disposal. Use whatever medium is most comfortable for you—pencil, crayon, pastels, markers, and so on. Shape makers can be helpful, but there are times for flowing, free-form designs. You can use a plate to draw a circle or the *mandala graph paper* offered (Figure 2.1). You may start drawing from the center or from the edges of the circle. A design can emerge, or you may simply draw a scene within the circle. When you are finished, give your mandala a title. Allow it to come to your mind with as little thought as possible. Drawing mandalas is a type of meditation. You may want to make this a daily exercise and date your work. It is natural to see progression and themes, but be careful of too much analysis.

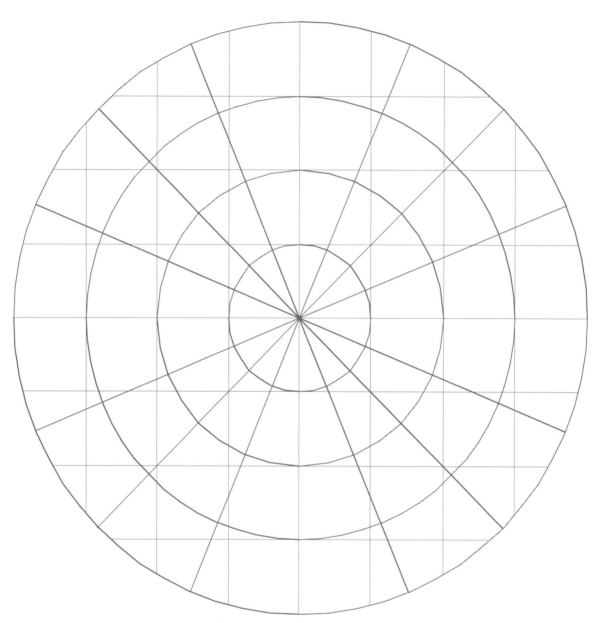

Figure 2.1 Mandala Graph Paper

RECOGNIZING AND REMEMBERING SPIRIT

If the way to Self lies deep within, conventional wisdom suggests the movement of Spirit is upward toward a source that validates, defines, and directs life—whether that be nature, art, people, or the Eternal. The first name that the early Hebrews used for God was *El Shaddai*, meaning "spirit of the mountain" (Noss, 1967). A "mountain god" would be easily recognized by tribal peoples who were familiar with animating many forms of nature with life. It does not seem suggestive of a transcendent, immanent monotheistic God that this people were credited with being the first to worship.

SPIRIT IMAGERY

The spirit of a high place is often what is needed to help people gain perspective and begin to make contact with their own most observant Self. The "Mountain Spirit" Exercise adapted from the *Initiated Symbol Projection Test* (Leuner, 1969) focuses on a spiritual encounter, rather than on identifying personal levels of aspiration and capacity for mastery as intended by Leuner.

Exercise 5

Mountain Spirit

Picture a mountain. It may be one you have heard about or seen in a photo or a place you have visited. You recognize it—it's height, the terrain, and the appearance of the peak—immediately. The summit of the mountain beckons you in some magnetic way, or it may appear impossibly out of reach, but know that you will find a guide, a helper, or even the *spirit* of the mountain along the way to assist you in your ascent. As you begin your journey upward, notice your surroundings and how it feels to be climbing. Sense yourself elevating higher and higher. Know that the spirit of the mountain is awaiting you. It may meet you on the path upward, at the peak, or even as you reach the top. You may need to go further on a beam of light, a ladder descending from the sky, or by stepping into a plane at the plateau (Assagioli, 1965/2000).

You can anticipate how the spirit will appear, catch a glimpse of it, or find it within your reach. Does it come to you as someone you have known, as a familiar character, an animal, or as an effect of light? Take your time to join this being that is all-wise and all-loving. Notice what it is like to be in its presence. Do you touch, make eye contact, or melt into it? Have your surroundings become unimportant, or does the lofty view change in some surprising way in the company of your spiritual docent? Is there any verbal exchange—something you need to say or understand or something the mountain spirit wants you to know?

Now push an instant rewind button in your mind to the point where the mountain spirit appeared. Give it a voice to describe its ethereal existence and its encounter with your human form. With just a kernel of an idea you can begin writing this waking dream and be surprised by the details that come forward.

Image/journal your own mountain and its spirit before reading the vignette.

Vignette 6: Jaleigh/Mountain Spirit

Jaleigh

I see one of those beautiful Swiss Alps capped by snow. I'm surprised as I start to climb because I move easily and freely. The crippling arthritis that set in after my car accident 30 years ago is gone. My dog is a

(Continued)

puppy again, and she is running by my side. I know who will be at the top of the mountain—my dear father who I've longed to see. But I won't be able to reach him . . . . My mother is standing in front of him. She is in the way, just as she was before he died. Now that she's dead, she still wants to keep him from me. . . .

If I give myself the power to walk freely again, with a flick of my imagination I can move her off my mountain . . . and there . . . she's gone. Now he and I are together, somewhere on the side of the mountain, below the snow but way high up. We just look together at the view. I'm content feeling his happiness, knowing how much he loved being in the country. With his arm around me, I feel totally safe. It is as though we can see forever—other mountains, hills, tiny houses, and cars. Objects pass by below so far away, distant, and remote.

I don't have to tell my father what's been bothering me. He knows I've been terrified ever since my husband called 911 after I took a handful of pills; and the policeman handcuffed me, humiliated me, and took me to the hospital. We're still gazing at the land rolling before us, but words flow mentally between our minds. He tells me I'm confusing the police cars of which I've become so frightened with my mother. He says it was only one officer who did not follow the protocol, but my mother *never* did. She lay in wait behind every corner, ready to slap me down with her words or her knuckles for the slightest infraction.

Without looking, I know there are tears running down his cheeks because he could not always protect me, and sometimes the more he tried, the worse her jealousy and wrath became. But a beautiful mountain stream is forming from his tears, and we watch it flow over rocks and cliffs. That awful past seems far away, and it is strange that something so beautiful could come from that much pain, washing away past hurt and current fears.

Mountain Spirit

I have been free of body for many years now. Just as we are looking at houses that seem so far away, I remembered how to look at aches, pains, and troubles and let them pass by. As I let go of worldly problems, I became a part of everything. I remembered that I was as much a part of my daughter, Jaleigh, as I seemed separate from her. And yet, if bliss can be multiplied, that is how my joy was to see her walk up a mind mountain toward me.

I almost feel earthly pride at my daughter's quick knowing to mentally shed the pain of her arthritis and that she did not resist when it was suggested to her that she had the power to keep anything from separating us. She feels my arm around her, but I feel I *am* her, and she *is* me. Together with one mind and one eye we look at the strange moves in our family's dance, trapped by ignorance of choices we did not know we had.

The tears she feels running down my cheeks are her tears. Joined in spirit, I can take the river of pain away from her and turn it into a waterfall that fractures light into a rainbow. So I ask Jaleigh to follow the waterfall and its river as it flows through a tiny town far below. And in that toylike town is a crier whom we can barely hear calling out, "Watch out, Watch out . . . a policeman might come with handcuffs!" And now Jaleigh knows that only her pride was hurt, that her spirit is up here on the mountain with me, and that the town crier is crying wolf because she has seen many police cars in the past and will see many in the future, and none will stop to hurt her.

IMMANENT SPIRIT

When conventional wisdom suggests that the way to Spirit is upward, it is only considering its transcendent aspect that is beyond memories, words, images, and Self. But Spirit is also immanent. It permeates every aspect of Being and interaction. A compass pointing toward Sprit would spin wildly because it lies in every direction. You cannot find Spirit, any more than you can find the ocean of air that surrounds and flows through you. The great search for Spirit implies that there is some place where Spirit is not (Wilber, 2004). In our efforts to find the Absolute we create objects out there, desperately whipping air into tornadoes that are awesome and beautiful, but terrifying. We avoid the injunction to *be still and know.* It is exactly in this knowing or reknowing that we recognize Spirit.

Witnessing the Physical

Knowing begins with noticing or noting. The following exercises are designed to help you discover the sleepless giant within that can report your dreams back to you upon waking. Your silent *seer* observes the stream of events that parade in the world outside as perceptions—in your body, as sensations, and in your mind as thoughts and images. Any feeling or pain that is attached to perceptions, sensations, and thoughts is simply noticed by this *mirror mind* that reflects all and absorbs nothing. Exercise 9 provides an opportunity to make a habit of tuning in your observant Self in the gross or dense realm of the physical world.

Exercise 6

Self Narration

Simply narrate your activities and movements as they are taking place. This opens the doors of perception to experience ordinary events as if for the first time.

- **Example 1:** *Narrate muscle mechanics* that are involved in putting this book down and picking it back up with *video talk*: "I'm holding this book open by clasping each side between my thumb and fingers. My forearms simultaneously lift up and shift to the side. I notice its weight before turning the book over on the bed by rotating my wrists and lowering my arms. Now with my thumbs on the bottom of each side, I lift my arms from the shoulders, rotate my wrists, and find my place in the text."
- **Example 2:** *Narrate yourself in the morning* when you wake up (Moody & Carrol, 1997): "I notice my slow and even breathing. I have the thought, 'It's time to get up,' and another part of me complains, 'I'm not ready.' I push the covers down until my foot is free. I pull myself up with my head and using my hand on the bed for support, I give a little push and both feet are on the floor. I feel my weight shift as I start to walk . . . "
- **Example 3:** Frequently *narrate yourself while driving* to increase attention: "I am holding the steering wheel firmly. My foot presses on the gas pedal, and my eyes shift to the odometer to make sure I'm driving the speed limit. I notice a car pulling up on my left, and I ease off the gas a little . . . "
- **Example 4:** Occasionally *narrate yourself while eating* finger foods to relearn how to make each bite burst with flavor and satisfaction (*Note*: Do not do this exercise with highly processed, sweetened foods.): I'm holding this apple in my hand, and it feels hard, round, and cold. I have to open my jaws wide and use pressure to take a bite when I hold the apple up to my mouth. I can feel a large chunk in my mouth, and delicious juice oozes onto my tongue. I suck out more juice and then bite the chunk in half, moving it around with my jaw while pulverizing it with my teeth. All the while, there is a juicy delicate apple flavor soaking my tongue, and I keep chewing until the entire piece is gone . . . "

Witnessing the Breath

Spirit has no boundaries. As awareness becomes more acute, the separate Self dissolves, and you become an opening for a stream of experiences. When you are just beginning the practice of noticing Spirit, it is good to look for an obvious leak in the perimeter between you and not-you. You can ask yourself, "Where is the point that the outside becomes my inside, and my inside becomes the outside?" The answer lies right under your nose. The very breath from which Spirit takes its name (*spirare* is the Latin verb "to breath") wanders to and fro without a passport, importing precious oxygen in its cargo and exporting the waste of carbon dioxide to the plant world. This *border crossing* at your nose can be used both as a focal point and a symbol of the porthole through which the universe is constantly marching.

Many forms of meditation and relaxation stress attention to breathing and prescribe proper ways to breathe, such as deep-belly breathing, cleansing breaths (inhale to the count of three and exhale to the count of six), square breathing (inhale to the count of four and exhale to the count of four), and more. When waking up to your internal Witness, aware breathing is best. Exercise 10 helps you attune to this Eternal Seer with exquisite attention to breath at the boundary of me and not-me without changing a thing.

Exercise 7

Aware Breathing

Aim your attention at the beginning of the in-breath and sustain your awareness until you are ready to breathe out. Notice if there is a slight pause between the in and out breath. As before, aim your attention at the beginning of the out breath and sustain it until you notice a pause or the desire to inhale.

Continue for several more breaths, but each time, be more mindful of all the amazing occurrences that happen during this seemingly simple process—What do the muscles in your nose do to orchestrate the drawing in of air? Can you feel the hairs inside your nose shift direction with each in and out breath? How much do your nostrils widen as you exhale? What is the difference in temperature between the air going in and the breath going out? Are you using your sense of touch or smell? Is the pause between breaths staying the same or lengthening? Can you apprehend the air before it enters your nose?

Keep your mind focused at the point where air transforms into breath. Although you could notice a myriad events as your lungs expand and push your diaphragm down, establish air entering your nostrils as a focal point. Whenever your attention wanders, come right back to this spot. Do not avoid noticing the lovely sensations of your diaphragm expanding and pushing your belly out; just come back to the focal point where air enters and exits your nose.

If your observations become too routine, simply note your breaths—*in . . . pause . . . out . . . pause . . . in . . . pause . . . out . . . pause. . . .* Notice the rhythm and subtle changes. Observe how you decide to stop this exercise. Do you say, "Okay I get it, I've had enough of this." "I want to find out what comes next." "I have other things to do . . . "?

Aware breathing is basic. Practice it for a minute or so whenever you think of it. Pausing to breathe mindfully just before you eat, while driving the car, or when you are anxious can improve attention or produce relaxation, depending on the situation.

To Be Mindful or Mindless

Mindfulness means "paying attention in a particular way, on purpose, in the present moment, nonjudgmentally" (Kabat-Zinn, 1994, p. 4). Much of the time we are preoccupied or postoccupied with a parade of *what-ifs, if-onlys, when-wills, have-tos, shoulds, awfuls, nevers, nobodies,* and *everybodies* that march through our minds severing us from the moment. Rarely are we actually occupied and mindful of the present except when engaged in activities that require or entice our attention and concentration. The archer shooting a bull's-eye, a pianist working out a difficult piece of music, and the caress of a new-found love can all produce total absorption in the moment. But when life becomes too easy or routine, habit steps in, turns on our automatic pilot, and robs of us of the present.

In times past, life was lived as an art as shown in the story of the kosher butcher (source unknown). It explains the Jewish (*kashrut*) law of killing an animal with the least amount of pain possible:

> A new butcher had arrived in a tiny eastern European Jewish hamlet.
> The people were asking, "So, how is the new butcher?"
> "Eh, so-so," Came the reply from one of his first customers.
> "Well, what is the problem? Didn't he sharpen the knife properly?"
> "Yes, he sharpened the knife."
> "Did he not say all the prayers before using the knife?"
> "Oh yes, he knows the prayers well."
> "Did he bring the blade to the animal's neck swiftly at just the right point?"
> "Yes, yes, he did that."
> "So. . . . What is the problem?!"
> "He does not wet the blade with his tears before striking the animal."

Unlike the new butcher, the old one was totally mindful of his occupation and its meaning.

One of the earliest sciences may have been studying ways to achieve greater awareness (of Spirit). Herb gathers, hunters, and medicine men and women would have needed exquisite concentration and inner guidance. Various methods of practicing awareness or meditation emerged. Perhaps the earliest were methods in which people focused on the very thing that would distract them, like heat in a sweat lodge or pain in a rite of passage.

Some types of meditation focused on forms—a shiny object, a phrase or mantra repeated over and over, or a complex mandala design visualized in the mind. Hopefully, this would ultimately lead to total peace through the elimination of all thoughts or internal mind chatter (Rowan, 1993). Such calm, although good, is not necessarily heightened awareness or mindfulness. It can take the form of a withdrawal from the world and attachment to stillness rather than bringing calmness to the present moment to understand interconnections in wide range of experiences (Kabat-Zinn, 1994).

In mindful meditation, thoughts, perceptions, and sensations are simply observed. Through this process, thought patterns change in ways that foster integration and understanding. The nature of thought itself and our relationship to it is contemplated. Rather than being ruled by tyrannical beliefs, ideas become servants until they are transcended altogether (Kabat-Zinn, 1994). Exercise 8 explains how to meditate mindfully by watching thoughts without being drawn into them.

Make a mental list of different kinds of **thoughts** so that you can note them with just a word when they occur—*judging, comparing, analyzing, wondering, remembering, doubting, planning, rehearsing,* or just plain *thinking.* You may also note **perceptions** in your environment—*hearing, smelling, touching, tasting, seeing* and **sensations** in your body—*heaviness, aching, tension, itching* . . . . Advanced mediators may notice perceptions, sensations, and thoughts without using mental words to note them, but in the early years of practice, labels help strengthen the role of the Witness or mirror mind that reflects and embraces all. You cannot fail in this exercise. If your mind wanders, the moment you realize this, you will have woken up to your Witness.

Exercise 8

Mindful Meditation

Take your seat mindfully, choosing your chair, cushion, or spot and posture with intention. As the ancient Zen proverb suggests, sit as though you are with an honored guest. Notice how your hands want to fall.

(Continued)

Palms down (containment), palms up (openness), and fingers folded with index fingers pointed (focus). Notice if your eyes want to be open or closed. If they are open, focus on a spot. It is likely that they will eventually close. Simply observe how this happens—Do your lids feel heavy? Do your eyes blink slowly? Does your vision become blurry? Periodically, close your eyes on purpose to find out if they want to stay closed, but if they want to open, focus back on your spot. Note if you are wondering, *Am I doing this right?* and let the thought go . . .

Take a few moments to breathe with awareness as you did in Exercise 7. Once your eyes close, your focal point is air touching your nose. Use aware breathing until you notice a state of quiet, receptive calmness, and mental alertness. This is the steady, nonreactive awareness and curiosity of mindfulness.

Now you can begin to examine various environmental perceptions and bodily sensations as they arise and pass away. If you notice an itch or need to move, do your best to focus on it and explore the urgency without yielding to it. This develops the ability to attend without desire and to release the energy of pressure. Often itches go away, but if you become too distracted and scratch, notice the mechanics of how you do that. Always come back to aware breathing.

Most challenging of all is to observe your thoughts. People are addicted to thinking and can become uncomfortable when there is no chattering going on in the mind. The goal is not to stop thinking, but to note the thoughts and any impact they have—*planning* = excitement, *what-if-ing* = anxiety, *questioning* = boredom, *criticizing* = guilt, judging = anger. . . . There are no bad thoughts—only adverse actions. Remember the scripture, "Fear no evil" from the 23rd Psalm. Your Higher Self is with you, holding the keys to the infinite. If a thought is too distracting, remind yourself that you are pre- or postoccupied; that there is nothing you can do about the issue at the moment; and that it is best to go back to your breathing focal point until your observant, quiet state returns.

Doubts about your skill, purpose, or the value of meditation can produce boredom and restlessness. Asking questions can disengage your attention from the doubt and turn it back on consciousness itself: "What part is questioning my ability?" "Who has had enough?" "Am I awake to my Witness?" "Am I really seeing this person or only hearing my thoughts about him or her?" "How connected am I to my Self or my Universe?" "Who am I?" Inquire without expecting answers, and enjoy the peace of silent responses. If any chattering doubts return, banish them with another question.

Detect your first impulse to quit. Stay with it for a little, asking, "How do I know it is time to stop?" If the answer is good enough, take your time to slowly become present in the room.

Just as your body needs a certain amount of sustained aerobics to gain cardiovascular benefit, repeated 30- to 45-minute practice sessions will produce heightened states of awareness. However, in the beginning, such lengthy periods may cause so much restlessness and impatience that formal meditation is counterproductive. Even a couple of minutes of practicing mindfulness here and there, in your car, while waiting for an appointment, or before falling asleep will begin to attune you to your internal, observant Seer and make your journey of Self discovery easier.

Who Am I?

As we become keen observers of our perceptions, sensations, and thoughts; they slow down, become more subtle, and change in texture. Such deeper or higher states of awareness begin to lift the veil that covers Spirit. The original source for Exercise 9 may be Assagioli's dis-identification activity. When practiced, it heightens a sense of permanency in observers and builds the ability to separate from their constant flow of sensations, emotions, and mental chatter. People should not be enslaved by changeable and contradictory experiences. To state, "I am I, a center of pure awareness (the witness) . . . is the key and the beginning of mastering our psychological processes" (Assagioli, 1965/2000, p. 104). This exercise has been adapted by many others and named "Capping" by Ken Wilber (2004, p. 23). It is not meant to replace any other form of meditation, but to intensify it.

2.16

Exercise 9

Capping Exercise

Review the following narrative, and then take your seat as you did for the "Mindful Meditation" Exercise. After a few moments of aware breathing, repeat the capping exercise to yourself. It is not important that you memorize or say it word for word. Do your best to touch on key (boldface) points:

- **Who am I? . . . I have a body, but I am not my body:** I can feel sensations in my body—pressure, warmth, tightness, tiredness, excitement, heaviness, lightness, pain. I can see my body and touch it, but I am not my body. Sensations come and go but do not affect that which senses—the vast free open Witness of them all.
- **I have thoughts, but I am not my thoughts:** Concepts, ideas, hopes, memories all arise, come and go, stay a bit, repeat, and pass. I can know my thoughts, but what is known is not the knower—the vast free open Witness of them all.
- **I have emotions, but I am not my emotions:** Desires, love, anger, hatred, fear, sadness, happiness, joy all arise, come and go, stay a bit, repeat and pass through me. I can feel my emotions but what is felt is not the feeler—the vast free open Witness of them all.
- **I am what remains:** a center of pure awareness. I cannot doubt that the Witness exists in this moment because the Witness is there to observe the doubt. I cannot see my Seer for it is doing the seeing. I am the simple Witness of my ordinary I: my I-I.

Reread this exercise periodically, and formally practice it. Other times, just utilize capping when you are mindfully engaged in any experience: (a) *I am feeling afraid, but I am not my fear. My fear may come and go, but I am the constant, unmoved witness of fear.* (b) *I have desire, but I am not my desire. Even though I have just eaten, I still feel hunger. I can know my desire and what can be known is not the knower. Desires come and go but do not affect what is constant and without need.*

TRANSCENDENT SPIRIT

To write about Spirit is a paradox because it cannot be caught in the net of words. But mediators and mystics come to *know* Spirit and share common experiences. At first, people are amazed by the amount of junk, fantasies, and concepts that flow through their awareness. When they are able to look at all this brain babbling without judgment, a milestone is reached. People report feeling balanced and centered. Some mystical paths make use of inner guides to find union with Spirit. For others, the Way of forms (focusing on an image, repeating a phrase, or noting thoughts) becomes the Way of formlessness—a silent, no-thought place where the Witness ultimately dissolves. Then the Self becomes an opening or clearing into which all experience can come and go. There is a waking-up to discover that real being is everything in awareness (Wilber, 2004).

At first, people come to reknow or recognize Spirit by exquisitely witnessing sensations and mental activity in the present. Then they remember Spirit by rejoining it and becoming unified with the steady stream of life arising moment to moment. You are no longer on one side of your face looking at the world out there (Wilber, 2004). As four gentlemen from England told us in the language of "Goo goo g'joob": "I am he as you are he as you are me and we are all together . . . " (lyrics from "I Am the Walrus" by Lennon & McCartney, 1967). Boundaries fall away in the choreography of a cosmic ballet in which one moment flows into the next, effortlessly.

Once you've arrived, you realize that this state of being has always been at hand. You still feel emotions, but embrace them fully and release the pain into the ebb and flow of life. Others' sorrows and joys are cradled by your pure presence. The nature of your total engagement may be gentle compassion with empathy for the many, iridescent intelligence with light for new discoveries, fierce discernment for exposing truth from falsehood, or healing radiance that causes disease to lose its meaning (Wilber, 2004). It can take many clicks of your ruby red slippers before you realize that you are no longer in Oz and if you fall asleep again, flying monkeys and wicked witches will be all the inspiration you need to find wizards and good spirits to reawaken again.

Because Spirit bathes you with life, transports you beyond yourself, and yet remains elusive, it will help to return to the in-between world of imagery to capture your own internal sense of it. The final exercise is adapted from the "Following a Stream" task in the *Initiated Symbol Projection Test* (Leuner, 1969) to reveal the movement of Spirit within and how it is carrying you in your life's journey.

Exercise 10

Flowing Water

Picture a stream or a river. It may be in the woods, a meadow, wetlands, a mountain, or near the sea. Even if it is a river or stream you have been to or seen in a picture, move close to it because flowing water is forever changing. Notice its width and depth. Has it become swollen with rain or reduced to a trickle from drought? Are there banks on the sides or does the water overflow its bed? Is it going downhill, uphill, or is it level? How clear or cloudy is the water? Is it fast and turbulent with obstacles attempting to block the flow, or is it calm and still? Does this waterway support much plant or animal life? Would you like to follow the stream or river to its source, find where it joins the ocean, drink from it, wade in it, float with the current, sit on the banks and absorb its beauty, or fish in it?

Image/journal your stream or river before reading the example:

"By the time it came to the edge of the forest the stream had grown up, so that it was almost a river, and, being grown-up, it did not run and jump and sparkle along as it used to do when it was younger, but moved more slowly. For it knew now where it was going and it said to itself, *There is no hurry. We shall get there someday*" (Hoff, 1982, p. 67).

This chapter ends where it began—in the 100-acre wood populated by Pooh and Piglet and honey pots, where even the river has allegorical meaning. A. A. Milne did not write his stories and poems for children, but for the child within. His *river* says much about how Spirit can flourish in each of us.

If your waterway suggests that you have not yet found your depth, that you are blocked by obstacles, and have unknown facets hidden by muddy waters, do not despair! An old saying suggests it is not wise to push a river because it flows by itself. If you stay with the energy that runs through you, you will arrive where you need to be. Even if you must return to where your stream of life began or imagine how it joins the worldwide ocean, there is something within you that is always there to nourish and heal your deepest aches. Spirit will be with you as you move forward to greet the personality parts in the next chapter that can mildly annoy or totally terrify as you tackle the white waters of your life.

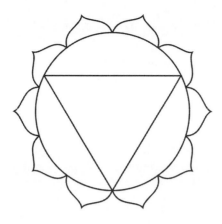

Chapter 3

Identifying Personality Parts

I saw myself for a brief instant as my usual self. . . . But I had scarcely had time to recognize myself before the reflection fell to pieces. A second, a third, a tenth, a twentieth figure sprang from it till the whole gigantic mirror was full of nothing but Harrys or bits of him, each of which I saw only for the instant of recognition. Some of these multitudinous Harrys were as old as I, some older. . . . Others were young. There were youths, boys, schoolboys, scamps, children. Fifty-year-olds and 20-year-olds played leapfrog. Thirty-year-olds and 5-year-olds . . . well-dressed and unpresentable, and even quite naked, long-haired, and hairless, all were I and all were seen for a flash, recognized, and gone. They sprang from each other in all directions, left and right into the recesses of the mirror and clean out of it. (Hesse, 1963, p. 179)

Originally published in 1927, Herman Hesse's classic work, *Steppenwolf*, tells the tale of an aging man who believes he is plagued by a struggle between his refined and savage sides, only to discover that—"two (personality) parts are too many . . . and more than two are not enough. Two can tear you apart (while) many can enrich and sustain you" (Rowan, 1990, p. 44).

Early in the novel, the protagonist, Harry Haller (Herman Hesse), mysteriously receives a "Treatise on the Steppenwolf" with a theory of personality that is light-years ahead of its time. It explains that no human, even a newborn, is so simple that its being can be explained as the sum of

---

The mandala on this page is the symbol for the 3rd (power) chakra. It is the downward-pointing triangle that brings spirit into matter; controlling the desires and energy of the lower chakras and allowing the spiritual richness of higher chakras to manifest in the material world. Interpreted graphically by Gavin Posey.

two or *three* principle elements—flesh and spirit, thoughts and feelings, instincts and culture. Even though there is an inborn need to regard the self as a unit, people are made up of a bundle of selves and everyone contains a chaos of forms, states, stages, inheritances, and potentialities.

To find peace, instead of narrowing and simplifying, people have to absorb more and more of the world and take all of it into their "painfully expanded souls." Births are separation from the All, and the return requires dissolving individuality and expanding the Self until it is able to embrace the All. Such simplistic divisions of self into human and wolf risk missing the multitudes of parts that return man to his maker or to the innermost Selves and higher faculties that we met in the previous chapters.

Hesse was no stranger to the burgeoning new science of psychoanalysis. In 1910, he began 11 years of therapy with Carl Jung's assistant, J. B. Lang. But in 1921, Hesse suddenly cancelled his analysis. Perhaps he graduated to mysticism and found more answers in the Eastern religions of which he had long been a student.

Through the power of fiction, Herman Hesse has Harry meet his feminine counterpart (anima), Hermine, who ultimately leads him on a magical mystery tour through the looking glass where he finds himself shattered into bits and pieces only to be resurrected and "condemned" to life and even marriage (integration) with his anima and shadowy wolfish parts. Harry must learn to see reality as a distortion of the ideal forms he reveres and to "seek the spirit that lies behind the mundane."[1]

In *Steppenwolf*, Hesse posed a fourfold challenge to psychotherapy: (1) to dismember the Self; (2) to find the missing parts; (3) to adopt a benign attitude toward them; and (4) to reassemble, contact, and incorporate as many of these fragments as possible so that the Self can begin to align with and reflect the All. One wonders what the pioneers of psychology who were introduced in Chapter 1 would think of such a literary feat.

---

[1] Hesse once complained to his dear friend Martin Buber (see Preface) that people misunderstood his work (Friedman, 1991). Although Hesse sought alignment of Self with the All, he was also interested in Buber's earthy mysticism, which aspired to find spirituality in everyday "mundane" encounters.

3.2

PSYCHOLOGICAL PIONEERS

Carl Jung (1875–1961) believed the psyche contained a multitude of parts called *complexes*, and he began discussing them as early as 1908. These were defined as groups of ideas clustered together; capable of gravitating between the conscious and unconscious; taking charge in turns; and containing a separate sense of *I-ness*. Such mischievous semi-autonomous systems are capable of interfering with the intentions of the Will and disturbing behavior (Rowan, 1990). " . . . A person does not have a complex. The complex has him" (Watkins & Watkins, 1997, p. 5).

Such common complexes—feeling inferior, superior, and so on—are different from Jung's anima and shadow archetypes. The latter are permanent, hidden, and fixed in the *collective unconscious*, while complexes are more mobile and malleable. The goal is for a person's unique individuality to rise above these subsystems from the depths of his or her archetypical self. In contrast, Hesse would have people dissolve their *individuality* to embrace the All and to seek the spirit that lies behind the ordinary.

Freud's theories of psychoanalyses emerged in the early 1900s, but he did not identify his personality units (the *id, ego*, and *superego*) until the 1920s. The *ego* is an integrative, organizing center that mediates between the id and superego with threats, counterthreats, domination, submission, wheedling, manipulation, attacking, and defending. The *superego*'s internalization of cultural and caregiver values serves a controlling function over the id's instinctual impulses. In 1927, when Hesse wrote, "no human . . . is so simple that its being can be explained as the sum of two or three principle elements . . .," (1963 ed. p. 57) could he have been referring to Freud's id, ego, and superego?

Assagioli (1888–1974) was the first to use the modern term *subpersonalities* to address the subdivided nature of the mind. When he opened his Psychosynthesis Institute in Italy in 1927, he echoed many of the ideas Hesse was espousing in Switzerland. Later summarized in his book, *Psychosynthesis* (1965/2000, p. 18), he writes: "Man intuitively feels he is one and yet finds he is divided unto himself." Every person has within him or her various self-models. They are diverse in nature and in constant conflict.

Assagioli's semi-independent subpersonalities form the nuclei of various parts that are fragments of what we believe ourselves to be, what we want to be, how we think we should appear, values that others project onto us, and internalizations of significant others. They exist at various levels of organization, complexity, and refinement. However, Assagioli also recognized a Higher Self within that feels both individual and universal. With its sense of freedom and expansion, perhaps it is able to embrace the All.

NEW AGE PSYCHOLOGY

Transpersonal psychology, a spin-off from psychosynthesis, teeters between therapy and mysticism and may come the closest to meeting Hesse's vision. As mentioned in Chapter 1, Assagioli embraced the term *transpersonal* when it was first used by humanistic psychologists in 1968. Institutes and associations for transpersonal psychology were formed in the 1970s. Their methods extend psychology from self-actualization to self-transcendence and employ standard psychotherapy techniques *or* meditative practices, whichever are appropriate to a person's level of psychospiritual development.

One of the major contributors to the transpersonal movement, Ken Wilber, defines a subpersonality as the experience of . . . "different vocal or subvocal voices in one's inner dialogue, . . . (which) vie for attention and behavioral dominance." They vary in degree of disassociation and level of development (Wilber, 2000, pp. 100–101). Alternatively, the *transpersonal Self* may be described as being aligned with Hesse's *All* with its capacity to use the personality to witness mental, emotional, and physical experiences to provide guidance for growth.

The mission of this chapter is to meet Hesse's first two challenges: to dismember the Self and find the missing parts. Adopting a benign attitude toward subpersonalities and making contact with them is covered later. The real Self is surrounded by personality parts designed for handling the details of everyday life. We can best make their acquaintance by exploring how these mental facets come to exist and how they are likely to behave.

ORIGIN OF INNER PARTS

Anyone who has observed a baby they did not know unabashedly staring at them with flirtatious eyes has met the spontaneous Self. Witness the toddler on stubby legs, hunched over, derriere in the air, searching the crevices of her log cabin for creatures to which she can exclaim, "I love you bug!" Yet, the existence of a center of pure awareness and Will in infants remains unproven. However, their ability to martial an army of caretakers to scurry about, deciphering whines and whimpers is undisputed. Adults must accommodate themselves to babies' eating, sleeping, and health needs. Perhaps these young ones are not only rulers of their own souls, but of their household as well.

All of this helplessness serves a purpose—the child masters its first developmental crisis: *trust versus mistrust* (Erikson, 1964). This *symbiotic Self* has entered a complex world. As it grows, it will need to remake the very people who have been meeting its needs into internal objects and delegate the tasks of self-soothing, control, and protection to them.

PERSONAS ARISE THROUGH ADAPTATION

Infants find that one personality works better for the important business of being fed and another for charming parents with playful coos and smiles. The child who is relaxed and independent at home can become "Betty Bashful" until she knows she can trust the newness of first grade outside her safety zone. A youngster with different body chemistry will find that school is her first opportunity for "Susie Socialite" to give star performances, while at home she manages better by being "Suzanne Serious."

As people evolve, their outer faces or personas change and become more varied. This is as it should be. The husband who complains that his wife has a different personality with her friends than at home and the mother who thinks her son is being phony around his pals do not understand the importance of adaptation in which an organism changes its form (behavior) to improve its chances of survival (acceptance) within a given environment (social setting).

FIXED PERSONALITIES (CHARACTERS) ARE FORMED BY IMITATION AND ACCOMMODATION

Identification is more powerful than adaptation in forming attachments between young ones and their caretakers—the people they depend on for survival. Traits acquired from imitating or accommodating to elders play a role in molding character. Varying degrees of superiority/inferiority, dependence/independence, and meekness/boldness are adopted. These qualities earn the title "Distracter" by avoiding *internal* anguish with such traits as passiveness, arrogance, or aloofness that stress others.

A facade takes over. Like an eye than cannot see itself, this false self has difficulty appraising the character it has acquired. Problems with self-analysis are compounded by constant verbiage about other people—"*He* should have known what I wanted." or "*She* made that mistake on purpose." Such monologues offer temporary relief from inner torment, even though they wreak havoc in the outer world.

Developing facets that must "do better"; "be loyal"; "believe the world is dangerous"—are all imitations of or accommodations to an extreme part of a parent by an approval seeking part of the child (Schwartz, 1995). Inherited temperaments to be introverted or extroverted or to be under- or overreactive will further mold character. Both biological tendencies and adopted traits give a person his or her unique flair and stance toward life.

HIDDEN (SUB) PERSONALITIES ARE INTERNALIZED DURING SOCIALIZATION

Each person must begin to internalize parental rules and delegate roles to inner parts. Subvocal in nature, they seem hidden compared to adaptable personas and observable traits. The very developmental "crises" (Erikson, 1964) that start maturation will trigger the formation of subpersonalities:

- *Trust versus mistrust:* Babies acquire a **self-soother** for times when parents are absent.
- *Autonomy versus shame and doubt:* Spurs toddlers to be self-governing and to control bowel and bladder functions. An internalized **controller** arrives with a litany of rules—*don't eat dirt; don't put fingers in electrical outlets; don't run inside.* After gaining a modicum of self-control, children want to extend their boundaries.
- *Initiative versus guilt:* Created from the crisis of young ones wanting to rule their world and the guilt of courting catastrophes. An inner **protector** forms to stop risky ventures by triggering instinctual fear. The ability to control and look after themselves readies children for formal education.
- *Industry versus inferiority:* Challenges tranquil energies that stare blithely at branches blowing in the wind to focus. Some young people are eager for the challenge while others need prodding. Eventually, an internal **pusher** will take charge of task completion and acquiring life skills.
- *Identity versus role diffusion:* Requires a personality part that can help adolescents belong and affiliate in social settings. Fully capable of grasping another person's point of view, they are able to internalize a **pleaser** that will navigate the complex geometry of in-groups and out-groups and redirect retreating or aggressive energies.

When misinformation is acquired through constant repetition or sudden trauma, benign trustees can turn into misers of convention, security, success, self-sacrifice, and perfection. They lose their sense of connection to the core Self and faith in its executive ability. If a *self-soother* is inadequate due to abuse or neglect, then some people may look to addictions or defying others for comfort. Caretakers and cultures that are too confining, plant seeds for rigid inner *controllers* that suppress autonomy with shame and doubt. Environments and parents can inflate *protector* parts, making people aspire to perfection to prevent all mishaps. Significant others and societies that devalue recreation and relaxation grow internal *pushers* that are driven to achieve, succeed, and acquire material goods. Social groups and families that demand or model subservience, promote inner *pleasers* that are martyrs and wary of emerging selfhood.

Inner Critics *Ingest* Parental and Cultural Demands

As young people learn to soothe, control, protect, and prod themselves, and join with others, they will also incorporate or *introject* perceived parental and cultural qualities. The Latin origin of this word implies that other people's features or voices are "thrown inside." Such demands can be even more illogical and unreasonable than those of an actual person because they originate from a small child's fantasy.

These alien chunks of borrowed personality have great capacity to generate inner turmoil, even though their initial intentions are often well meaning. Their ultimate goal is to suppress impulses before they come under fire from outsiders. An inner **critic** is formed, always ready to assist the directors of self-control, protection, pushing, and subservience—*You are worthless, at fault, inferior, unlovable . . .*

Vignette 1: Sasha

Sasha was taking advanced classes for her university degree, and her very common fear of public speaking was becoming more of a problem. As she focused on the gut-wrenching feeling in her stomach, she heard an inner voice say, "You best be quiet. You won't use the right words, and you'll make a

(Continued)

mistake." A memory came of being the last one chosen to be on the school team, and the voice said, "You're not worth being picked."

Then she remembered the source of the ultimate feeling of worthlessness—her mother telling her she was a piece of crap. Sasha had been the feisty one in her home, but her mother's words silenced her when she attempted to defend her father or siblings. After a while, Sasha formed an internal "mini mom" that triggered a frightened part in settings where there was a remote possibility of coming under verbal fire. Although this inner voice's brutal words tied her stomach and tongue into knots, as a child, it saved her from fiery, dreaded maternal assaults.

Sasha's story has an interesting twist. When dealing with waiters or coworkers beneath her in the chain-of-command, she could be demeaning and demanding. Sasha had found another escape route from being "a piece of crap" by acting more powerful than others. The false self that lorded over people when it was safe to do so identified with her mother by following her dictate to "be better than."

Introjects are foreign voices that become naturalized citizens of the psyche because they think they can do a better job of preventing the child from being abandoned or attacked than the real Self. They usually develop to help an individual cope with a specific problem or situation (Watkins & Watkins, 1997). Although these monologues are cruel and tiresome, they remain in residence because the person has lost touch with his or her core that knows alternatives to these self-defeating statements. When Sasha's true Self was coached to validate her critic by saying, "Long ago, it really was dangerous to speak out" (hypnotically implying that now it *is* safe); she felt a new freedom. No matter how familiar their voices become, introjects always remain objects that frantically try to direct—*Don't say too much; don't say too little; keep busy; pray the right number of times . . .*

Introjects come from culture as well as from caretakers. Women can have inner martyrs telling them to be ladies-in-waiting, always ready to give unsolicited help. This can mystify the ruggedly independent part of men, which neither asks for, nor offers, assistance that could insult people still wanting to figure things out on their own (Gray, 1992). Poignant country music lyrics convey the burden placed on the pleaser in one young woman who imagined that leaving her boyfriend would kill him in a "Whisky Lullaby" (Brad Paisley, 2003).

Some religious or ethnic groups give the impression that making anything less than an A could indicate intellectual deficiency or that a random, wicked thought could imply moral depravity. Even formal education can instill an *inner stickler* that experiences accelerated stages of bereavement (shock, disbelief, pain, anger, but not acceptance) when it spies a misplaced apostrophe (Truss, 2003). The salt introjects rub in their own wounds offers motivation to find alternatives to their misguided messages—*You goofed.* The distracting voices that produce rigid traits bring strange comfort and little desire to change the refrain—*They are at fault.*

EMOTIONAL ENTITIES EMERGE FROM THE DEEP

The most obvious facets in young people are instinctual energies that form the kernels of *emotional entities*. Bubbling up from the (mammalian) midbrain like lava from a volcano, they seem to be vectors with velocity and direction: Sadness sinks, fear recoils, anger thrusts, love flows out, happiness rises, and tranquility rests. As children grow, experiences of mistrust, shame, guilt, and inferiority compound raw instincts. The internal critic's self-doubt is added to the mix, and some young people constrict themselves to avoid disgrace. But there are also be many positive incidents of success, excitement, and acceptance. Both experiences of wounding and wonder can be encapsulated in *emotional buttons* triggered by certain persons and life events. Internal directors to control, push, and appease are needed to manage these emotional entities.

Emotional Entities Are Transformed by Trauma

Personas, character traits, and subpersonalities develop over time. Instinctual energies are inborn. However, during trauma new emotional entities can be created instantaneously due to sudden changes in neurotransmitters, which freeze images, thoughts, feelings, and sensations occurring at the time of the event (Shapiro, 2001). The terror and rage that is experienced is locked into separate emotional entities, and new voices form to direct them with such dictates as—*You're at fault, not safe, or trapped*. Thinking they have to protect the Self in this way, they contaminate the core Being.

Vignette 2: Alice

The corners of Alice's mouth turn down in utter disgust. She cannot rid herself of haunting images of her stepfather sliding his hand between her legs in the family car. Worse yet, an inner voice called "Mr. Nasty" taunts her by saying, "You enjoyed it!" Unlike many young girls, Alice told her mother what her stepfather had done, and she found out there are worse wounds than molestation. Her mother's twisted interpretation of events—"You know you liked it"—flooded her brain with a chemical reaction that wrapped disturbing images and sensations in words that made no sense. Alice's disclosure did stop further incidents, but Mr. Nasty lurked inside making her feel responsible for her stepfather's perversions. Paradoxically, this condemnation also gave her a sense of control. If she punished herself sufficiently, she might be good enough to keep future events from happening. As a bonus, the blame she heaped on herself kept her rage at her mother at bay while she still depended on her.

Alice's Mr. Nasty had the subvocal words that continually triggered an emotional entity to reexperience images, sensations, and disgust. No one ever told Alice when she was young that her mother's thinking was distorted, so Mr. Nasty's sense of his power to protect became inflated. She could not hear the soft whisper of her true Self that knew this inner critic was trying to help her be good (and safe) by making her feel bad. Therefore, it was hard for Alice to become Self-reliant instead of relying on Mr. Nasty.

Emotional Entities Become Emotional Personalities

When trauma is severe enough, an emotional entity can break off or disassociate into an *emotional personality* (EP) that carries a sense of *not-me-ness*. Emotional personalities were identified in the 1940s by psychologists studying World War I combat soldiers who had experienced extreme, life-threatening situations. When triggered, an EP reexperiences overwhelming events as though they are happening in the present with visual images, sensations, and motor activity related to the incident. These flashbacks may not be exact duplications of the occurrence. They can include fantasy, misperceptions, exclude parts of the event, and carry a sense of timelessness and changelessness.

This reexperiencing is not a normal memory with a verbal narrative. While EPs are active, people may not be able to access their usual memories, factual knowledge, and even skills; they may assume defensive postures and walk backward (Nijenhuis, Van der Hart, & Steele, 2004).

If trauma is early or severe enough, an EP can form its own identity in what is called Dissociative Identity Disorder (DID). The person may develop a propensity to create other EPs called *alters*. Each alter assumes demeanors appropriate to their identity and their memories. Even understanding of current events will be related to the time the alter was acquired, rather than present-day reality. Such victims of trauma also have an *apparently normal personality* (ANP) whose function is to avoid traumatic memories, detach, numb experiences, and provide partial or complete amnesia (Nijenhuis et al., 2004).

The ANP is a master at keeping EPs separate by applying the gamut of dissociation: losing a sense of self (depersonalization), detaching from the external world (derealization), reliving a complete overwhelming event (flashbacks), or developing separate identities (alters) that operate under the guise of amnesia. The ANP's agenda is to keep EPs out of sight and out of mind where they remain broken pieces of self that are too isolated for teamwork, disputes, or inner monologues. They compete for attention in an isolated way.

Vignette 3: Donna

Donna had been in treatment and diagnosed with DID. She neither liked nor wanted to believe this diagnosis but memory lapses, strange writing in a foreign hand, and involuntarily walking backward into walls made her a willing participant in therapy. While Donna calmly explained to her counselor that she did not believe she could have been molested and penetrated by the father she idolized (who had protected her from her cold, attacking mother), her arm involuntarily grabbed a pen and scrawled, "She's lying." This was only the beginning of many strange occurrences that did not always match textbook descriptions of how people with DID were supposed to behave.

Donna's alters became more insistent that the incest had occurred. They knew better than to speak to Donna who found their ideas too threatening, and she claimed amnesia for the information they conveyed to her counselor. Donna's denial was based on her father's calm negation that he ever abused her and on what she believed were incongruities between the places where her alters said the abuse occurred and her memory of the location of her bedroom in the house of her youth. Grasping at straws, her counselor asked if she would like to talk to a distinguished older man who had been in treatment for molesting his daughter. Donna was intrigued.

The interview and Donna's questioning of the admitted incest offender was progressing smoothly. Then Donna asked him how old his daughter was when he first molested her. When he replied that she had been about 10 years old, Donna became contorted. Limbs twisted into impossible shapes, and a high-pitched voice screeched, "He's lying; he *should have* started when she was younger!" Donna—the attractive middle-aged woman who was a pillar of society, was married to an attorney, and performed countless volunteer hours for her synagogue—transformed into an eerie alter who complained that if Donna's father had not started molesting her when she was a baby, then it would never have come to exist to help the weak, miserable child (that Donna had become) through countless hours of pain.

The gulf between Donna and this unnamed alter was huge. Like an ordinary introject, alters develop to cope with a specific situation, but once created, they are highly motivated to continue their existence. Because Donna's ANP used amnesia to deny her abuse, she could not go inside herself to appreciate this part's strength and willingness to be there for her when she was so young. Although Alice's Mr. Nasty was an inner voice that she could calm by silently saying, "You're repeating accusations that Alice's mother made," Donna's alter had formed at a much earlier stage in her development and during circumstances of continuous, horrific abuse. It had no understanding of present-day reality and was convinced that Donna depended on it for survival.

CORPORATE SELF

Now that the origins of the directing voices, distracting messages, and emotional energies of the triune personality have been explored, their identities and interactions can be described more fully. An extension of the metaphor of *The Corporate Self* presented earlier (Figure 1.6) focuses on the directors, inside agitators, and workforce; while the functions of the corporate officers are minimized (Figure 3.1).

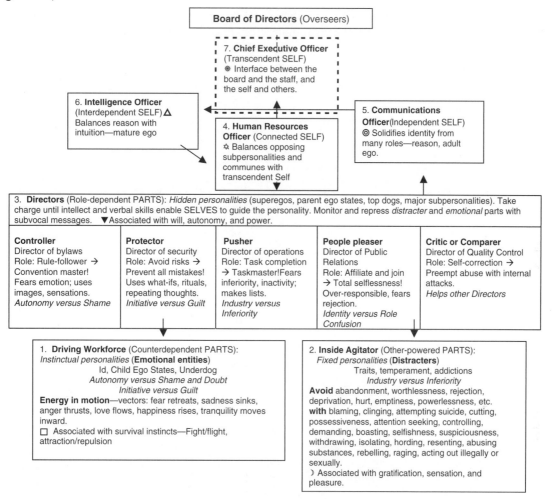

Figure 3.1 The Corporate Self: Organization of *Parts* and *Selves*. *Note:* Analogy to corporate structure from Carter McNamara (2003). The *Board of Directors* is totally spiritual and beyond the scope of this work. Numbers 7–1 correspond to the *chakras* (energy centers) found in Yoga—☀ △ ◉ ✿ ▼ ☽ □.

DIRECTORS MANAGE EMOTIONAL ENERGIES AND DISTRACTING TRAITS

The *corporate directors* or hidden personalities were first named "the superego" by Freud and more recently, "the Parent ego state" by Eric Berne (1964). Fritz Pearls (Perls, Hefferline, & Goodman, 1951) called them "top dogs" that were righteous, authoritarian, and prone to threaten catastrophes. Whether directors carry cultural values or more personal parental demands, they appear to have a good understanding of power.

In the Yoga tradition, they would seem to emanate from the 3rd chakra (energy center) located in the solar plexus (just below the diaphragm) that rules will, autonomy, and, of course, power. Interestingly, this is also the location of a person's navel—a convenient place for family values to travel through an imaginary umbilical cord that can never be cut.

Director personality parts have gained a *third-person perspective*. Like an audience watching players in the theatre of the mind, they are able to internalize the roles they are viewing. Faulty stories and dictates are acquired from caretakers who, themselves, may have been dominated by one or more of these hidden parts. A discussion of the misguided messages that commonly attach to each director follows next.

Controller

The job of mastering body functions and the basic rules of society was originally assigned to the *controller* or *director of bylaws*. Having a good appearance and mature behavior are essential. Angry outbursts, crying spells, emotional displays, and sexuality are unacceptable! The rule of thumb is to look *normal* and stay away from unconventional ideas. The controller will trigger vivid imagery, repetitive thoughts, and queasy sensations to keep distracters and emotional energies in line.

Vignette 4: Jaleigh

Jaleigh, who we met in Chapter 2 (Vignette 2 and Vignette 6), was tormented by the sight of police, their cars, and the sounds of sirens ever since her husband had called 911 when she had taken a handful of pills during a marital dispute. Jaleigh vented easily about her husband's failure to realize that she was not making a real suicide attempt, the terror she felt when the officer (inappropriately) locked handcuffs on her arthritic limbs, and the dehumanizing manner of the psychiatric ward staff. She was not used to looking inside. Her therapist gave her a choice of several malevolent props to represent the *inner* part that kept replaying these terrorizing images. Jaleigh picked a toothy rubber rat to portray the vicious tormenter.

Her therapist spoke for the rat, "Every time you hear a siren, I flood you with memories of what happened—that nasty officer, those handcuffs, sitting alone in the car, the way the staff treated you. . . ."

"But why does it do that?" asked Jaleigh, finally ready to look inside.

Her therapist encouraged, "Go inside and ask it (the ratlike part)."

Jaleigh's raised eyebrows erased confusion from her face. "It wants to keep me from 'stepping over the line.' It's afraid I'll go off and take another handful of pills!"

Jaleigh started yelling at the rat to stop giving her such a hard time—her usual modus operandi. Quickly grabbing another prop, her therapist, placed an angel bear in her hand and said that the real Jaleigh could not help the rat by yelling at it. She suggested simply telling the rat that she knew it was terrified Jaleigh would do something wrong.

Now fully into the drama, the rat was moving about saying, "But she gets so out of control!"

The therapist mentioned that the rat sounded apprehensive, and Jaleigh spontaneously had the angel bear pet it and lovingly tell it that she knew it was worried.

It took considerable determination on the part of Jaleigh's therapist to keep her focused on the director that was creating such inner havoc instead of the mean-spirited police and hospital staff who had mistreated her. This director, whose job was to keep her following the rules of society, had become terrified by a distracter part that grabbed a handful of pills to hijack a marital dispute. Now Jaleigh's controller would click on internal cuffs at a glimpse of a police car or the sound of a siren. If she reverted to blaming her husband and law officers for her problems, she would remain caught in an endless cycle of trying to control factors she could not change, instead of simply noticing the voices of her dictatorial director—"Don't step over the line." It is no wonder that this part played such a strong role within Jaleigh, because her mother was a controller, *par excellence*, monitoring every move she made.

Protector

The *protector* or *director of security* was originally assigned the task of stopping ventures that are too risky for young people who are learning how to master the world around them. As children test the interplay of cause-and-effect reality, they also learn social rewards and punishments. This is a confusing time. Children, who do not know the extent of their own power, can be prone to guilt. When President Kennedy was assassinated, the White House received many letters from youngsters confessing that their misdeeds had caused the horrible event.

With its ever-ready weapon of shame, the protector is on the prowl—monitoring and evaluating danger, and looking for imperfections. When a protector becomes inflated, it cannot distinguish between the precision needed to prepare a rocket for launching and the inexactness inherent in everyday life tasks. The protector's job is to prevent a person from having observable flaws, taking *any* wrong action, making mistakes, and on and on.

Often protectors specialize, particularly in the case of Obsessive Compulsive Disorder (OCD). Many check repeatedly to ensure that doors and windows are locked or that ovens and irons are off. Others are concerned that all household items be in perfect order, lest visitors think they are slobs or that they have succumb to a paralyzing depression. Other security directors engage in continual *germ warfare:* Surfaces and bodies cannot merely be wiped or washed but must be decontaminated. Some protectors are closely allied with controllers and fear an emotional part will go berserk and harm those they love most or act out in some obscene fashion. With the twisted logic that directors are so good at employing, they prevent such a catastrophe with murderous or sexual images. There are very creative protectors: One constantly looked for snakes under his bed or sofa, another was on cat patrol wherever she drove—it was her duty to save all felines from becoming roadkill. Then, there was Julie . . .

Vignette 5: Julie

Julie was excited about her new kitchen floor. Unlike the vinyl and linoleum of old, it was colorful, shiny, and engineered with a combination of polymers to be resilient to stains. But the long, hot Florida summer came and Julie made a discovery: The particular flooring *she* had chosen felt sticky in the heat on bare feet. Try as they might, Julie's friends and family could barely notice this stickiness, but Julie's protector was concerned that she had made a grave consumer error. Then, buying new sheets became a problem—would they be soft enough? Her protector listened late into the night for noises suggesting that household items might be faulty, forcing her to face the challenge of finding appropriate replacements. Anxiety breeds anxiety, and Julie became riddled with dread until she began taking medications that effectively dampened her fears.

One might wonder about Julie's upbringing. Had she been blasted by constant criticism and demands for perfection? Her father was a rigid man who knew how to pinch a penny, but this could not explain all of Julie's problems. What was unique was her ability to play piano by ear and discern sounds others missed.

Today, Sensory Integration Disorder (SID) is recognized in people who are hypo- or hypersensitive to outside stimuli. Hypersensitive people are literally bombarded by environmental stimuli. A protector would be put on high alert trying to make sense of overwhelming sensations. The inner commotion might be interpreted as germs or slithering reptiles. Special demands for outer order might be made to quell inner chaos. Sometimes, the repetitive thoughts and rituals of OCD may be secondary to an underlying SID.

Although Julie never faced her critical voices through talk therapy, others have found relief without medication. There are methods that help people learn to desensitize themselves to the onslaught of stimuli that contribute to OCD and SID. One woman took charge of her overzealous protector by picking up a sharp object every time it told her she might stab her beloved husband to show it that she could hold a "weapon" and do no damage. The man whose inner terrorist kept warning him there might be a snake slinking under the sofa, found a brave part that would stick his arm just where the serpent was supposed to be, proving that no harm waited. But protectors are not limited to OCD.

Vignette 6: Jenny

Jenny waltzed into her new therapist's office, feeling immediately at home with the stuffed animals that lined the shelves of one bookcase. She spotted Eeyore, explaining that she had a shrine devoted to him at home with all-things Eeyore. (One Internet site has over 1,400 Eeyore fans worldwide, which may only be the tip of the iceberg, considering that many do not have a passport to cyberspace. The reason for this Eeyore following will become apparent shortly.)

Jenny's therapist encouraged her to take Eeyore with her to her seat as she began explaining that she wanted coping skills for her mother's impending death. It did not take much detective work to discover that Jenny had a gloomy (Eeyore) part inside that kept flashing warnings: "The time is coming! It won't be long now (before she dies)." Her therapist asked Jenny to go inside and find out why Eeyore was constantly making such predictions. Still caught up in Eeyore-logic, Jenny announced, "So I won't be so scared and hurt when she does die."

To help Jenny dis-identify with Eeyore, her therapist began discussing how Winnie-the-Pooh would handle the situation: He'd just be there for a dying parent (as he was always there for his friends), notice the changes that were taking place, and make new discoveries. Jenny pointed out that it seemed like Eeyore and Pooh had each been cut in half and stuck together, giving a perfect description of how the core Self can become contaminated. Now, identified with her true Self, Jenny explained, "Eeyore has been giving me a double-edged sword—he is trying to prepare me, but the way he does it is very painful." This realization gave her great calm.

Jenny is an adult in her mid-twenties and like many other grown-ups who fret, complain, and try to prepare for (and protect themselves from) the worst, she feels a strong affiliation with Eeyore.

Pusher

The desire to master body functions is almost innate. A *pusher* or *director of operations* will be needed to acquire the myriad of academic skills needed to survive in the world. Its special weapons are forebodings of being left behind, of being inferior, and of accomplishing nothing. This puritan does not like the positive emotions—happiness, love, and tranquility—any of which could prevent a person from keeping his or her nose to the grindstone.

The director of operations can have people make endless lists, give them repeating nightmares that it's time for final exams and they have not cracked a book, and keep them up late, trying to pack extra hours into a day. As it takes over more of a person's inner life, the pusher becomes power hungry—compulsively accumulating wealth or advancing career options, yet forever feeling as though nothing has been accomplished. It is so important to give laid-back parts some freedom that when people do not, they can draw a spouse or child into their lives to be lazy for them; or they may give up in a state of total exhaustion (Stone & Stone, 1989).

Vignette 7: Betty

Betty (Chapter 1, Vignette 2) was in her usual dither. An exceptional first grade teacher, she was frustrated that the school had been slipshod in putting a new child in her class (without giving her any prior information) so that she could properly prepare for him. She was starting to unfurl a list of to-dos when her therapist asked Betty to "go inside" and ask her taskmaster (silently) if it thought there were limits to what Betty could accomplish.

Betty reported, "It's saying, 'You're making an excuse.'"

Her therapist prompted, "Ask it why it thinks Betty would make excuses."

Betty smiled. Now she knew who the taskmaster was. "My sister is always calling me asking—*Have you done this; have you done that?* When we were young and my father got sick, she took over as the mother hen, and I offered the family comic relief. But, when I did not do my part, those were her words—"You're making an excuse."

Since Betty had been in treatment, she had suffered a horrible case of shingles, and after they passed, a plague of wicked, never-ending migraines. Through all this excruciating misery, Betty pushed on, refusing to give in to the pain. A week after this session, Betty came to therapy in a full leg cast. She had fallen and sustained a clean break just below her knee; her body had finally succeeded in slowing her down.

Pleaser

Unlike the pusher that wants to accumulate knowledge, achieve, and compete; the *pleaser* or *director of public relations* is concerned with the important tasks of affiliating and belonging. In the female form, she is cheerful, nurturing, and loving; but she can rescue the needy, *always* be available, and give until depleted. The male pleaser is steadfast, understanding, humorous, and responsible for everyone and everything.

These caretakers have difficulty setting limits, saying *no*, and are drawn to (or create) helpless, needy, chaotic spouses and children. Pleasing parts attempt to control angry emotional energies that are inclined to become fed up with their servitude. They confuse independence with isolation. Fears of abandonment, rejection, and being unlovable are their ultimate weapons, and they can switch roles, becoming helpless, needy, and ill to keep loved ones tethered to them. Without help, a person's pleaser will prevent him or her from experiencing the very connectedness he or she seeks.

Vignette 8: Tony

Tony is a people pleaser. He came to therapy because his wife wanted to consider reconciling after they had been separated briefly. Although Tony had found the separation excruciating, he had survived it and wasn't sure he wanted to endure more heartbreak with this same woman.

(Continued)

His first concern was the anxiety he felt around other people. He quickly identified a part that told him not to say anything that might arouse anger or disapproval—a tactic that helped him avoid the ire of his judgmental parents. With his therapist's help, he was able to dialogue with this part and discovered that when he simply told it, "You're feeling worried," he felt more at ease—identifying an inner Self, "At Ease."

In time, a woman at work began showing an interest in Tony. Still discovering the benefits of being on his own, he somewhat reluctantly ventured back into the dating world. Tony would report to his therapist that he could actually witness the people pleaser taking over; especially robbing him of intimate moments with thoughts like, "You might not be touching her right. . . . I wonder if she likes what you're doing now."

Tony had connected with a core Self, capable of observing and learning the words to calm his pleaser so he could truly bond with others.

Critic

Unlike the controller, protector, pusher, and pleaser, the *critic* did not evolve from developmental crisis gone awry. This inner bully is an amalgamation of every despairing comment, ruthless remark, and even constructive criticism deposited into the files of the *director of quality control*. It preempts further torment from those outside with constant correction within. Sasha (Vignette 1) interjected a "mini mom" to tell her she was a piece of crap, making her mute in settings where authorities might render more verbal attacks. Then there was Alice (Vignette 2), whose "Mr. Nasty" kept punishing her until she became a mousy girl with downcast eyes, unlikely to experience further sexual experiences of any kind.

Physical appearance, intelligence, and lovability are all fair game for the critic. It reviews behavior hours or days after an event, making embarrassment linger. A constant comparer and expert tag-team player, it works in league with the other corporate directors. When Jenny's gloomy protector (Vignette 6) tried to prepare her for her mother's death with constant reminders that "the time is coming" and "it won't be long." It also told her that "she would not be good for anything" and that "she would be hopeless and helpless" (after her mother's death). Was this the voice of her protector flashing out warnings or her critic afraid that her all-powerful, picky mother had left her with no legs to stand on? In the following vignette, identify the point where the critic deftly steps in.

Vignette 9: Karen

Karen (Chapter 1, Vignette 6) had not had any visits from the Reverend Oscar Charles Dawson (OCD) in a long time, but she was concerned. Her husband was planning a trip out of town in a few weeks, and being alone at home was the circumstance that incited the first barrage of brooding about all the heinous acts she might be inclined to commit. The Reverend Dawson was summoned into the session to elicit the particulars of how Karen might kill herself: Would it be with a knife in the kitchen, a razor in the bath, or ramming her car into an oncoming truck on the road? Without her husband at home to save Karen from herself, who knew what she would do!

Yes, these red alerts made sense. Karen's mother had always been timid and watchful, cautioning her not to stand out in the mountain community where she grew up. But then Karen announced—"I shouldn't even be having these thoughts! What kind of depraved person gets such violent images?"

Just as Karen was about to understand how the Reverend Dawson was desperately trying to internalize the protector role acquired from her mother, the voice of the critic emerged. In other therapy sessions, Karen had felt compassion for the Reverend Dawson's frantic maneuvers. But now, on the eve of her husband's departure, the corporate superegos were not ready to trust her inner Self to simply enjoy time alone and explore all the nooks and crannies of freedom. They pulled out their big gun, the critic, with vague allusions to pervasive evil.

INSIDE AGITATORS DISTRACT

The *inside agitators* or *fixed personalities* are commonly recognized as dependent, arrogant, and avoidant **traits**. In some cases, these tendencies engulf the whole personality. People become the characters they are playing in the theater of mind, giving them a *second-person perspective*. Identifying with the demanding, docile, oppositional, or suspicious features of a caretaker, they can only see through their eyes. This means they are *other powered* and need outside sources for security, worth, and power. They tune out director personality parts with their (third-person) you-better, you-have-to rules and project those outward—"They better . . . , They have to . . ."

They distract any corporate parts that are sad or fearful with binging on alcohol, drugs, and food; shopping; gambling; and other enticing behaviors. Even self-mutilation (which releases endorphins) and suicidal thoughts (which hold the promise of escape) are within their repertoire. They transform anger (triggered by the loss of power) into long-lasting blame, bitterness, and resentment—a strangely self-satisfying ploy. Their use of self-gratification, sexuality, sensation, desire, and (impulsive) movement ties them to the second chakra that Yoga masters locate in the abdomen or lower back near the sex organs.

When directors become dictatorial in the demands they place on emotional parts to be in control, to perform, and to please; distracters offer relief with comforting indulgences or blaming. This creates a vicious cycle because it gives directors more ammunition for criticism. These inside agitators can take over the corporate self with avoiding tactics, substance abuse, and addictions to people by clinging.

Vignette 10: Eli

Eli's mother had abandoned the family when he was young. His father tried to raise him single-handedly, but ultimately, he was placed in foster homes, some of which were arbitrary and cruel in their punishment. He longed for weekend visits from his father.

In his late 50s, Eli sought help for the impossible love-hate relationship he had with his girlfriend Jezzy. Eli was a people pleaser to the core and would paint Jezzy's house, manicure her lawn, and pay some of her bills, hoping for a few crumbs of affection. This uneasy balance almost worked, until he realized she had been unfaithful to him in a wanton display of sexuality—a side of herself that she only gave begrudgingly to Eli.

The horror stories of Jezzy's abuses were never ending, but occasionally he'd ask, "Why do I put up with her?" Eager to hear the subvocal voice that made Eli a slave to Jezzy, his therapist would start to make an intervention. Before she could form her words, Eli would say, "Let me tell you just one more thing Jezzy did."

Past attempts to leave Jezzy were made by finding other women using Internet dating services. She could sense Eli was distancing, and like a bloodhound, Jezzy would sniff out the other woman and tell her that Eli (her boyfriend) was married and being unfaithful. Just as he clung to Jezzy, Eli sought other woman to be his life raft to avoid the waves of feelings of abandonment that might wash over him.

Like Tony (Vignette 8), Eli aims to please, but his dependent traits are powered by a need to find security and distract him from terrifying fears of abandonment. Tony has merely internalized a part that will help him belong by warning him not to say *anything* that would cause disapproval. He might have easily mastered the developmental task of affiliation, but an internal critic pushed his pleaser into overdrive to diminish unceasing parental scolding. However, his earliest needs were met well enough that he is not tightly tethered to others. Eli's identity is based on having a woman to cling to, while Tony's internal pleaser is triggered into action depending on the circumstances.

WORKFORCE SUPPLIES ENERGY AND EMOTIONAL FUEL

From the 1920s to the 1960s, the emotional personality parts bore the name *Es* (German) or *Id* (Latin) to represent a person's most primitive instinctual urges of sexuality, aggression, and the desire for instant gratification or release. This Freudian view is similar to the Yogi conception of the first chakra at the base of the spine that is related to raw energy and peoples' instinctual nature. Eric Berne (1964), who expanded on Freud's theories, did not necessarily see emotional parts as stemming from inborn instincts and drives, but from internal childhood feelings encapsulated in a "state."

This text views emotions, born from instinctual *drives*, as the driving force of the corporate Self. Even childhood feeling states can supply tiny stores of bubblelike energy cells that easily pop under certain circumstances. The basic emotions of fear, sadness, anger, love, happiness, tranquility, and the many varieties thereof, supply a multitude of energizing and calming feelings. Controlling directors and disruptive distracters may, indeed, try to manage or numb these energies, but they will continue to rise, sink, flow, recoil, thrust, and rest at any opportunity; which merely keeps directors and distracters employed.

In the theater of the mind, these survive-at-all-cost energies take the first-person perspective, thinking they are the only players on the stage. They barely know other parts exist, much less understand their points of view. This is why they require so much management, originally from caretakers and then from internalized directors, which earns them the title of being *counterdependent*[2] in their fight for a premature independence.

Even though babies have some ability to be self-regulating, until higher facilities of intuition and reason can use subvocal language, it may be too much to expect these Higher Selves to take on management functions. Emotions that have been unduly stifled can explode into monstrous rage. Stress, early trauma, or a genetic deficiency of brain chemicals may require medication to rebalance moods. But generally, spirited talking, crying, shaking, striking out, and even yawning will release blocked feelings so driving energies can return to their mission of fueling the corporation.

Vignette 11: Sasha

Sasha (Vignette 1) was awaiting her husband's arrival at the airport. She keenly observed the greetings people exchanged as they met at the concourse: A young woman was swept up in her lover's embrace, a child threw a tantrum while his father turned to hug his wife, and eyes lit up as two friends caught sight of each other. Then Sasha saw her husband—his cell phone (the badge of being a corporate vice-president) was perched between his ear and shoulder, and as he came closer his arm stretched forward, palm toward her to ward off any advance she might make. She did not say anything, but inside felt a deep

(Continued)

---

[2] The figures in Chapter 1 that show how the Self "involutes" from symbiosis to transcendence, name stages to show the progression toward and beyond independence: symbiosis → counterdependence → other powered → role dependent → independent → interdependent → integrated → transcendent.

hurt and anger; she had been robbed of the punctuation that was supposed to mark such marital greetings. Her therapist asked if she could talk to the part that was hurt.

The ready reply came, "I just feel like throwing things when I get ignored!"

The emotional part was given an ample supply of stuffed objects—handy missiles to aim at the opposite chair. Her therapist supplied the sound track: "That's no way to treat your wife. . . . How could you ignore me like that!"

Sasha joined in: "I want what I want, when I want it!" But, then a sheepish look came over her face.

Her therapist asked what part of her had just stepped in. Sasha replied that she knew she was being *unreasonable*. The word "unreasonable" caused her therapist to think that a logical Self had intervened rather than a controlling director, and she began coaching this true Self. Grabbing a small doll with permanently affixed tears, her therapist placed it in within Sasha's reach. She asked Sasha to go inside and tell her hurt part she knew it had good reason to feel wounded as a child; that it is totally understandable that it would be triggered now. (This crying doll is a prop that has earned its reputation for connecting people to sensitive energies.)

Sasha took the doll on her lap and said, "Why she's crying! She's so hurt and she is inside of me."

A trickle of tears began to well up and, with encouragement from her therapist, Sasha began to breathe and make noise, and then the snivels became sobs. As Sasha held the doll, her therapist held them both, feeding words for Sasha's inner Self to repeat, "You were looking forward to seeing him so much, and then he pushed you away, and it brought up all that worthlessness."

"I just want my husband to understand," she pleaded. Her therapist asked her to go inside to see if she could locate her true Self that does understand—completely, totally, and in a way that, perhaps, no other human ever will grasp.

NAMING PARTS TO RETURN
TO THE TRUE SELF

Like many clients who seek therapy, Sasha first presented the common but amorphous goal—*I want to find myself*. As the journey of her life unfolded, she had lost a sense of who she was, and no wonder: The triune governors of her personality, meant to serve Higher Selves, had become her masters. A director designated for feedback and self-correction had morphed into a critical dictator (Vignette 1) with subvocal messages that told her not to dare to speak in large groups lest she become the target of a phantom, faultfinding authority figure. Her repertoire of confident behavior had become a demeaning, demanding distracter, ever ready to give a quick shot of self-worth when it could lord over subordinates (Vignette 1). A wounded emotional entity (Vignette 11) poised to exude love had been rebuffed by a hand gesture, sank into a well of despair, and ricocheted back as the rage of rejection, keeping her controlling director well-occupied—muting anger into sarcastic snipes and cool glances.

It is easy to see how these directors, distracters, and emotional entities could spin into a mental merry-go-round, making people lose their ways. But inner Selves are not so easily daunted. They had turned that merry-go-round into a gyroscope that pointed Sasha to a therapist's office where she could step through her own looking glass to start the first steps suggested by Herman Hesse in the chapter quote of "dismembering the personality and finding missing parts." Sasha's core Beings had begun to adopt a benign attitude by validating her inner critic's attempt to protect her in a time when it was dangerous to speak out (Vignette 1); seeing through her arrogant distracter's vain attempts at vanity (Vignette 1); and comforting a wounded part's pangs of rejection (Vignette 11). These Selves might never incorporate and integrate so many parts so that Sasha would "become one with the All," but as she rediscovered her knowing, calm Core, she would, indeed, find her path and continue her journey through life. With their deeper perspective, transcendent, centered intuitive Selves can use the exercises in Chapter 4 to identify many personality parts to dis-identify with them and disarm inner voices with compassionate dialogue.

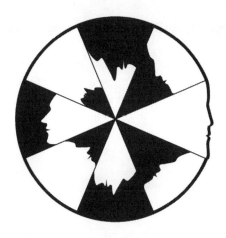

Chapter 4

Exercises for Identifying Inner Parts

Who's on first!
I mean, *What's* the fellow's name?
I just *don't know.* . . .

In one of the most famous baseball comedy acts ever to take place, Lou Costello's persistent efforts to find out the names of the players on the mythical St. Louis Wolves team causes total befuddlement.[1] The simple question, "*Who's* on first?" yields maddening answers. The chaos increases when a second baseman is identified by the question, "*What's* the fellow's name?" In a sigh of exasperation, Costello unveils a third mysterious player—"*I don't know.*" In mind games matching this kaleidoscope of players who elude identification, people often wonder what personality part is *on base* making subvocal comments.

The mandala on this page was designed by the author and interpreted graphically by Gavin Posey to show fragmented fixed personalities that interact with the world and hidden parts that direct from within.
[1] The complete text can be found by typing, *Abbott and Costello, Who's on First*, into any search engine.

This chapter begins in the spirit of Abbott and Costello to help identify the infielders and outfielders of the mind: inner **directors** that control and criticize; **distracters** that evade harsh messages; and **emotional entities** full of energy and impulses. To be a good coach, it is necessary to recognize these peculiar players and to know when Who, What, or I Don't Know is on base to help them assume the best possible stance.

PERSONAE—ADAPTABLE PERSONALITIES

People acquire many masks to improve their chances of acceptance in a multitude of settings. They do not have one persona or public relations personality, but many personae. The personality you wear when you are relaxing with your family may be very different from the one you assume as your professional self. Although not technically a personal part, it is important to become familiar with these adaptations. The Exercise 1 will help you realize how varied your outer roles have become. More important, you can discover which facades you value and any you want to avoid. By their very definition, personae are visible. Unless an identity is illegal or the target of contempt, changing faces should be facile, depending on the social setting.

Exercise 1

Identities

Simply write, "I am a(n) . . ." followed by a noun. Think of the many life roles that you play and list them—family positions (son, mother, grandfather, uncle, sister . . .) your occupation, avocation, (artist, writer, coach, dancer . . .), nationality, race, ethnic group, family name, gender, sexual orientation, religion, hobby (gambler, golfer, Trekkie . . .), interests (Red Socks fan, cat lover, movie buff . . .), physical distinctions (redhead, physically challenged, senior citizen . . .), earned titles (veteran, friend, divorcé, survivor, felon, alcoholic, smoker . . .), astrological sign, and so on.

After compiling a long list, notice which identities are most important to you—your occupation, family position, or avocation. What does that tell you about yourself? Do any of your identities seem to consume you so that you cannot drop a role when you are no longer in the appropriate setting? Do you need to learn how to become a good spouse or develop more interests so that one identity doesn't make you dull and dreary? Are you having boundary issues because you are still being a mother at work, thinking about work at home, or using street language with your parents? Are you missing some personae and finding it difficult to adapt in social settings? Are you resisting changing your role as your children become adults or your parents become dependent?

PERSONAE AND OPPRESSION

Do you have any identities of which you are ashamed? Imagine yourself standing in front of a large audience as you announce, "I am . . . (a rape survivor, a Jew, a transsexual, . . .)." You hear a thunderous applause. Then give this audience a talk about the three greatest advantages and disadvantages of having this title, what you want people to understand, and what changes society needs to make so you can be open with who you are.

The best way to fight oppression is by being visible whenever it is the tiniest bit safe to do so. If you are a person with a past, whether it is as a victim or as an offender, you have survived. Mentioning your experience casually at appropriate moments will help you reclaim yourself and open doors to the diversity in society for others.

If there are any former activities in which you no longer want to partake, imagine confessing them to the same large audience and telling them your plan to stop smoking, shoplifting, or defeating yourself in some other way. Feel the group's compassion and goodwill pouring out to you. If possible join an actual support group for this issue.

DISTRACTERS—FIXED PERSONALITIES

Parental characteristics are first imitated as a means of remaining attached to those on whom people depend. They form into organized patterns of behavior or traits that become our modus operandi for interacting with others. Temperament, which is also a part of a person's demeanor, is largely inherited. Unlike personae, which change as the situation demands, the mosaic of traits adopted (or inherited) from others will make up an observable facade, fraught with strengths and weaknesses in facing the world.

One of the "Guided Affective Imagery" (GAI) tasks developed by Hanscarl Leuner (1969; Exercise 10, Chapter 2) is ideally suited to produce imagery that reveals a person's manner of interacting with the world. The less you know about the exercise, the more telling it will be of inner truths.

Exercise 2

Dwelling Visualization

Imagine being in a meadow. Notice the color, length, and type of grass. Are there any other forms of vegetation or animal life? What time of day is it? What is the temperature? What feeling do you have as you lie down, sit, or walk in the meadow? Now begin moving through the meadow and shortly you will come to a dwelling or home.

Even if it seems familiar, this dwelling will be unlike one you have ever seen. Notice how it appears on the outside. How is it constructed? What color is it? Are there windows? What kind and how many? What is the door like? Does it have a handle or a knob? Is it hard to enter? Find a way into the dwelling. What is the first room you see? If there is a kitchen, look in cabinets or the refrigerator to find out if there is food. Is there furniture? How is it arranged? Are there bedrooms and bathrooms? How many? What kinds of beds do you find? Are there closets? What is in them? Is there an attic and basement? If so, see if you can discover anything of interest.

Image/journal your own dwelling before reading the vignette.

Vignette 1: Louise

Louise found herself in a pleasant meadow with a large tree. There was a horse running free and a fence. When asked to imagine a dwelling, she saw a shack in the distance. As she came closer, she noticed it was made out of wood. There was a dog at one side and a front porch. The shack was leaning. She easily entered the living room that was barren of furniture. The kitchen was to her right. The cupboards were empty but, when she opened the refrigerator, there was a carton of fresh milk. This seemed strange because Louise did not think there was electricity running to the shack. She found a bedroom to the left with a bare, double mattress and a TV that did not work. The closets were vacant. There was a second bedroom in the back of the living room. It had twin beds neatly made up with brightly colored comforters.

When Louise was told that the house symbolized her in some way, she was not surprised. She is the only one in her family who had made something of herself. Everyone relies on her, including her mother. All the relatives know when she gets paid, and the calls start coming. Louise felt this was why the shack was leaning and had been cleared of all its furnishings. Yet, the fresh milk suggested that *she* is the eternal source of nurture for the whole family. Louise also knew that the beautifully made up twin beds in the back bedroom are for her niece and nephew who are currently in foster care. They are innocent children who would be welcome any time.

Freud and others considered a house to be a symbol of the personality. Louise's tendency to give until she is depleted but still offer sustenance is well captured by her house. The spontaneous presence of the horse in the meadow might suggest love in Louise's life (Gottlieb & Pešić, 1995). The next vignette portrays a very unusual, but highly accurate self-image.

Vignette 2: Melanie

Melanie found herself in a meadow with light green grass and a few stray deer. When told she would find a dwelling, she reported seeing a cave. She said nothing blocked its entrance, and once she was inside, she found a brown bear that she believed represented the man she currently lived with. She said the bear was just there, not frightening and not interacting with her (much as he was in real life). She said the cave had just one large opening with no side chambers and that it was damp and dark inside. She could not find the source of the dampness—there was no spring to quench her thirst, nor was there any food.

Although her therapist was puzzled by this primitive dwelling, when she told Melanie that it was supposed to represent her in some way, Melanie said it made sense: She believed she did not have anything to offer people, and the only way she found men was by being sexually available. The vaginal symbol of a damp, dark cave represents the raw essence of her current behavior repertoire. The deer in the meadow may express her hope to have a dear one in her life.

When personal style is more problematic than promising, people can make alterations in outer garments, even if they have become suits of armor. Waking dreams are the perfect way to begin to envision changes. Melanie imagined a new home, the opposite of the one she had blindly created. She described it in first person.

I'm a fortress with two-foot thick stone walls. All visitors must be clearly identified. Only the most worthy are allowed to enter the castle at the center of the fort. The guard does not reject people on the basis of their position or wealth, but has the power to discern their integrity and truthfulness. There are many rooms in this splendid palace. Each room is dry and warmed by an enormous fireplace. There is a well-stocked kitchen and richly decorated sitting rooms and bedrooms, all designed to make the deserving guests feel welcomed. Yet, there are private chambers and secret passageways that guests could never find when time for solitude is needed.

Although Melanie's new home has many chambers, this does not suggest the presence of a multitude of subpersonalities, but instead, the capacity to have room for different people in her life and to be comfortable with herself. It shows an ability to be nurturing, attractive, and warm without becoming depleted. Had Melanie been asked to describe herself as beautiful and worthy she might have resisted. Creating a handsome well-endowed *symbol* for her personality was a far easier task and one that could unconsciously guide her future endeavors.

DISTRACTER VOICES

Distracter personality parts are vocal, but can be hard to recognize. People do not embrace hidden critics that wag contemptuous fingers at other inner parts. Complaining, blaming voices that focus on others' flaws offer strange comfort and are easily owned. They have the ring of truth (from the eye of the beholder) and are hard to stop once their discourse begins.

Vignette 3: Alex

Alex had not seen his therapist for a long time. He returned on his wife's orders because his mood had become dark and crabby. This man, who could excel at almost any occupation or avocation, was becoming mired in the *Mickey Mouse* theories that students majoring in elementary education are obliged to learn. He knew he was becoming lax in completing his assignments and slipping below what should be a 4.0 average.

He was on a roll with his litany of complaints about college classes, when his therapist pulled out a deck of tarot cards divided into piles. From the *distracter pile,* she asked him to pick cards that reminded him of his dark parts. He chose an exploding tower, a blindfolded person with crossed arms and swords extending from each clenched fist, and a person looking at seven cups containing alluring, frightening, and mysterious contents. He explained that these cards represented how ready he was to blow up, do battle, and look for diversions.

From another pile, he was asked to pick cards for the parts of him that are able to rise above petty annoyances. Alex explained that when he was *in the zone*, the card with the crowned sword held high above the mountains and the woman embracing a lion showed his firm resolve and his gentle compassion. From a third pile, he picked the Emperor, that reminded him of his controlling critical father, and a skeleton riding a white horse to represent his OCD, which was the original reason he sought treatment.

Alex said the dark cards were saying that he had to put up with a lot of crap (in college). His therapist suggested that the zoned-in cards might go inside and tell the dark parts (silently) that they knew how very tedious and trivial this course work was for him and how he felt as if he might bail out. Alex reported that the Emperor had jumped in and said he was a quitter.

His therapist encouraged Alex to use the zoned-in cards to reflect this concern, "You're afraid he'll quit, that he'll play the fool like he did as a child when school was too easy."

The Emperor retorted, "Yes, or that he'll leave like he did in nursing school, convinced that his professors didn't know anything!"

The Tower card (explosive part) chimed in, "I could just torch the place—the whole school of education!"

But the zoned-in cards spontaneously spoke, "You've matured a lot; you're really different now."

Not used to hearing encouragement from within, Alex said he felt like he was barely holding it together. His therapist asked him which card was "holding it together." After a brief moment's reflection, Alex replied that it was the critical Emperor.

His therapist mused, "I wonder when . . . you will be able to trust your true, zoned-in Selves, to help. Do you remember what they said to the dark cards?"

Alex was able to remember their words, which reflected but did not absorb: "We know this course work is so very tedious and trivial for you and that you feel as if you could bail out." He stopped himself short of adding a "but"—none was needed.

Alex's therapist knows nothing about tarot cards. She acquired them as a tool to encourage children to tell self-revealing tales. In need of a vehicle to help clients' inner parts and Higher Selves come alive, she was inspired one day to yank them out of her toy closet. Although Alex's focus on others can detour his treatment, his verbal skills keep therapists engaged and him in command of sessions. The cards were, indeed, effective in cutting through his verbiage and in helping him gain (as he said) a kinesthetic sense of his interior terrain. Distracter parts (that noticed his teachers' professional incompetence) distract Alex from achieving. He is a more sophisticated version of his ever-critical father. But Alex has begun to rediscover his true (zoned-in) Selves that can focus on goals and remain calm in the face of frustration. Exercise 4 on p. 4.8 offers practice identifying *Distractor Voices.*

DIRECTORS—HIDDEN PERSONALITIES

I think, therefore I have inner parts. With apologies to René Descartes for any plagiarism, discovering the directors that run our personality, is as simple as recognizing the voices we hear inside our heads all the time.

DIRECTOR VOICES

To internalize rules and roles, directors absorb information from people on whom youngsters depended and from society as a whole. These subvocalizations can become hardwired into the nervous system due to sudden changes in body chemistry during a traumatic event or from constant repetition. Distortions can occur and plant the seeds from which controlling, protective, pushy, compliant, and critical hidden personalities grow. Exercise 3 identifies the loud, redundant monologues these parts are inclined to deliver.

Exercise 3

Director Voices

Think of a current situation or memory that is upsetting. Ask yourself, "What bad thought does this situation give me about myself? How does that person 'make me' feel?"

When I feel . . . , I think I'm . . . For example:

- When I feel guilty, I think, "I'm bad or tarnished."
- When I feel sad, I think, "I'm lost, incomplete, or alone."
- When I feel angry, I think, "I'm not in control, a fool, or trapped."

Negative beliefs about yourself often start with the words, "I am" and are invested with "I" energy. You can begin to dis-identify with these thoughts by turning them into the very statements that were originally directed toward you, which started with the words, "You are . . . ," "You have to . . . ," "You cannot . . ." Use memories of upsetting situations or persons to identify cutting comments and diatribes that are triggered in your mind. Check any inner commentary that you *hear* in your worst moments on the list below:

Controller Voice
- ☐ You can't handle it, be trusted, or stand it.
- ☐ You cannot show emotions or speak up.
- ☐ You have to control things (yourself); you have to fix everything.
- ☐ You can't . . . ; you shouldn't have to . . .

Protector Voice
- ☐ You're not safe.
- ☐ You're trapped; you cannot tell, or speak up.
- ☐ You might (will) fail, get hurt.
- ☐ You cannot make a fool of yourself.
- ☐ You might get sick, not get better, die.
- ☐ You could do something awful.
- ☐ You cannot handle new, unfamiliar situations.
- ☐ You're responsible for others or everything.
- ☐ You (your judgment) can't be trusted.

(Continued)

☐ You can't trust others.
☐ You are (will be) ruined or damaged.
☐ You have to be perfect; you cannot make mistakes.
☐ What if . . . what if . . . what if . . . ?

Pusher Voice

☐ You have to . . . , you better . . . , you should . . .
☐ Have you done. . . . Have you done . . . ?
☐ You have to have what you want when you want it.
☐ You have to find excitement, a purpose, enough of what you want.
☐ You have to get it (done) *now.*

Pleaser Voice

☐ You have to please everyone.
☐ You (your needs) are not important; others come first.
☐ Others might not like how you sound, look, act . . .
☐ You could be abandoned.
☐ You need others; you're incomplete on your own.
☐ You're empty or alone.
☐ You have to make others love, understand, care for, or approve of you.

Critic Voice

☐ You're worthless, defective, disappointing, a failure, different, weak, dirty, or at fault.
☐ You're helpless, powerless, or a fool.
☐ You can't find love, caring, understanding, attention, approval.
☐ You don't deserve love, happiness, or to live.
☐ You're not good, smart, or attractive enough.
☐ You should have . . .

Keep a journal of the mental monologues that cloud your mind. If this chatter starts with "**I** should have . . ." or "Maybe **I**'m not . . ."; switch the wording to "**You** should have . . ." or "Maybe **you**'re not. . . ." You will know you are at the mercy of an inner director, and the act of writing will take away some of its steam.

Exercise 4

Distracter Voices

Exercise 3 can be slightly altered to identify the elusive distracter voices from the previous section. The word "**You** . . ." has been replaced with the word "**They**. . . ." Notice that the controller, protector, pusher, pleaser, and critic can just as easily face outward as inward. Instead of having an inner critic that says, "I don't know what I'm doing," a judgmental part might fume, "They don't know what they are doing!"

Be especially alert to ruminations that contain the words, *He should. . . . She never. . . . They always. . . .* "Should," "never," and "always" are red flags that signal a distracter is on the loose. Addict monologues have been added to the list below, because distracters love to soothe pain. Mark any words of blame control or judgment that sound familiar:

- ☐ **Controller Voice:** *They can't handle it. . . . They shouldn't be emotional. . . .*
- ☐ **Protector (perfectionist) Voice:** *They can't be trusted; they have no right to. . . .*
- ☐ **Pusher Voice:** *They have to . . . , better . . . , should. . . .*
- ☐ **Pleaser (clinger) Voice:** *They have to love, understand, be there for me.*
- ☐ **Critic (judger) Voice:** *They're disappointing, foolish, failures, weak, dirty, at fault.*
- ☐ **Addict Voice:** *This will be the last time I'll. . . . It won't matter if I. . . .*

Record rantings that begin with the words "They," "he" or "she," . . . This is especially effective in deflating a distracter. Even if its words offer false pride or tempting comfort, the act of writing is labor intensive and can condense a recital of grievances. Your rational Self may become engaged in the process of putting words on paper and be able to see through faulty logic.

EMOTIONAL ENTITIES—INSTINCTUAL PERSONALITIES

Emotional entities are best noticed through body sensations. The voices that seem to accompany them—"I don't know what to do" "I'm alone" "I'll never find anyone" "I might get hurt"—are really missiles from misguided directors saying—"You don't know what to do" "You're alone" "You'll never find anyone" "You might get hurt." It is their words that cause the heart to sink and the stomach to feel tight. They make muscle fight muscle: some trying to release emotions and others attempting to prevent just that. Tension in the eyes may be holding in tears; tightness in the temples can be clamping jaws together to prevent screaming or yelling; stiff shoulders and necks are often held in anger, rage, or hostility. Identifying the dictatorial words that accompany tension and learning how to dialogue with them (to be explained in Chapter 5) will take the pressure off emotional parts and give them relief.

Anger, the energy that thrusts outward, is expressive. Even though it may be covering a deeper hurt and fear, it can use words. Sasha in Chapter 3 (Vignette 11) had a part that said, "I feel like throwing things when I get ignored." But mad feelings can be tricky. Distracters—adept at noticing the *failings* of others—keep resentment, bitterness, and vengeance in their arsenal. One of Alex's dark parts (Vignette 3) said, "I could just torch the place." Was this a justified anger at having to learn trivial education theories or a rage that helped him avoid the critical ranting of his internalized father that mocked, "He'll leave like he did in nursing school. . . ." For less verbal parts, it is possible to use a *voice-over* technique to help them release budding tensions before distracters have a chance to crystallize tightness into tenacious bitterness and resentment.

Exercise 5

Teaching Emotional Entities to Talk

Scan your body to notice where you feel tightness, tension, or numbness. Increase tensions by deliberately contracting the muscles involved and add sound. Say, "No" "I won't!" "I'm resisting!" See how much noise you can make as you suck air in, growl from the back of your throat, or squeeze out a high-pitched sound. Slowly relax your muscles and open yourself to any feelings that surface whether it is a desire to cry, strike out, vomit, laugh, or scream. If it fits, use the words, "I'm sad, frightened, or mad!" (Wilber, 2004, pp. 114–119). Feelings can be released through a blocked area and travel on their merry way to infinity.

Young children need to be taught to verbalize feeling. They are given words for emotions—**sad,** rejected, hurt, disappointed, **afraid,** cautious, shy, suspicious, worried, embarrassed, terrified, startled, horrified, **angry,** furious, frustrated, disgusted, irritated, impatient, jealous, envious, guilty, ashamed, confused, **happy,** safe, relieved, excited, confident, satisfied, grateful, and loving. It is just as important for adults to identify the feelings that accompany quivering tummies, tightened throats, and tensed forearms. When an inner voice repeatedly predicts, "Your boyfriend is going to leave you," and ties your stomach in knots, a deep Self can whisper, "Your warnings are *terrifying* that emotional part—is that what you want?" This gives such energies an advocate until turning to the source of truth within becomes a regular practice.

IDENTIFYING INNER IMAGES

Realizing that endless dictates ("Stay in control," "Say the 'right' thing," "Do more work") and enticing editorials ("They don't know anything," "care enough," "hurt you on purpose") come from fragmented inner parts is a huge step. This allows people to regain their sanity by talking to themselves and turning incessant monologues into dialogues ("So what if I'm not in control," "I've matured since my quitting days," "Maybe I need to know others' viewpoints").

Is it important to go beyond inner voices and seek images that accompany them? *Identity* is the key word. The more fully personality parts are recognized, the better people can dis-identify from them. We are dominated by the things with which we identify. Saying, "I'm discouraged," or "I'm angry," places people under the rule of those emotions. A slight change in grammar—*A part of me is discouraged or angry*"—preserves the core Self and helps reconnect to the Inner "I" "We can dominate and control everything from which we dis-identify." (Assagioli, 1965/2000, p. 19). Putting a face on the words that inner controllers, protectors, pushers, pleasers, and critics use furthers the process of dis-identification. Parts revert to inner objects that can be faced, questioned, and redirected.

Concerns might be raised about the distinction between dis-identification and disassociation. In disassociation, an alter is created during early trauma that has a sense of not-me-ness with a separate identity that fights for control of the body (see Chapter 3, Vignette 3). It may not even want to cohabitate with other parts. Alternatively, subpersonalities have misguided messages, poor coping strategies, and stuck emotions. They are not trying to replace the Self, but to provide control, comfort, or energy where they think it is lacking.

Giving personality parts subtext, images, and *descriptive* names is for the purpose of making them more recognizable, not to create competing identities. Attaching thoughts and behavior patterns to graphic representation takes place under the auspices of a mature Self and is not a distraught reaction to an overwhelming childhood event. With the issue of disassociation laid to rest, subpersonalities can blossom into recognizable personifications.

EMOTICON IMAGES

You do not have to be an artist to find a face for personality facets that fill you with doubt and dread. Newly arrived from cyberspace, emoticons (sequences of keyboard characters often found in e-mails and chat rooms) are designed to turn an emotion into an icon. They express attitudes and personalities through simple combinations of colons, parentheses, brackets, dashes, slashes, and so on—often saying more with less.

Exercise 6

Faces of Inner Parts

Director Emoticons

}:^[	(8-\	>8-[	~:-I	>:^<
Controller	Protector	Pusher	Pleaser	Critic
"Don't ask for directions."	"You could get an attack and not be able to breathe."	"You haven't done enough."	"You might have upset someone."	"You're no good."

Return to Exercise 3 and note the comments you say to yourself in your worst moments. Create an emoticon that might go with each monologue. The ones above are suggestive of controlling, protective, pushy, pleasing, and critical directors.

(Continued)

Create your own faces in the blank boxes below by using combinations of the following keyboard characters—:; [] {} ~ ^ * ~ @ + I 8 0/—turned horizontally or vertically (whichever works best). Underneath each face, write the misguided messages that you frequently repeat to yourself—"You should have . . . " "If you say how you feel, others will . . . " "You could make a fool of yourself!" Then name the feeling caused by subtext.

(8>\				
Example: "You can't make a mistake."				
Afraid, worried				

Now, return to Exercise 4 and create an emoticon to represent distracter personality parts that try to blame, judge, and control others or tempt you. A few faces have been designed for you, but add your own.

Distracter Emoticons				
#:^0	>:-)~	|B'-()		
"He shouldn't curse!"	"Smoking pot calms your nerves."	"She has to love me!"		

Design an emoticon for your core Self that is untouched by dictatorial directors, wayward distracters, or emotional entities. Refer to Chapters 1 and 2 and use whatever names come to mind.

0:-)	;-D	8:-)}}	8-)	
Core Self	Still strong voice	Wise old man	Logic	

It may take time to gradually acquire a set of emoticons to represent the major players in your personality. Catch hidden directors in the act of making demands. Notice when you want to blame, judge, or avoid others and capture all these expressions with keyboard characters. Even when you cannot label an emotion, you may be able to record it as an emoticon face. Be sure to make an emoticon for your core Self.

When emoticons are drawn on the lower half of an unlined three-by-five card, they can be folded in half, and stood upright. Place them on a cleared surface in a way that represents their dominance in your inner psychic life. This can change daily. Also, pose these facets in the positions you would like them to take. Gradually, your core Self may take a more forward or central position and director, distracter, and emotional entities may turn to face a witness Self so they can benefit from its compassionate observations. The only rule is that you cannot destroy a part of yourself.

Vignette 4: Celia

Celia had had a rough 2 weeks. Her son asked her to stay with him during his court-ordered therapy session with his father via the telephone. Her stomach did a summersault just hearing the voice of the man who damaged her face and threatened to "get her some day." She bolted from the therapist's office. This man had been absent from her life for 2 years and had moved out of state, but it felt like he was coming through the walls. The legalese of domestic violence charges, restraining orders, divorce issues, and now this phone call beat Celia down, just as she was starting to be her vivacious, fun-loving self.

She sheepishly told her therapist, "You're going to think I'm crazy, but I hear voices in my head all the time. . . ." "If only I could get them organized." After being reassured that this was completely normal and even healthy, Celia proceeded to identify their various commentaries, and sketched emoticons to give an additional dimension to their remarks:

|8-C	(88-O	|:^ [	>:-<	;-)
"Rhonda Rerun" "What if he does this . . . ?" "What if he does that . . . just like he used to?"	*"Clara Clairvoyance"* "You have to know what is going to happen!"	*"Ms. Fix-It"* "You could have done something to keep the assault from happening."	*"The Should-er"* "You should have left sooner and not put your son through all this."	*"Ms. Whatever"* "OK, I've had enough of this nonsense . . ."

It became clear that "Ronda Rerun" was trying to prepare Celia for an any-case scenario by replaying old tapes that actually kept her immobilized. "Clara Clairvoyance" was another protector racking her brain to fathom the future. The pushy "Ms. Fix-It" did not have any suggestions, but kept poking and prodding, and the critical "Should-er" could bring out a tearful, defenseless part. Every so often, "Ms. Whatever" would pop up, turn the whole sorry business off, and Celia would have a life again. Celia started laughing, "This is so ridiculous. . . . It's such a circus."

Laughing at yourself or your inner parts is a true sign of enlightenment—of literally becoming lighter and shedding unhelpful misguided messages. Celia wondered how looking at this audio-visual display of personality parts was any different from hearing inner voices. Little did she know that *listening* to such thoughts, made her the target of their *what-ifs, have-tos, and should-haves*. Realizing that *a part* of her was saying, "What if . . . ," was the first step in dis-identifying with that voice and divesting it of power. Instead, she was now becoming identified with her witness-Self that can observe inner dramas, without becoming their victim.

DRAWINGS

Emoticons provide the bare skeleton of a face. This subtlety can add the needed touch to give life to subvocal messages. But for the artistically inclined, personality parts can be drawn to gain even more distance from them.

Exercise 7

Pictures of Inner Parts

Refer again to Exercises 3 and 4 and write a few of the phrases you use to torment yourself or blame others. Allow an image to come to your mind to represent a particular missive. Draw your own image before reading the vignette.

Vignette 5: Rebecca

After her second therapy session, Rebecca was excited to discover the personality parts that were creating havoc in her inner life. She returned a week later with a crayon-and-marker drawing, clearly showing the commotion that was pulling her in different directions. A part called "Cuffed" with green shackled arms, said little more than, "Click. . . . You're screwed." There was a blue "Judge" with folded arms that

(Continued)

scolded, "Tsk . . . Tsk . . . " "What were you thinking?" "Haven't you learned yet?" "Don't you know!?" "Mrs. Desirable," with her pretty face and makeup, seemed to go beyond the judge and snubbed, "You are so disgusting—kill yourself." Worse yet was "The Terrorist," a hollow-eyed ghoulish type that threatened not to speak his name and (perhaps) encouraged avoidance. No wonder "Past Bloom," a dying rose, hopelessly moaned, "It's not going to get better," and "Daddy's Girl" in pigtails with a tear-stained cheek pleaded, "I need help." Where were the bright spots in this dreary collage? "Miss Ohh" wearing glasses to put things in perspective said, "Wow . . . (this problem) doesn't really matter in comparison to the big picture." Finally, "The Presence" consoled, "I'm always watching, always here to comfort your crying heart."

Rebecca's drawing (Figure 4.1) shows the full panorama of the triune personality, ready to be guided by inner Selves. There are the **directors:** "Cuffed" controls, "The Judge" warns, and the critical "Mrs. Desirable" tries to squelch Rebecca, possibly into nonexistence, before she can be hurt by more vicious mudslingers in the real world. The nameless "Terrorist" encourages avoidance and may trigger **distracters** to relieve anguish. "Past Bloom" and "Daddy's Girl" are wells of hopeless,

Figure 4.1 Rebecca's Drawing (Exercise 7)
1. Controlling, protective, critical **directors:** Cuffed, The Judge, Mrs. Desirable.
2. Avoiding **distracter:** The Terrorist.
3. Hopeless, sad **emotional entities:** Past Bloom, Daddy's Girl.
4. Inner **Selves** to guide and comfort: Miss Ohh, The Presence.

4.14

sad **emotions.** They look to the past for comfort, while just above is "The Presence," an observant **Self** that will always be there, but may be too awesome for guidance yet. More immediate, in the very center of the composition, is "Miss Ohh," an intuitive **Self** that can put puny problems in their place. Just looking at Rebecca's drawing has helped many of her therapist's other clients recognize that they, too, have their own inner cast of characters.

TAROT IMAGES

It is not cheating to rely on the art of others when casting about for images of personality parts. If you have a wall hanging that gives you comfort or brings a smile to your face, it may be a good illustration for your core Self. Be aware of any pictures that remind you of your inner critic or a desperate, clingy facade.

A ready-made collection of artwork can be found in a tarot deck. Speculation on the origin of the word tarot is vast. There was an Egyptian mother goddess named *Tarut*. The Sanskrit word *Toran* means truth. Although some people have negative associations with cards used to tell fortunes, you will not be employing them for such a purpose.

The standard Rider-Waite deck was published in 1910 by Rider & Company in London. They were designed by Edward Waite and Pamela Colman Smith to communicate ancient principles through symbols. Although there are many varieties of tarot, it may be best to start with the Rider-Waite deck, which presents a balanced view of human nature and is not biased toward cats, angels, or fairy tales.

The Deck

A tarot deck consists of 78 cards. There are 22 major *arcane* (secret natures) with pictures symbolizing strength, temperance, sun, moon, star, and so on. These represent universal patterns of human thought and emotions that must be endured before a person's full potential can be reached. They are *mirrors* that reflect both unique individual interpretations and consistent, common reactions.

The rest of the deck is divided into four suits or lower natures—swords, cups, wands, and pentacles (or coins)—which correspond to the familiar spades, hearts, clubs, and diamonds. Each of the suits stands for a particular approach to life: (1) intellect, air, ego—swords; (2) emotion, water, feminine principle—cups; (3) action, fire, masculine principle—wands; and (4) security, earth, physical—pentacles.

The aces express the most positive force a suit has to offer; the middle cards examine all aspects of an approach in daily life; and the tens take the theme to its logical conclusion. If an ace introduces love, the ten will show the joy and peace of family life. The kings, queens, knights, and pages express ways of being in the world appropriate to their rank.

This collection of personal potentials, liabilities, life approaches, and maturity levels provides a wonderful array of images with which to identify facets of the personality. The less you know about tarot cards, the more useful a projection tool they will be; therefore, this description has been intentionally vague. Tarot decks can be purchased in almost any bookstore and on the Internet. Images can be found on Wikipedia: http://en.wikipedia.org/wiki/Rider-Waite_tarot_deck.

Exercise 8

Many Mirrors of Tarot

Use masking tape to cover any card names. It is important that your responses not be influenced by conventional card labels. For many people, the card titled "strength" suggests compassion, patience, or

(Continued)

---

calm. Using your intuitive reaction, divide the deck into four piles: (1) **Inner Selves**—cards that suggest sources for guidance and support; (2) **Directors**—images that make you feel judged, controlled, and pushed, or show the need to please others; (3) **Emotional entities**—expressions of undefended feelings of hurt and fear; (4) **Distracters**—depictions of diversions from a goal or temptation. Lay any cards aside that do not fit into these categories. The cup suit can be confusing. Many of these cards are useful when placed in the director pile for inner pressures to please. When you are upset, use the following steps:

(1) Identify the misguided message a personality part might be using for humiliation, nagging, or taunting from Exercise 3.

(2) Choose cards from the **director** pile that might illustrate these words. If you are feeling bitter, resentful, or tempted to stray from your chosen path, you can start by choosing cards from the **distracter pile** that show those urges. Lay them face up on the table in any position that seems right to you.

(3) It is not always necessary to choose cards from the **emotional entity** pile, but when these feelings are overwhelming you, find an image to represent them.

(4) Choose one or more cards from the **inner Self** pile that would be unaffected by your turmoil. Also lay them face up on the table.

(5) The cards in the **inner Self** pile offer guidance and support, but do not advise. They simply narrate—"I know you're trying to help Alex run away from tedious, trivial work" (see Vignette 3); "You have every right to feel fear. . . . I've always been there holding you every time you were terrified (hand holding a star)."

Step (5) will be covered in more detail in Chapter 5. For now, simply prepare a deck with masking tape to cover words and divide it into director, distracter, emotional entity, and inner Self piles for times when inner terrorists and champions need to be identified. Notice how Alex (Vignette 3) and how Dulci (Vignette 6) began to expose major players in the battlefield of their minds and used the tarot as a tool to plum the depths of their psyches.

Vignette 6: Dulci

Dulci (Chapter 1, Vignettes 1 and 5) had made some improvements during her time in therapy. She did not languish so long in bed, spoke up more, and was even beginning to find some independent interests—but she did not know exactly what she was supposed to feel, and happiness was certainly not an option. She visited her therapist on the sixth anniversary of her father's death. As usual, Dulci was glum but could not find the words to say why. She did not like it when her two youngest children were visiting their father or even when they were away at school. Her therapist gave her the **emotional entity** pile from the tarot deck to find an image that captured her feeling. Dulci picked a red heart with three swords plunged through it. She explained it represented her and her two children who were a "Stronghold" against the world.

Her therapist queried, "And when your father was alive . . . ?"

"Then we were a real fortress, and now, a huge piece is missing."

It was no wonder that Dulci was just beginning to recover from her father's death and that she became unsettled when her children were away from her, even at school. Looking for strength, her therapist gave her the **inner Self** pile and asked her to find a card to represent something within her that knew all was okay in spite of her fears. Dulci chose a graceful young person with pointed toe and sword held high to the side. She said it was a part that showed "Readiness" to fight to keep her and her children safe, if the need arose. She also chose a calm, radiant sun that gazed over a child joyfully astride a white horse. She said that the "Sun" sees, watches, and touches everything—an apt image for the observant part of Dulci (Chapter 1, Vignette 1).

Her therapist probed further, looking for what kept the "Stronghold" from trusting the watchfulness of the "Sun *Seer*" or the responsiveness of her *Readiness* Self. She searched the **director** pile for a part that was telling her to be on guard constantly. None could be found. But there, in the **distracter** pile, was the devil himself. Dulci explained that he tells her if she stops worrying about her children, she will be condemned to eternal damnation. She said he had always been there. Her mother told her to do the right thing, and now this part was saying, "Do the right thing or you will be screwed!" This was "Eternal Pressure" indeed.

Her therapist placed "Eternal Pressure" on one knee and the "Sun Seer" on the other so Dulci could begin to experience their opposing messages: "I have to make things right or I've failed" "I can watch over everything and respond." Her eyes darted from one image to the next. For just a moment she heard the "Sun Seer" whisper, "You only have so much control . . . " But "Eternal Pressure" was ready to whop her with, "No, no, no . . . you will have failed if anything bad happens." At least Dulci had finally, spontaneously, heard the "Sun Seer" with the help of vibrant tarot pictures.

Cyber Images

People who are not artistic, and sometimes put off by tarot cards or find emoticons lacking, can discover vivid portrayals of divisive parts and uniting forces in cyberspace (which sometimes may only be understood in the mind of the beholder). It is not surprising that a search engine found an image for a Higher Self called "Yoda." But fascinating cyber portraits can be found for personality parts dubbed "Psycho Witch," "Mr. Nasty," and "Poor Pathetic Me." Download an image of Edvard Munch's, *The Scream*, for protective parts that give warnings of impending catastrophes. If you have no sense of your inner Self, an image search for "Calm Center," "Supreme Self," "Wise Mind," or "Knower" can provide provocative results.

PROPS

The tarot deck with its many symbols of vitality and vulnerability is open to interpretation (Who would think that a pierced heart could represent a stronghold?), and would seem to offer an endless supply of inner images. Yet for some people, the cards miss the mark.

Vignette 7: Joyce

Joyce is a successful young businesswoman who had been emotionally abandoned by the father she adored when he remarried; she was nine. Then her mother left her in the care of an elder sister who tormented her if she did not clean fast enough or do things just right.

When she was 18 years old, Joyce married a man who began saying no one would want her and that even her family did not care because they did not call often. When he began having girlfriends, Joyce thought if she could just be a good-enough wife, her life would improve—but it only declined down a slippery slope into bizarre love triangles.

Ultimately, Joyce, the dutiful, working wife became independent and left with her young daughter. In time, there was a new boyfriend but old tapes played: "You're not good enough," "People will leave you," "You cannot trust anyone . . ."

Joyce looked in the tarot deck for an image to represent the intruding voices that made it impossible to accept the supportive new man in her life. The cards in the director pile were not menacing enough, and those in the distracter pile were overkill.

(Continued)

Joyce was then offered a choice of the rubber rat, a witch, or an ugly corncob doll to identify her tormenter. The rat with its associations to the father who betrayed her was an apt object for the inner self that gnawed at Joyce. An angel bear made a logical counterforce to reflect but not absorb the rat's nastiness: "You're very good at belittling Joyce—at telling her the worst."

People have menageries of objects in their homes to represent personality parts and inner Selves that create unity. Children's toy chests, collector's items, jewelry boxes, holiday decorations, tools, and even kitchen utensils can symbolically represent divisive facets and the Self.

Exercise 9

Scavenger Parts and Selves

Review Exercises 3, 4, and 5 to gain a sense of the directing, distracting (tempting), and emotional parts of yourself. Be on the lookout for objects in your home and office to represent these personality parts. Even desktop items like a hole punch or stapler can represent a biting critic. Notice any trinkets or conversation pieces that suggest your inner strength, wisdom, and guidance. Gradually collect and place such items on a cleared surface. Arrange and rearrange them to show how various parts and Selves gain and lose power as your true Self becomes more prominent.

IDENTIFYING NAMES FOR PARTS AND SELVES

Glancing over the vignettes that populate this and the previous chapter yields a crop of descriptive names for **personality parts** and harmonizing forces: "Stronghold," "Eternal Pressure," "Readiness Self," "Sun Seer," "Cuffed," "Judger," "Mrs. Desirable," "The Terrorist," "Past Bloom," "Daddy's Girl," "Miss Ohh," "The Presence," "Dark Parts," "Zoned-in Self," "The Emperor," "Inner critic," "Mr. Nasty," "Ratty Part," "Angel Bear," "Eeyore," "Pooh," "Taskmaster," "At Ease," "People Pleaser," "Oscar Charles Dawson" (OCD). . . . In contrast to these designations, **alters** in people with dissociated identities have common names making the personality that might pop out at any given moment appear ordinary. A woman named Susan had several alters that were called "Marla," "Serene," "Marianne," "Alan," "Denny," "Elka," "Alena," "Roselle," "Lion-Mom," "Chan," "Christa," "Richard," "Marlene," "Muriel," and "The Other" (Watkins & Watkins, 1997, p. 70). Only "Lion-Mom" and "The Other" were not ordinary aliases.

The reason for naming personality segments and Higher Selves is *not* to give them an identity but to clarify their purpose. In some cases, this can be a generic function such as controller, protector, pusher, pleaser, critic, distracter, tempter or inner child. Naming subpersonalities raises awareness of what is happening internally and helps them separate from the true Self.

Celia (Vignette 4) had referred to the voices that made her anxious as her "crunchy parts" before she used emoticon images to break them down into "Ronda Rerun," "Clara Clairvoyance," "Ms. Fix-It," and "The Should-er." She did not even know she had a "Ms. Whatever." Naming divisive personality parts does not empower them but, instead, makes them more recognizable and *pulls away the curtain* to expose the fragmented facets behind the voices of the great and powerful *wizards* within.

Vignette 8: Odette

Odette is in her late 50s. She has recently been keeping company with a 60-year-old male friend, whom she proudly, more often than not, wallops at chess. Together they enjoy dinner, movies, and conversation. But she became distressed when she learned that he had paid $80 for tickets for his ex-girlfriend and himself to attend a concert. Because she knew this man had many issues with women, she had decided not to give her heart to him. Puzzled by her distress, she consulted the tarot deck to find out what part of her was causing the upset. In the **director** pile, she spotted a shabbily dressed person, toiling away at some menial task.

Odette thought, *"That's me, some lowly person who can be shoved aside."*

But this seemed more descriptive of her feelings. What part was telling her she did not matter? Then she noticed a regal-looking king, robed in red, with a scepter. Deciding that the only fitting name for any *royalty* that would make her feel so low was "King Assholiness," Odette dismissed him with a smirk. It did not take this wise woman long to get back on top of her game.

Reminded that her friend's behavior revealed his own quirks and said nothing about her self-worth, she was ready to focus on him with multiple choice quizzing: Did you buy those tickets (a) to show your ex what a good guy she lost, (b) because a part of you still wants to cling to her even though she has thoroughly humiliated you, or (c) because spending money freely makes you feel good about yourself?

This technique of *turning the spotlight* on others is covered thoroughly in the book, *Making Hostile Words Harmless* (Cohen-Posey, 2008). For now, giving a name to the subpersonality (King Assholiness) that made her feel low, helped Odette dethrone her true opponent. She realized that her friend's philandering did not have to impact her.

Exercise 10

Christening Parts and Selves

Review Exercises 3, 4, and 5 to gain a sense of your directing, distracting (tempting), and emotional parts. Look at any emoticons, pictures you have drawn, or tarot cards that represent their nature. Pick a name that seems appropriate for each part. What names would you give to the two troubling parts that Rita identified in the following Vignette.

Vignette 9: Rita

As Rita had predicted (Chapter 2, Vignette 5) Roy's tryst with his childhood sweetheart had ended. Although he called Rita, and they went on a few dates, he was not romancing her as he had done in the past. They planned a dinner date for her birthday. Roy was frustrated that she could not meet him in *his* time frame, and he contacted her en route by cell phone and ordered her meal. When she arrived, their dinners had been served and Roy was already eating. As Rita listened to this braggart, she saw that he only cared about himself. Her blood reached the boiling point. They exchanged words that could never be retrieved and cut the tenuous ties between them.

Still furious when she came to see her therapist, Rita ranted about the incident and how her friends had supported her in the depths of her despair that *she wanted to blame on Roy.*

Her therapist pondered, "I wonder if any part inside is adding to your despair."

Rita readily agreed that an inner voice was saying that she allowed Roy to make a fool of her. Helping Rita access her core strength, together they asked the critical voice when Rita had a sure sign that Roy was a lost cause.

Although it wanted to say she *should* have known from the beginning, the real Rita agreed that the sudden appearance of Roy's childhood sweetheart and his quickie marriage less than 3 months after his whirlwind romance with Rita, certified that Roy was not a man to be trusted or tampered with ever again. Rita silently agreed with her inner critic; when Roy brought up the shady childhood sweetheart business, she should have let him go. The nagging seemed to evaporate.

Then her therapist asked, "What part did not want to let go of Roy?"

Rita knew that voice also—the one that only noticed the wonderful things about Roy and ignored his subtle controlling. This was a part of Rita that did not think she could stand on her own and wanted to pretend Roy was her happily-ever-after man.

Rather than feeling angry that Roy could not be her savior, her true Self was able to help this pretending part see that Roy was all bluster and no substance. As Rita started expecting Roy to be who *he was* instead of who *she wanted him to be*, he began to shrink in size, appear vulnerable, and look pitiful. She knew that any time anger toward Roy surfaced, it was a sure sign the desperate part had asserted itself and was trying to turn Roy into her rescuer, just as he tried to make her over with the *right* hairdo and acrylic nails.

Rita teaches preschool and is thoroughly familiar with A. A. Milne's characters that inhabit the Hundred-Acre Wood. How might she use them to typecast her inner parts and Selves? Who is the clever critic who tells her she should not have been fooled and the hesitant creature who makes her feel needy and desperate? Those familiar with the story would quickly recognize Rabbit and

Piglet. Pooh is very much alive and well in Rita, able to find a way round Rabbit's rebukes, to support Piglet when he feels overwhelmed and always ready for new adventures.

LITERARY CHARACTERS

As Rita's vignette shows, literary characters create powerful portraits for inner parts. A. A. Milne, who wrote more for the child within every adult than for children, was thorough in his representation of personality parts. Eeyore is gloomy, fretful, and knows enough to be critical. Piglet is fearful, hesitant, and, sometimes, displays bravery born of caution. Kanga is fierce and protective. Roo is playful and curious, and gets into trouble. Rabbit takes charge, is outspoken, feels self-important, and displays conventional wisdom. Owl pontificates, thinks he knows a great deal, and understands little. Tigger is bouncy and energetic and doesn't know his own limits. But, what about Winnie-the-Pooh? Being "a bear of little brain," he doesn't get tangled up in knowledge and is able to see through to the essence of things. He likes doing nothing and going nowhere, which means "just moving along, listening to all the things you can't hear, and not bothering." From this nowhere (now here) place, Pooh creates tunes, invents games, discovers the *North Pole*, and gets honored for his bravery (Hoff, 1982).

Traditional, well-known, legendary, or mythological stories are well suited to capture the nature of divisive personality parts and sources of inner strength. In this day and age, few people are familiar with the major players in such epic tales as the *Iliad* and the *Odyssey*, but they were ideally suited to a scholar experiencing a midlife crisis of Homeric proportions.

Vignette 10: James

James had been married for more than 15 years, had two sons, and was the police chief of a small town. While cruising in cyberspace one day, he happened on a *Combined Gender Identity and Transsexuality Inventory* (COGIOTI). The computerized interpretation was both shocking and a relief. The results showed that James was probably a transsexual.

The very fact that James was interested in taking the test may have been the best indication that he was questioning his identity. He had his master's degree in philosophy and had previously pursued careers that he perceived as feminine in nature. Although he loved law enforcement, he wondered if he had chosen this path in an attempt to deny the gentler aspects of his nature. The COGIOTI gave James permission to express a part of himself that he had only seen glimpses of in his youth and early adulthood, yet it brought up grave implications for his marriage, career, place in society, parental role, and even (he thought) his relationship to God.

James' therapist asked him if there were a character he had come across in his love of literature that might help him with his problem. Saying he was partial to the classics, he began describing Odysseus and other characters from the *Iliad* and *Odyssey*. In one of Odysseus' ventures, while homeward bound, the wise but curious captain had instructed his sailors to plug their ears with wax and bind him to the mast of his ship as they approached the island of the mermaidlike Sirens, who lured boatmen to crash into the seaside cliffs with their enchanting singing. It was here that James envisioned Odysseus, shackled high above his deck, ready to tangle with feminine powers of legendary proportion, yet willing to give him words of wisdom: "You are the sum of all your parts; be who you are."

Only a hero with courage of this magnitude could applaud James on his own journey. Perhaps Odysseus' mission to return to his faithful wife and, yet, find a safe way to experience femme fatales was giving James a subtle message in his quest to express the other gender—*Go as far as you can without destroying yourself.*

Exercise 11

Typecasting Parts and Selves

Think of a favorite story from childhood or even a television show you are currently addicted to. Do any of the characters remind you of parts that demand perfection, absolute control, or unceasing work; distract with temptation, bitterness, or blame; or wear their hearts on their sleeves? Usually such dramas will have a wise hero or a narrator who sees all. When you hear subvocal messages that push and pull at you, identify them with a literary character that clarifies or exaggerates their agenda. Think of a figure that would be untouched by their message, even if this means importing persons from other stories— Yoda or the Good Witch of the West are well known for their calmness in the face of calamity and their words of wisdom. What observations would such knowing beings make about bothersome browbeaters to help you reflect and not absorb their message?

DRAMATIC PATTERNS

One of the best ways to summons the Calm Center to the foreground is by exaggerating controlling, demanding parts. One young man who felt destroyed when a girl rejected him was asked to play his *desperation* and shook his imaginary self by the shoulders saying, "You've got to get people to like you!" Out popped (what he called) his "attitude" saying, "Dude, you sound desperate!" He reported feeling a weight fall from his shoulder.

Another young woman who struggled to start conversations with anyone she did not know, parodied a frantic part—"You could say something really stupid" and "The full weight of the conversation rests entirely on your shoulders!" Her *Realistic Self* spontaneously shook her head, saying, "That's not right."

The more absurd the scene becomes, the more reasonable a person starts to feel. A mother who felt anxious picking up her son at the school where her ex-husband taught was told by her therapist to kneel on bended knee and plead, "See what a good mother I am. . . . Don't believe what my ex-husband says about me. I know you take his word as gospel." After that display, a *Solid Self* stood up, seemed to shake imaginary slime off of its limbs, and announced, "Who cares what they think!"

MAKING THE WHOLE GREATER THAN THE SUM OF THE PARTS

The personality sits like Pandora's box. It appears solitary, but when the lid is lifted, out fly various **dictatorial parts** (intent on controlling, protecting, pushing, pleasing, or criticizing); a variety of **distracting traits** (struggling to subdue anxiety with blaming, clinging, boasting, avoiding, or using substances); and **emotional energies** (expressing pent-up pain or exuding peace). Just as the myth suggests, at first glance, the triune personality seems full of affliction, sorrow, and mischief—but the name *Pandora* means "all gifts." In truth, every personality facade or facet has a contribution to make when given proper guidance.

The one entity that did not escape Pandora's box was hope and, like hope, the Self remains within. It may take a crushing defeat before people lift the lid once more and turn to the Self with its far-reaching powers of observation, compassion, and reflection. In Abbott and Costello's game of life, the Self knows when "Who," "What," and "I don't know" are on base, and this ultimate coach can gently evoke the most effective postures. Chapter 5 is an instructor's manual for narrating and questioning errant players' misguided messages. The *team* becomes a cohesive whole as the Self engages personality parts in empowering dialogues.

Chapter 5

Engaging Personality Parts with Dialogue

In the beginning of the eighteenth century, many communities began to blossom in the harsh Eastern European landscape, each with a "miracle worker" at its center. These *rebbe* were persons of extraordinary spiritual gifts whose devotion was dependent on the congregation of Hasidim that gathered around them. In turn, it was their task to raise the spirits of their followers toward divine light; to be the eyes and caretaker of the community; and to teach their followers how to talk to God through song, dance, and wonder.

Within 200 years after its founding, almost half of Eastern European Jewry belonged to the Hasidic movement (Friedman, 1991, p. 38). Like a campfire suddenly doused by a downpour, these communities vanished as quickly as they came in the horror of the Holocaust. But embers remained—sparks that jumped to America and Israel, which again attracted lost souls to their warmth.

Stories live on . . . stories of lesser and greater miracles. It was the Day of Repentance and the Hasidim were gathered in prayer. Among them was a 13-year-old lad, so backward that he could neither read nor write, much less dare to speak to God. In his pocket, he toyed with the flute he used to herd his sheep. But something was wrong:

> Even on this day of endless entreaties to the Almighty, the prayers were taking too long. The
> Rebbe paused, a strained look on his face, his eyes cast upward. The shepherd boy, yearning to

The mandala was designed by the author and interpreted graphically by Gavin Posey to represent how personality parts become balanced and turn to dialogue with the central Self.

pray like the others, pulled out his flute and called to God as he did to his flocks. The startled congregation turned around to silence him. A smile brightened the Rebbe's face; he resumed the service and brought it to a joyous conclusion.

Later, the curious congregants were told, "I sensed the gates of heaven were closed to our prayers—that they were lacking in sincerity and I did not have the force to inspire the necessary reverence. I feared a year of misfortune would follow for our people. However, one heartfelt blast from the lad's flute pierced through all the heavenly gates and thereafter our prayers were permitted to follow."[1]

A rebbe was an arch expert in ways to break through the "gates of heaven." Sometimes it took tears of a broken heart; other times looters or thieves might be chosen as prayer partners to pick the locks of Heaven, allowing holy petitions to enter.

These Hasidic communities of Eastern Europe are metaphors for the personality parts and Self that comprise the multifaceted person. The *inner rebbe* values energies that barely have a voice, judgmental voices that might stifle subpersonalities they do not understand, and mischievous parts whose expertise to break and enter can turn a frozen lock. This rebbe has enough magnetism to attract diverse parts and *turn* them toward their Core while infusing them with respect to value one another.

---

[1] A classic Hasidic story, only the last sentence comes from Berg's (2003, pp. 4–6) modernized Hasidic-like tale.

MIND AS METAPHOR

Martin Buber, with his *Philosophy of Dialogue* (see Preface) and interest in a "social reality," was profoundly impacted by the Hassids. After completing his doctoral dissertation on German mysticism at the age of 26, he found a more earthy mysticism with the Hasidim. Awareness of *otherness* replaced becoming one with the All; discovering *uniqueness* was favored over achieving universality; ever-painful meetings with others were exchanged for *unity*.

Appreciating others and meeting in spite of opposition was the basis of community and planted the seeds for Buber's most famous book, *I and Thou*. Each person must find the divine in common, everyday experiences to restore harmony to the world. Hassidic communities with the "central Thou" of the rebbe enhanced this possibility. Through dialogue the spiritual leader renewed each Hassid, keeping him or her fully alive. Buber explored the possibility of genuine community in academia and other social settings. New ground for envisioning community emerged when therapists fractured the monolithic self into ego states (Watkins & Watkins, 1997) and other theorists began exploring systems models.

FAMILY SYSTEM

In the 1950s, family therapists were breaking away from traditional analysis and becoming interested in the social reality of domestic units. Although people are autonomous they are also "locked into" and governed by those around them. Murray Bowen (1913–1990) was one of the earliest proponents of this "systems" model and his approach bore a striking resemblance to the role of the rebbe with his Hasidism.

The therapist sits with the family, often choosing the members who are most "individuated" or in touch with their uniqueness. If the husband makes a comment to the therapist, the counselor asks the wife what thoughts she had when her husband was talking. Then, turning back to the husband or another family member, the therapist asks what he was thinking when his wife (or mother) was talking. Unlike other family therapies, the participants do not talk directly to each other, but only to the mediator who asks many questions to elaborate the thinking of each person into a clear presentation. If tears or emotions erupt, the therapist calmly asks what idea stimulated sadness or anger.

The thoughts (not feelings) of everyone present are externalized, allowing others to listen with greater depth than they could when talking to each other. The therapist is always in control of the session by asking questions and involving each person. People who have been nontalkers become talkers. Everyone is included, and balance is maintained with the therapist at the center, like a hub surrounded by spokes of a wheel. Bonding and expression of affection occur later, at home.

This style of leadership allows the individuality of each member to blossom in relation to a validating center. Contact is made, person to person, with an appreciation of each individual's uniqueness. The torch is passed, and one or more family members become strong enough to lead the family. The magnetic, spiritual force of the rebbe and the neutral, questing leadership of the therapist are apt models for the Self that is the true executive of personality parts.

MATERIAL MIND AND DIALOGUE

The therapist coaches people to access their central Thou or Self. Leadership of a myriad of inner voices begins by addressing them one at a time. To do this, the Self (1) *turns* toward an activated part, (2) labels the *type* of idea or feeling suggested in subvocal thoughts ("You're making dire predictions" or "You sound afraid"), (3) asks questions ("How will your predictions help?"), and (4) allows responses to emerge.

The challenge of these dialogues is to *turn* subpersonalities from their interest in controlling people or emotional energies toward the central Self that reflects without absorbing misdirected, distracting agendas. Outside support from a counselor is initially needed to feed lines to the Self that will keep the dialogue from becoming a debate. Misguided personality parts can become derailed by tasks of handling the details of everyday life. It is assumed that these voices simply need an occasional connection with the Self to become its allies in seeking meaning, purpose, and harmony.

FROM MONOLOGUE TO DEBATE

The concept of a *material mind* is a contradiction in terms. The brain has matter—neurons, blood vessels, fat cells, and so on. The material of the mind can only be known through inner voices and images. Random thoughts are part and parcel of monologues that switch course and ramble indefinitely. Mental chatter like Tony's (Chapter 3, Vignette 8) is typical.

Vignette 1: Tony

"I'll never get all this work done. . . . This is too much for me. . . . They just keep piling it on, and I don't know how I'm going to make my deadlines. . . . Meanwhile, my debts are piling up. How will I ever retire in 20 years? My 401(k) certainly won't hold me. I just don't know what I'm going to do. I'm so exhausted. . . . I don't even feel like getting out of bed and going to work. . . . "

A runaway monologue can cause depression, panic attacks, phobias of all kinds, angry outbursts, hopelessness, and helplessness. Life intervenes. Friends and family offer reassurance or discourage volatility. Gradually, Tony, like other people, will adopt the habit of talking to or debating himself:

First Voice:

a. I'll never get all this work done.

c. The workload seems worse than before.

e. And how am I going to get my bills paid.

g. (Struggling to get up) God I'm tired!

Second Voice:

b. *You*'ve done it before; just take one step at a time (encouraging).

d. Well, just do *your* best . . . but you've got to get out of bed (suggesting, ordering).

f. *You*'ve done that before, too, and you're getting annoying. Now cut it out and get out of bed (reminding, criticizing, ordering)!

In debate, a second voice seems to enter the mind, addressing the first voice with the word *you* (statements b, d, and f). Although it has the person's best interests at heart, it is intent on imposing its position—promoting constructive action. Resistance leads to frustration, and this unknown, benign intruder becomes more vocal and volatile. Not all internal debates become nasty. Often consoling words like—"It doesn't matter what others think of you" or "It's okay if you make a mistake"—can hush anxious forebodings.

A therapeutic technique that makes use of debate, instructs people to shout loudly in their minds, "Stop!" when an unwanted thought is heard—"I should have never retired, I was so stupid for not staying with the department. . . ." "*Stop!*" Extra punch can be added by wearing a rubber band on the wrist and snapping it whenever a disturbing thought arises.

Debates are an improvement over monologues and occur naturally, but they pose several questions: Who are the participants in the debate? If the first voice speaks with the pronoun *I*, is that the "real person?" Is one side usually negative and the other positive? Is there a way of keeping debates from spiraling downward? Are encouragement, suggestions, reassurance, commands, explanations, attacks, and so on the most effective ways to help frightened, angry, or discouraged personality parts?

PREPARING FOR DIALOGUE

Before answering these questions, a preview is offered to show how this kind of debate can be turned into a dialogue. Tony's therapist coached him to translate his random thoughts into observations and questions. Tony had identified an inner observer called "At Ease." He was aware of a "People Pleaser" personality part that frequently made him anxious and an entity he called "Dark Man" who could raise his ire. At Ease had come to know those subpersonalities well and could often calm them when they became distressed. In the earlier monologue and debate, a new voice puzzled him:

a. Voice: *You'll* never get all this work done. . . . *They're* piling it on; it's too much for *you.*
b. At Ease: You sound gloomy (identifying which part is speaking), and you're making dire predictions (labeling the type of thought).
c. Gloomy Pusher: (Does not seem to be saying much.)
d. At Ease (continues thinking about this part): You sound like Tony's mother. You get stuck thinking of the worst possible outcomes (labeling intentions).
e. Gloomy Pusher: (Still quiet, more relaxed.)
f. At Ease (feeling compassionate): I know you're afraid for Tony (labeling feelings).
g. Gloomy Pusher: (Feels comforted.)

Tony and his therapist lapsed into normal conversation about his financial concerns without benefit of dialogue and out popped the gloomy pusher:

h. Gloomy Pusher: Maybe *you'll* manage to get *your* bills paid, but how will *you* ever have enough retirement money?
i. (Therapist's *suggestion*): You could buy a house, and in 20 years, you won't have to worry about paying rent.
j. Gloomy Pusher: But in 20 years the *polar icecaps* will have melted, and Florida will be underwater.
k. At Ease (takes command): That's your best prediction yet! It sounds like your mother saying, "There's no hope for salvation" (labeling type of thought and its source)!
l. Gloomy Pusher: But it really is true! All the carbon dioxide is warming up the planet exponentially.
m. At Ease: So now you've gone from rousing anxiety about retirement to the fate of the world (labeling feelings). How do you think this will help Tony (questioning purpose)?
n. Gloomy Pusher (seems more subdued, but not quite calm): Isn't there something *Tony* can do?
o. At Ease: You don't think Tony is doing enough to pay his bills or save the planet (questioning underlying demands)?
p. Gloomy Pusher: Maybe *he's* doing all he can for now.
q. At Ease: (notices Gloomy is calm and relaxed).

FROM DEBATE TO DIALOGUE

The difference between debate and dialogue is found in the role of "At Ease" or the Self. It does not have an agenda or try to impose a point of view. This mysterious partner turns to the facet that has been activated, fully opens itself to what is being vocalized, seeks the meaning of the part's message through making observations and asking questions, and listens with all its presence for responses to emerge. Although not the first to speak, it is the central Self that actually initiates dialogue. Notice that the therapist started the second part of this dialogue with a suggestion (i), almost turning it into a debate.

Grammar of Personality Parts

A more obvious contrast between debate and dialogue is that the inner voice instigating issues (a) speaks in second or third person by using pronouns *you, he, she, his, her, they,* or an actual name. *"I'll* never get all this work done" becomes *"You'll* never get all this work done." This grammatical maneuver causes the gloomy part to disengage from the inner "I." The process of dis-identification (see Glossary) is begun. Instead of dominating, the discouraged subpersonality is turned back into an internal object that can be faced, questioned, and redirected. The Self is free to observe, understand, and know; unencumbered by a facet referring to itself as *I*. The mysterious identity of the inner voice that describes thought patterns and probes (statements d, f, k, m, and o) is revealed as the true Self.

Now the question is raised—Who is this gloomy subpersonality addressing when it predicts (a) *"You'll* never get all this work done?" Figure 5.1 "The Community of Self" shows the central Self

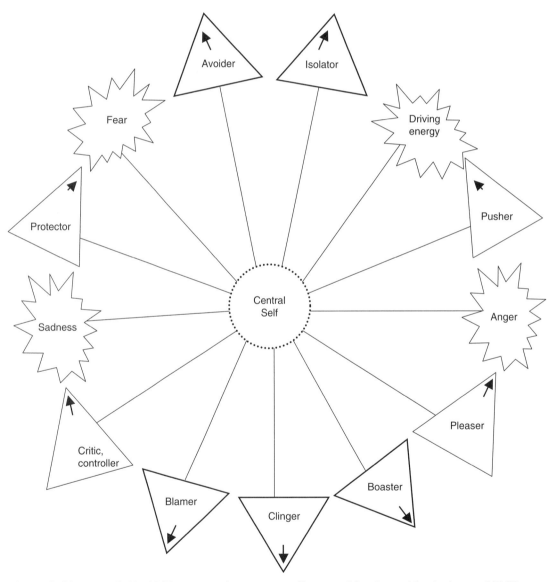

The Central Self is surrounded by (1) **Distracters** ◁ intent on controlling or avoiding the world and others and (2) **Directors** ▷ that try to rule (3) **emotional energies** ⚙ with sub vocal messages. While Personality parts are busy handling the details of life, The **Central Self** is free to find balance and harmony, view the big picture and discover meaning and purpose. It is always available to dialogue with a part in distress.

Figure 5.1 The Community of Self

surrounded by three personality components. **Distracting** parts take the pressure off of **emotional energies** by trying to control others. The use of the third-person pronoun *they* or referring to people and objects in the world (employers, polar icecaps, carbon dioxide) suggest their presence.

Directing personalities focus on emotional energies, trying to control them with subvocal messages. They become stuck in various roles:

- *Controllers* fixate on sad or excited feelings in an effort to keep them from becoming too extreme. Their rules are endless—"Crying is a sign of weakness" or "Don't be too happy or you'll get disappointed."
- *Protectors* think they are helping fearful parts by giving warnings of impending catastrophes—"You'll get dizzy if you stand up for too long." Of course, this creates self-fulfilling prophecies and more terror.
- *Pleasers* dictate—"Put your own needs aside and make others happy." They attempt to control angry demons, but create resentment.
- *Pushers* (Tony's gloomy voice) order—"You better do something! You won't get your bills paid." They overlook any constructive action that has been taken and insist on more.
- *Critics* are always ready to help any other dictating director.

Grammar of the Central Self

In the transition from debate to dialogue, the Central Self draws the attention of directing or distracting parts away from emotional energies or worldly objects by refocusing them on the Central Self. Figures 5.2 and 5.3 (small sections from the "The Community of Self" in Figure 5.1) illustrate this concept.

In Figure 5.2, the Pusher is playing on emotion with talk of pollution and polar ice caps melting, while in Figure 5.3, the Self's persistent observations ("You're making predictions" and "You've gone from rousing concerns about retirement to anxiety about the fate of the world.") have rotated the Pusher 90 degrees, leaving Tony's energy unhampered by the fretting, Gloomy Pusher.

It is very important that the Self speak back *to* any personality part that emerges with a voice that uses the second-person pronoun *you*—"That's your best prediction yet . . ." The Self should speak *about* the individual in the third person using his or her name—"You don't think *Tony* is doing enough . . .?" versus "You don't think *I'm* doing enough . . .?" The Self remains neutral, objective, and above the fray. It is a constant, unlabeled, inner Being that refers to the person that must be

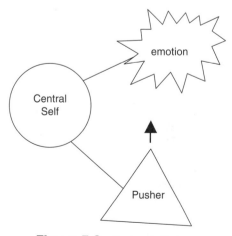

Figure 5.2 Pusher in Debate

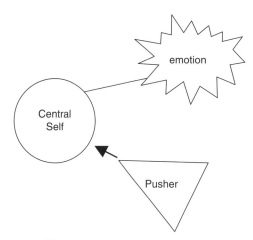

Figure 5.3 Pusher in Dialogue

named in the course of doing business with the world. It is interesting that when the Gloomy Pusher (in the example) finally turns to face the Central Self, it also talks *about* Tony—(g) "Isn't there something *Tony* can do?" and (i) "Maybe *he's* doing all *he* can." It has ceased to bash vulnerable energies with "*You*" statements—(a) "*You'll* never have enough retirement money." and (c) "*You'll* be underwater."

A One-on-One Process

The Central Self deals with directors and distracters one at a time. It does not have to keep them all pointed inward simultaneously as the mandala that starts this chapter would suggest. In the following vignette, after calming a critical protector, Inner Being turns to face a feisty distracter.

Vignette 2: Rita

Rita (Chapter 4, Vignette 9) had made great strides in depending on herself and not looking to men for life support. But her past antics had come back to haunt her. Before starting a new school year, she received a reprimand at work for talking too much about her personal life. She had begun having panic attacks before leaving in the morning. Her therapist asked what voice seemed to start her anxiety. Rita found A. A. Milne's characters fitting for her parts and Self—Eeyore is the protective critic that ends up exciting Piglet's instinctual fear; Rabbit can be righteous and irate; and, as always, Pooh is her inner calm:

a. Eeyore: You might mess up at school. They're going to watch you like a hawk.
b. Pooh: You're warning Rita to be careful and discouraging her (labeling type of thought).
c. Eeyore: Yeh . . .
d. Pooh: (Notices that Piglet is feeling calmer.)
e. Rabbit (a new part jumps in): Rita shouldn't have to take orders from a rookie teacher when she's been an aide for so long!
f. Pooh: You resent it when you assume someone is looking down on Rita (labeling feelings). . . . I think you might be Rabbit (identifying a part).
g. Rabbit: She worked her butt off. . . . She deserves respect!
h. Pooh: Exactly what would this teacher need to do to show Rita respect (question clarifying *respect*)?
i. Rabbit: When Rita came in late, that rookie could have said she understood Rita was finishing school projects at home and shown some appreciation.
j. Pooh: Why do you think the teacher didn't do that (empathy oriented question)?

5.8

k. Rabbit: I don't know! Maybe she just wanted to show who was boss.

l. Pooh: Suppose you sincerely asked her why she was upset when you were delayed by finishing projects at home. What would she say (role-play question)?

m. Rabbit: She'd say, "Oh we have so much stuff to get done before tomorrow, I just don't know how we're going to do it all!" (whiny voice)

n. Pooh: It sounds like she was feeling a lot of pressure, and her own issues got in the way of her being appreciative (labeling teacher's feelings). Do you think that's possible?

o. Rabbit: I suppose so (finally calming down). But I've told her that we'll take it one step at a time and get it all done.

p. Pooh: You really tried to reassure her (labeling intentions). Which do you think would work better—reassuring this novice or telling her that you know she is under pressure when she is acting stressed (clarifying options)?

q. Rabbit: It actually feels stronger to say, "I know you're under a lot of pressure." All the reassurance in the world wouldn't settle that woman down.

r. Pooh: (Observes that Rabbit seems happy, relieved, and less likely to worry inner parts about the teacher's reaction or to try to control her.)

In this vignette, the protective Eeyore seems subdued by being made aware that he is predicting: (b) "You're warning Rita." Although Piglet does not take part in the dialogue (fearful energies are rarely vocal), his presence is noted (d). When a resentful, blaming tendency is activated (e), the Central Self turns to it. Considerable feedback of thought processes and questioning are often needed to rotate distracting parts inward from their daunting task of trying to control others. Such efforts are effortless for the Central Self that is only interested in observing and understanding and knows that change will come in due time from the grace of genuine internal engagements.

STEPS TO THE DANCE OF DIALOGUE

Identify-Narrate-Question (INQ) protocol is a fitting name for the dialogue initiated by the executive officers of the Corporate Self, INQ:

I—Distressed parts that have issues are first *identified*.
N—The types of thought patterns and associated feelings are labeled or *narrated*.
Q—Concerns, their meaning, origins, and purpose are clarified with *questions*.

These steps do not take place in the order just given. The identity of a subpersonality may not be discerned until thinking tendencies or feelings have been exposed. Sometimes flourishes such as statements of compassion and truth are added during the process.

Hidden within the acronym INQ is the process of going *IN*ward, suggested by the first two letters. Once a narrating statement or clarifying question is formulated, it is asked silently to the part in distress. It is difficult to isolate each movement in the dialogical dance; one step unfolds from the next. Each one merits further clarification in the vignettes that follow.

IDENTIFYING DISTRESSED PARTS AND INNER BEING

Chapter 4 is devoted to identifying subpersonalities with scripts, emoticons, pictures, tarot images, objects, names, exaggeration, and symbols. Aimee in Chapter 1 (Vignette 7) imagined a depressed part as a little gnome sitting on her shoulder and a subpersonality that terrorized her about germs as a niggling, clawing lion. In Chapter 3, Alice (Vignette 2) heard the voice of "Mr. Nasty," who chided her with taunts that she liked being molested. Jaleigh (Vignette 4) chose a rubber rat to represent the part that tormented her with images of being handcuffed by a police officer after she made a suicide attempt. Karen's (Vignette 9) "Reverend Oscar Charles Dawson" (OCD) made regular visits to warn her of heinous acts she might commit. Sasha (Vignette 11) held a crying doll on her lap to connect with a hurt, rejected emotional energy.

Chapter 2 provides exercises to gain glimpses of powerful Selves. Jaleigh (Vignette 2) remembered an "angel" that helped her give birth and also imagined a mountain spirit in the form of her wise, loving, deceased father (Vignette 6). In Chapter 1 (Vignette 7), Aimee was well acquainted with her "Stoic Self" who spontaneously calmed her with the words of the prophet Jeremiah.

In this chapter, personality facets and Selves have also been identified. Tony (Vignette 1) found a new part he called "Gloomy Pusher." When he looked *inside*, this woeful subpersonality had a dejected expression while his "Dark Man" appeared agitated. In his journal, he captured the essence of "At Ease," his true Self, as a small, Buddha-like figure sitting under a tree. Simply looking at this drawing made Tony smile. Rita (Vignette 2) chose parts from A. A. Milne's Hundred-Acre Wood that were perfect caricatures of her coterie of parts and Self.

Subpersonalities are discovered, not invented; and, sometimes, *christened* as the next vignette shows.

Vignette 3: Melanie

Melanie (Chapter 4, Vignette 2) came up with a wonderful name for her clingy part that plagued her with questions—"Why doesn't your boyfriend love you? What is your ex doing with his new girlfriend? Why does he put up with her smoking when he never let you?" In her journal, this part's nom de plume became "PITA" or "Pain in the Ass." As she narrated and queried its incessant whimpers, her core Self grew stronger: (N = Narrate; Q = Question.)

a. PITA: Why doesn't Mel's boyfriend love her like her ex did?
b. Self: Why do you want Mel to stay with him if he doesn't love her (Q—purpose)?

c. PITA: She enjoys his company, and she can make *him* realize that she won't hurt *him* like his old girl-friend did.

d. Self: You want Mel to convince him he won't get hurt, and you also compare him to her ex-boyfriend (N—convincing and comparing).

e. PITA: Yes. . . . Her ex really loved her. *They* would go back and forth saying, "I love you," before *they* got off the phone. But then *he* pushed Mel out of his life, and *he* fell for that dopehead. *He* wouldn't even let Mel touch drugs. What are *they* doing now? . . . Do *they* want a baby. . . . Do *they* . . . ?

f. Self: You keep running a tape of Mel's ex and his new girlfriend over and over in her mind, speculating about their life (N—guesses). What is the reason for doing that (Q—purpose)?

g. PITA: It will make her stronger to have it thrown in her face.

h. Self: When you speculate about her ex, she seems to feel sad and weak instead of strong (N—consequences).

i. PITA: Maybe it will help (sounds more unsure).

j. Self: You sound hesitant (N—change in tone).

k. PITA: (Quiet.)

Although slightly derogatory, the acronym PITA has the ring of a pitiful part wanting to hold tightly to others and avoid the (imagined) terror of independence. But Melanie is beginning to change. She no longer imagines herself as a damp, dark cavernous opening desperate to fill itself with any stranger, rather than feeling empty (Chapter 4, Vignette 2). She has learned to say *no* and set limits. As her core Self becomes stronger, she may lose her dread of independence that she confuses with abandonment.

Notice that Tony's "Gloomy Pusher" (Vignette 1) and Melanie's "PITA" (Vignette 3) use slightly different grammar. Because a Pusher is in the director level of the triune personality, trying to dictate wayward emotional energies, it speaks *to* inner entities with second-person "*You*" statements—"You better get your work done . . ." or "You have to do something." PITA is a distracter that is trying to help Melanie avoid her fear of abandonment by controlling and speaking *about* people in the outside world. Therefore, its language is littered with third-person pronouns *he, she, him, her, they*, and *them*—"She can make him . . . , He pushed Mel . . . , He fell for . . . , He wouldn't let . . . , What are they . . . , Do they. . . ."

RECOGNIZING PARTS THAT *POP IN*

In Vignettes 1 and 3, the core Self only needed to identify one personality part. It is important to distinguish when a new voice has entered the dialogue and to recognize emotional energies whose nonverbal presence can be difficult to detect.

Vignette 4: Tara

Tara was facing an ordeal that had become much too familiar in her life. She had filed a grievance against her supervisor. At the forthcoming meeting, a union steward and company executives would be present. Friends from Tara's spiritual group suggested that her work conflicts were re-creations of early childhood scenarios. Tara, who had a basic mistrust of the paternal hierarchy, summoned her inner earth-mother goddess "Gaia" to find out if there was any merit to her friends' theory: (I = Identify; N = Narrate; Q = Question.)

(Continued)

a. Part: Here you go again—back in the same old hornet's nest with corporate and a union rep.

b. Gaia: I guess you're putting Tara on alert. What does she need to do (N—purpose, Q—meaning of being *on alert*)?

c. Part: She needs to say as little as possible so her supervisor doesn't have an opening to reprimand her for anything else.

d. Gaia: *Avoiding* communication is a hard order (I—avoidant protector, N—purpose). If she doesn't say anything, that can be cause for additional complaints (N—consequence).

e. Avoidant protector: Okay (seeing Gaia's point). . . . When she does communicate, she needs to document anything out of line that that drunken sot says. . . . They can always get you!

f. Gaia: You're giving Tara a constructive plan to document and warning her of the worst (N—conflicting goals). Which is more helpful (Q—options)?

g. Avoidant Protector: (Quiet but feels uncomfortable.)

h. Gaia: I know you really feel powerless (N—feelings) and that's why you make dire warnings (N—possible intentions).

i. Tara: (Hard Crying) There is no winning. It's like it was with my dad. He was always beating on me for something.

j. Gaia: Oh, that's "Little Tara" who feels so helpless (I—emotional entity). Of course it's scary (N—feelings).

k. Avoidant Protector: The company executives will support her supervisor!

l. Gaia: You seem more comfortable being angry at the company than feeling Little Tara's fear (N—feelings). Do you think she is as powerless as she was as a child (Q—feeling origins)?

m. Avoidant protector: No, but . . .

n. New part: Tara must have done something wrong!

o. Gaia: This is a switch (I—critic). Why find fault with Tara instead of the system (Q—purpose)?

p. Critic: Tara needs to accept that the system is perverse and be quiet.

q. Gaia: You're advising Tara to *expect* the system to be flawed (N—intentions), but why should she be quiet when they cross the line (Q—purpose)?

r. Critic (calmer): It is okay for Tara to speak as long as the angry avoider doesn't take over at the meeting.

s. Gaia: You seem more trusting of Tara (N—feelings). Maybe her protector was fighting you for the right to speak, and the less it has to struggle, the more she'll find her true voice (N—possible consequences).

t. Critic: (Calm and quiet.)

A part of Tara said, "She needs to say as little as possible" (c), and by narrating that this was an "order to avoid" (d), her true Self was able to identify an avoidant subpersonality. Unlike a typical superego protector that focuses on controlling emotional energies, it distracted fearful instincts by avoiding and blaming parties in the outer world—(e) "They can always get you!" Narrating and questioning this rigid defender, quieted it enough to expose painful emotions.

When sadness surfaced—(i) "It's like it was with my dad"—the "Protector" made another attempt to distract by focusing on company executives—(k) "They'll support her supervisor." Gaia blocked this avoidance with (l) "You seem more comfortable being angry than with feeling fear," and a harsh critic stepped up to the plate to suppress distraught feelings—(n) "Tara must have done something wrong."

The true Tara was able to notice the shift in energy so that "Gaia" could question this critic's purpose (o) "Why find fault with Tara?" and point out intentions, feelings, and consequences (q) "You're advising. . . ." and (s) "You seem more trusting . . ." "The less she has to struggle, the more she'll find her true voice." Many therapy approaches spend time focusing on the inner child, like "Little Tara," to help her find her voice. However, when directors and distracters stop battling each other and resume their intended roles of giving feedback and providing a unique personal style, the inner "I" is free to speak for the Self with knowing flexibility.

NARRATING INTENTIONS, FEELINGS, AND CONSEQUENCES OF THOUGHTS

Narrating subvocal messages clarifies the roles of puzzling inner facets. This is the internal art of observing and labeling. Inner voices can be narrated in blow-by-blow **descriptions** of the **intention** behind their ideas and messages. Thus far, careful observation of mental chatter has revealed intentions to:

Predict: "It's too much for you."
Doubt: "You cannot do it all."
Order: "Say as little as possible . . ."
Remind: "Your boyfriend used to . . ."
Scold: "You shouldn't have . . ."
Convince: "You can make him . . ."
Speculate: "What is he doing . . .?"
Advise: "You need to . . ." or "They should."

Narrating requires concentration. In Chapter 2, the art of noticing was begun with Exercise 6, "Self Narration," to experience ordinary event as if for the first time by noting what muscle movements are involved in picking up this book and putting it down; what steps are needed to rise from bed in the morning; what actions and observations are made while driving, and so on. Exercise 7, "Aware Breathing," practiced paying exquisite attention to the boundary where air becomes breath. Noting exhalation and inhalation with the words *out* and *in* is one of the simplest forms of narration. Exercise 8, "Mindful Meditation," dives into the heart of narration by paying attention to thoughts, on purpose, in the present moment, nonjudgmentally (Kabat-Zinn, 1994). The parade of *what-ifs, if-onlys, when-wills, have-tos, coulds, shoulds, awfuls, nevers, nobodies,* and *everybodies* is simply observed—always returning to the focal point where air becomes breath each time a thought occurs. Practicing Exercises 6 through 9 will enhance the witness Self's ability to narrate personality parts, which are driven to compare, judge, ponder, and evaluate.

Labeling the feelings that thoughts cause is easier than narrating the intention behind an idea. Although the mystery of which came first—the chicken or the egg—may never be solved, psychology proposes that thoughts *do* cause emotions. The mental chatter produced by personality parts can be reexamined to reveal the sentiments they incite: "It's too much for you"—pressure, "They should . . ."—frustration, "You might mess up"—timidness, "You cannot do it all"—hopelessness, "You should have . . ."—regret, "Say as little as possible"—helplessness, "Your boyfriend used to . . ."—sadness, "You can make him . . ."—righteousness, "What is he doing now?"—jealousy.

Pointing out the consequences of a particular line of thinking links feelings to the ideas that produce them. Personality parts often engage in faulty logic or do not fully pursue a line of reasoning. In some of the previous vignettes, various Selves narrated the effects of misguided musing: "Not saying anything could result in Tara having further reprimands at work" and "When you try to silence Tara, her angry protector becomes more likely to sound off" (Vignette 4). Giving feedback about an inner voice's intentions and the feelings or other consequences that are caused, increases awareness throughout the whole internal community. Often, one simple narration will soothe a troubled part.

Vignette 5: Angie

Angie frequently had panic attacks that made her heart pound, her breath quicken, and her head spin. They were triggered by noticing or dreading the slightest change in body functioning. Before panic had robbed her of her joy, her friends had called her "Giggles" because of her sparkling personality: (N = Narrate; Q = Question.)

(Continued)

a. Negative Part: You'll be exhausted after you pick up your daughter and won't be able to enjoy her.
b. Giggles: You're making predictions that upset Angie (N—type of thought and feeling).
c. Negative Part: (Quiet.)
d. Giggles (Observes that the negative part appears sad that it is upsetting Angie): It seems like you don't want to upset Angie (N—feelings).
e. Negative Part: (Still and quiet.)

SPEAKING SILENTLY TO TROUBLED PARTS

"Giggles" had to ask, "What is this negative part doing, and how is it affecting Angie?" to compose a narration (b) "You're making predictions. . . ." This may be written in a journal or worked out in the mind. The second part of narrating is more important than finding words to label the type of thought and the consequences or feelings that result. The Self *goes inside* and speaks silently to the troubled part. If a narration was written in a journal, it should *not* be read, but, instead, memorized and uttered within. An image of the dictatorial, distracting, or emotional part being addressed can be of assistance, but is not necessary. Angie could not *see* her negative part but sensed its sadness.

Brain mapping studies show that by simply counting out loud, motor areas of the cortex used in normal, wakeful states are activated. Counting silently energizes the frontal lobes, which also become dominate during meditation and other types of focused concentration (Hamer, 2004, p. 123). After formulating a message, inner Being can use its still strong voice to silently speak calming words. Then, still facing inward, it listens and observes to discern if a connection has been made or if the subpersonality is still making distressing (subvocal) comments. In most instances, the Self must make several narrations before the turmoil a part is stirring subsides.

Vignette 6: Hanna

Hanna had become familiar with the nagging subpersonality that tried to dash her dream of changing careers on the rocks of despair. A new opportunity was presenting itself on the horizon, and her critic was full of bluster:
(N = Narrate.)

a. Critic(s): You could fail, you know!
b. Real Self: You're frightening Hanna (N—feelings).
c. Critic(s): You have plenty of reason to be scared: You might not make enough money, waste your time, not be motivated enough, not be organized, not be competent . . .
d. Self (breaks into the monologue): You have so many *doubts* about Hanna (N—type of thought).
e. Critic(s): Why should *we* believe you're capable? You always had things done for you, and you've made a few bad mistakes in your love life!
f. Self (notices that there seems to be more than one critic): You don't see Hanna's strengths *because* so much was done for her when she was young, and you place importance on her premarital escapades (N—causes).
g. Critic(s): Maybe, but what if *she's* making excuses by hiding behind the way *she* was raised?
h. Self: It's so hard for you folks to believe in Hanna. You were robbed of knowing who she really was (compassionate narration).
i. Critic(s): (Quiet, calm, feels connected.)

In this vignette, the critic is initially speaking to a young Hanna whose fears have been encapsulated in an emotional button. Her clever Self goes beyond the usual narrations to point out the *causes* for her critic's disbelief—(f) ". . . so much was done for her. . . ." The first signs of this doubter turning toward the central Self are its reference to Hanna in the third person—(g) ". . . *she's* making excuses" and the use of the word *maybe*.

Addressing Emotional Energies

Although it would seem that repeatedly narrating negative verbiage could frustrate the real Self, the more the critic persists, the clearer its character become. Rather than feeling impatient, core Beings often experience and express compassion as they sense dictatorial parts trying to hang on to their power. Deep caring is particularly important when addressing emotional energies.

Vignette 7: Odette

Odette who proved she could enjoy herself and still love her deceased son (Chapter 3, Vignette 3) still grieved. Her son died in a motorcycle accident in his late 20s. Odette kept the TV on constantly to keep from hearing a "Controlling Mother" part that constantly incited sad energies: (N = Narrate.)

a. Controlling Mother: If only you had kept him from leaving that night . . . , If only you made him sell that bike. . . .
b. Knower: You fill Odette with regret (N—label the feeling).
c. Controlling Mother: You should have argued less with him.
d. Knower: You're blaming Odette for failing to control death itself (N—scolding).
e. Sad energies: (Crying begins.)
f. Knower (Starts to notice sad emotions surfacing): It's fine to cry. . . . You can make noise . . . breathe (compassionately narrates and encourages release of emotions). This is gentle grieving (Narrates and labels release).
g. Controlling Mother: She will never be normal again. She will never stop crying.
h. Knower: You're afraid to let Odette grieve. You're afraid she won't ever stop (N—feelings) but you also make Odette cry by telling her she should have prevented her son's death (N—consequences).
i. Controlling Mother: (Quiet and calm.)

The witness Self must make a special effort to notice and comment on the presence of emotional energies. Most adults have controlling parts that will allow little more than the shedding of a few tears and fleeting sensations. Odette's "Knower" wisely counsels sad energies to make noise and breathe (f) to bypass well-ingrained dictates.

QUESTIONING TO CLARIFY THE MEANING, ORIGINS, AND PURPOSE OF THOUGHTS

Narrating the type of thought and resulting consequences or feelings can increase awareness of what a part is doing and how it is impacting the internal community. However, sometimes it is necessary to probe further and clarify meaning, origins, or motivations of distorted views by asking questions. This is especially true when an inner director is trying to control emotional energy.

Vignette 8: Emily

Emily and her husband were devoted to their delightful 1-year-old son, but Emily was distraught that her marital bliss was declining and mystified by the reason. Her circle of friends was steadily shrinking, and her husband seemed unhappy when she spent time with them. She quickly discovered a subpersonality that had allied with her spouse:
(N = Narrate; Q = Question.)

  a. People Pleaser: You better not upset your husband. He might yell at you if you go to the store with your best friend, and he'll give you the third degree about what you did.

  b. Real Self: What would be bad about him getting upset (Q—meaning)?

  c. Pleaser: You dread seeing people you care about yell and get mad.

  d. Real Self: Where do you think that worry comes from (Q—origin)?

  e. Pleaser: Little Emily used to feel awful when her stepdad would yell at her sister for picking on her (begins crying).

  f. Self (speaking to Little Emily): When you were very young a voice inside said it was your fault if your sister got into trouble (I—origin of a part).

  g. Little Emily: (Crying and nodding.)

  h. Real Self: You still have that voice, and it makes you feel guilty (N—feelings). I wonder what will happen if I give you a hug. Cross your arms so opposite hands touch your shoulders and give them alternating taps . . . about twenty. . . . That's my way of hugging you (narrates butterfly hug).

  i. Little Emily (Crying stops . . . becomes calm and quiet.)

Labeling and narrating any thoughts that surface and then using alternating shoulder taps (h) is a special technique called the "butterfly hug." Tapping puts attention on and stimulates the (rational) Self to help personality parts reprocess maladaptive information—(f) "It was your fault your sister got in trouble." This method will be used in other examples and explained in more detail in Chapter 6.

Asking, "What is bad about . . .?" (b) is a typical way to **clarify** the **meaning** of an idea. But the quest to understand can be more difficult. Personality facets are masters at using vague terms, making the need for clarity a priority. In Vignette 4(b), Gaia asks an avoidant protective part what Tara would need to do when she is on alert to specify exactly what this order demands. Similarly, in Vignette 2(h), Pooh asks Rabbit what the rookie teacher would have to do to show respect and to find out what Rita is seeking.

Emotional energies usually reside in younger personality parts. Asking, "When did you first get that idea?" or "Where do you think that worry comes from?" (Vignette 8,d) can **clarify** the **origins** of misinformation. Children often feel responsible for the unhappiness of everyone in their world. While painful, this guilt gives them the illusion that they can fix others. Emily may need to reprocess emotions that she assumed for not preventing her sister's punishments before she realizes she is equally powerless to make her husband feel secure when she spends time with others. In Vignette 4(l) Gaia asked, "Is Tara as powerless now as she was as a child?" to point out the origins of her helpless feelings and how these stuck emotions prevent her from accessing abilities she has acquired as an adult.

As the core Self becomes adept at using questions, **clarifying** the **purpose** of a line of reasoning occurs spontaneously.

Vignette 9: Penny

After several weeks of therapy, Penny thought she had mastered the panic attacks that terrorized her. She had started dealing with relationship problems with her boyfriend and children when the "Panic

Terrorist" stuck again (as they often do when people are out of practice using techniques to float past and distract themselves from symptoms). She looked to her "voice of reason" for help:
(N = Narrate; Q = Question.)

   a. Terrorist: You don't breathe right. . . . There must be something wrong with your lungs.
   b. Reason: You are pushing Penny's panic button with your assumptions (N—type of thought).
   c. Terrorist (Quiet . . . more tentative): But she could have something wrong with her lungs.
   d. Reason: Why does Penny's breathing become normal when she gets up and walks around (Q—exceptions)?
   e. Terrorist (Quiet . . . more subdued): Maybe Penny is dying.
   f. Reason: What would be bad about her dying (Q—what dying means to Penny)?
   g. Terrorist: She might go to Hell or never achieve true happiness before she dies.
   h. Reason: What does Penny have to do to achieve happiness (Q—meaning of "true happiness")?
   i. New Part: Penny needs to get her house fixed up. She'll never have enough money to do that!
   j. Reason: You sound a bit pushy (I—pusher), and you're ordering her to repair her house before allowing her to be happy (N—intentions) . . . Do you think this command will help her (Q—purpose)?
   k. Pusher: (Quiet and calm.)

Penny's voice of reason began with a leading question to point out how quickly her breathing normalized (d). Then she asked a daring, but very important question: (f) "What are the implications of death for Penny?" and "Why does this grim reaper hold so much power over her?" Although she could have asked what the chances were of Penny dying or pursued her fears of going to Hell, the significance of "true happiness" called for clarification (h). Apparently, a pushy dictator was ratcheting up surges of panic producing adrenalin—"She needs to fix her house." In this case, just asking the purpose of the hidden pushy part ("Do you think your command to get repairs done will help her?") was enough to silence it (j). However, had it retorted, "Penny needs me or she will become lazy and do nothing," the voice of reason would have merely pointed out the consequences of this flawed thinking—panic attacks (resulting from orders) paralyzed Penny more than any innate idle energies. The sources for thinking she might become indolent could also have been explored.

In theory, all personality parts are trying to help the core Self but they are led astray by misinformation and loss of communication with inner Being. When a part realizes its agenda serves no useful purpose, it may become quiet, as did Penny's pusher.

Other vignettes in this chapter have asked purposeful questions with promising results. Tony (Vignette 1, f) realized he was doing what he could when "At Ease" asked a gloomy protector, "How will it help Tony to worry about the fate of the world instead of retirement?" Melanie (Vignette 3, f) exposed a bizarre line of logic by asking an annoying part called "PITA," "What is the reason for reminding Mel over and over of her ex boyfriend?" The consequences of PITA's attempt to "make Mel strong" were quickly shown to have the opposite effect. Tara (Vignette 4, o, q) discovered that an inner critic was trying to squelch the voice of a vengeful, distracting protector by asking, "Why find fault with Tara instead of the system?" and "Why should Tara be quiet when the corporation crosses the line?"

As they become more familiar, questions to clarify the purpose behind an idea or a line of reasoning all seem to be cut from the same cloth—"Do you think . . . will help?" "How do you think . . . helps?" "Why are you bringing up . . . now?" "What is the reason for . . .?" "What other part are you preventing from speaking?" "Why . . . instead of . . .?" "Why should this person . . . when . . . happens?"

EMBRACING ALL PARTS

There is one ultimate question that crosses the abyss and connects with the most stubborn personality parts—"Do you think you are no longer wanted or have a purpose (in the psyche)?"*

5.17

Vignette 10: Joyce

Although Joyce (Chapter 4, Vignette 5) had chosen a rubber rat to represent the inner voice of the father who betrayed her and the sister and ex-husband whose accusatory words gnawed at her, in her journal, she preferred to write dialogues simply between a "part" and "Me." She conversed each morning when she awoke, resolving yesterday's crisis, and put words on paper afterward to record the dialogue. An issue between herself and her mother, her one last connection to her family, remained unresolved: (I = Identify; N = Narrate; Q = Question.)

a. Part: You shut your mom out. . . . You aren't a good daughter. You don't even mind her being gone now.

b. Me: You're scolding Joyce and telling her she is lousy (N—intent and feelings).

c. Part: Yes! (Sounds very self righteous.)

d. Me: Will this criticism help (Q—purpose)?

e. Part: I'm not here to help. I'm here to make you think you're a bad person so you don't let your guard down.

f. Me: It still sounds like you're trying to help Joyce be on guard (N—intent).

g. Part: I don't care about you.

h. Me: *Do you think I'm asking you to give up your power or trying to destroy you (Q—purpose)?

i. Part: I'd be crushed (feels like it's crumbling).

j. Me (feeling compassionate): I like your strength; you've always had my back (N—intentions).

k. Part: I can only be strong in *my* own way.

l. Me: I know you're afraid of change or to trust me to be strong (N—feelings).

m. Part: (quiet.)

n. Me (observes part is taking it in—not yet in agreement, but not fighting): It's good to resist and I know you want the last word (N—intent).

After narrating scolding (b), Joyce asks a question (d) to clarify purpose—"Will criticism help?" This negative facet (probably in an internalized clone of the father, sister, and husband who had abandoned and abused Joyce) persisted in rejecting all attempts to reach out to it. Curiously, it definitely has a male gender (n). Joyce finally asked the question that strikes at the heart of every personality part's worst fear—"Do you think I'm asking you to give up your power or trying to destroy you?"

When an inner entity becomes particularly obstinate, it may be fighting for its existence—not realizing that the central Self only seeks contact with, not elimination of, parts or even integration. This dialogical method prefers to simply make connections, and, when possible, a compassionate embrace with all the worthy opponents that lie within. It is expected that a distressed challenger will arise again, but each time the central Self recognizes and responds by narrating and questioning, the internal community will become more cohesive.

STATING THE TRUTH TO TEST FOR CHANGE

While Joyce's "Part" was doggedly resistant, other subpersonalities seem too compliant. Many times, it is good to use a statement of truth to discern if actual change has taken place.

Vignette 11: Theresa

Theresa's divorce did not stop her from being responsible for and sympathetic to the husband who never seemed able to hold a job or pay his bills. She had ignored a judge's advice to let child support payments go through the court, and now, her ex-husband was several thousand dollars in arrears. Although her own

5.18

finances demanded that she follow the court protocol, she unwittingly felt obliged to ask her former husband's permission to follow legal protocols:

(I = Identify; N = Narrate; Q = Question.)

a. Fixer: You must help your ex-husband if *he* thinks you're obligated.
b. Intuitive Self: Your demands hold Theresa hostage to his whims (N—type of thought).
c. Fixer (Quiet) . . .
d. Intuitive Self (Observes fixer seems relaxed. Makes a statement of truth to test for reactions): It's fine to have child-support payments go through the court (listens within; I—new part) . . .
e. Ms. Haughty: You bet you can make support payments go through the court (angry, edgy voice)!
f. Intuitive Self: Why do you have your back up (Q—purpose of Ms. Haughty's reaction)?
g. Ms. Haughty: Theresa has to distance from her ex-husband or the Fixer will return.
h. Intuitive Self: When you make Theresa distance from people, she acts superficial and out of character (N—consequences).
i. Ms. Haughty: I want to find a middle ground.
j. Intuitive Self (makes another truth-test statement): It's fine to have child support payments go through the court. (Listens. . . . All parts are quiet within.)

Theresa is an amazingly intuitive woman who can often read strangers like a book, yet she has difficulty trusting her instincts with people about whom she cares deeply. Her intuitive Self narrated the Fixer's intentions precisely—(b) "Your demands hold Theresa hostage" and gave her clear insight into the "Ms. Haughty's" agenda—(g) "Theresa has to distance . . ." When Ms. Haughty stated, "I want to find a middle ground," it seemed she wanted to integrate, transform her character, or change her role. However, in the present moment, this part has simply turned to the Central Self and allowed it to lead with its still strong voice. Ms. Haughty may come back with her superior attitude, trying to distract the Fixer from saving the next handsome underdog who crosses her path, but inner Being will become adept at narrating these facets' intentions with arresting speed, giving Theresa force and certitude.

DIALOGUE IN A CHILD'S MIND

The "language of parts" comes naturally to children. Talking about the *part of them* that worries about monsters, is afraid to try new things, or forgot to do their chores reduces a problem tenfold and provides a new way to attack it. Of course, the "language of *Self*" must also be included by casually mentioning that they may or may not know that they have an *inner "I"* that can chase monsters away, that is excited to learn new things, and that can remind them of what they need to do.

Young people are eager to draw pictures of angry, sad, and timid parts but may need prompting from the emoticon images (Chapter 4, Exercise 6), which can produce interesting designs for their calm, comforting Selves. A plethora of action figures that represent tormenting facets and knowing Selves can be easily extracted from toy chests. Parents can coach a child's true Self to narrate and question distressed voices, or they may simply talk them through a problem.

CALMING ANGRY, INSTINCTIVE ENERGY

Because the squeaky wheel gets the grease, anger and attitude are often a parent's most pressing concern. With children of all ages, the best inner dialogue work cannot stand alone to vanquish youthful furies. Parents' directives must be backed with action to provide an incentive to internalize rules and take charge of instinctual energies. However, when accompanied by behavior management tactics, the language of parts helps the child's inner "I" become the parents' ally.

Vignette 12: Jeff

Five-year-old Jeff was having frequent and extreme outbursts since his parents had separated. His mother used several variations of the following speech to teach anger control:

a. A *part* of you has trouble understanding why I say *no*. That part makes you mad.
b. That angry face helps your mad part let out your anger faster. . . . You can go in your room, and your angry part can draw a picture to show how upset it is, or you can stand right here and jump up and down until the angry part wants to stop. . . .
c. There might be things right now that make that angry part want to act up more, but you still have your old calm Self inside.
d. Maybe you have an action figure that behaves like your calm Self and stays cool even when everything is going crazy around him.
e. I wonder who you want to be the boss of you—the angry part or your calm Self?

Just as with the first steps of adult anger management, points (a) and (b) provide young people with safe, acceptable ways to release and reduce anger. Rage results from a loss of power, and children have this experience over and over as they are made to follow rules that *cannot* make sense to them until they are older. There should be no implication that the angry part of them is bad. It is natural! Steps (c) through (e) may be mentioned after a tantrum has subsided. Angry energy must dissipate before some children will admit that they have a serene Self, much less consider allowing it to be in charge. *Brief Therapy Client Handouts* (2000, p. 8.11) reviews release-reduce-reexamine-request steps for managing anger.

Although teens have greater powers of reason than young children, their struggles for independence inflate adolescent attitudes, which have little regard for the needs of others. After a blowup has passed, a parent might choose to coach using the following dialogue.

Vignette 13: Teen

Generic Teen Attitude (I = Identify; N = Narrate; Q = Question.)

---

a. Parent: It sounds like you have a part that makes you mad. (N—feeling) Maybe it's telling you . . . (Parent speaks teen's angry part with a sassy attitude): *I don't know why you cannot do what you want to do when you want to do it*! (I—demanding part).

b. Parent (coaching): I wonder how the real you will deal with that part? It might ask the mad part, *Can you disagree with your parents without sounding angry? Is that impossible, hard, or an interesting challenge* (evocative questions)?

When parents have a dramatic flair, they can ease a tense situation. Much like the central Self, they are not attempting to change the young person's attitude, just to demonstrate how their child's real Self can narrate feelings of inner voices and subtly suggest options. Parents can create opportunities for such dialogues by saying, *We need to talk before you use the phone, go out with friends, or watch TV.*

SOOTHING FEARFUL, WITHDRAWING ENERGIES

Some children are biochemically predisposed to be more fearful than others. Repeated questions can be early indicators of Obsessive Compulsive Disorder (OCD) or they may be typical youthful anxieties that will pass. Many children use *transitional objects* such as a blanket or a stuffed animal to represent the comfort of a significant adult. Parents can make use of such security symbols by having children choose toys that represent the brave parts of themselves.

Vignette 14: Kenny

Since school started, 8-year-old Kenny has been delaying bedtime with a barrage of questions. He picked a stuffed kitty for his frightened part and a GI Joe for his brave Self:
(N = Narrate; Q = Question.)

a. Mom (repeating Kenny's words): The kitty is saying, *A hole might go through the earth.*

b. G.I. Joe (mom's voice): It seems like you're scaring Kenny (N—feelings). Where did you get the idea of a hole going through the earth (Q—origin)?

c. Kitty: Kenny saw it on TV.

d. G.I. Joe: Is there anything bad about the hole (Q—meaning)?

e. Kitty: The earth might blow up.

f. G.I. Joe: Will it happen tonight? What is the chance (Q-meaning)? Lets see if it happens in the next three minutes.

g. Kenny (smiles): Kitty's okay for tonight.

The Next Night

h. Kenny: What if I don't know how to do my job when I grow up?

i. Mom (*I hear the kitty. G.I. Joe better talk to him*): Kitty do you know that Kenny is only 8 years old (Q—meaning of age)?

j. Kitty: Yes.

k. G.I. Joe (mom's voice): Does the 8-year-old Kenny know more than he knew when he was 2 years old (Q—meaning)?

l. Kitty: Yes—he can dress himself and ride a bike.

m. G.I. Joe: Will the 20-year-old Kenny know and do things 8-year-old Kenny can't do now?

n. Kitty: I'm not sure because his mom won't be there to help.

(Continued)

o. G.I. Joe: You must be a *doubting* Kitty (N—feelings). Even though Kenny can throw a ball better than his mom, you make him think he's going to stop learning to do new, fun stuff at 8 years of age (N—type of thought).

p. Kitty: Maybe Kenny will learn some things, but he'll still need his mom.

q. G.I. Joe: Oh, you must be a Velcro Kitty that likes to stick to things (N—clinging feeling). I remember when you wanted Kenney's mom to help him go to the bathroom. Do you still want her to help you with that (Q—purpose).

r. Kitty: No!

s. G.I. Joe: It's normal for Kitty parts to give kids doubts and make them want to cling, but G.I. Joes like me are inside too and *know* Kenny will learn a lot and want to do things by himself, like using bathrooms.

t. Kitty: Oh . . . (quiet, no more questions).

Just as with adults, protective, terrorizing subpersonalities are vague. Kenny's mother (through the voice of G.I. Joe) helped clarify the *meaning* of a hole in the earth—(d) "is there anything bad about the hole?"—and how imminent the danger might be—(f) "Will it happen tonight?" The next night she helped her son's brave Self ask questions to clarify the meaning of how children develop as they grow—(k, m) "What does 8-year-old Kenny know? . . ." "What will 20-year-old Kenny know?" Then, she narrated feelings of doubt and clingy insecurity—(o, q) "You must be a doubting . . . Velcro kitty" Finally, going beyond the Identify-Narrate-Question (INQ) protocol, she normalized his tender feelings and evoked confidence—(s) "It's normal to doubt . . . but Kenny will learn and want to do things. . . ." G.I. Joe became a transitional object that symbolized the secure Self that lies within every child.

ADOLESCENT ANXIETY

Kenny had an inner voice that wanted him to cling to maternal support. If young people have not found the strength of their own being by the teen years, dictatorial subpersonalities will desperately turn to peers for approval, rousing adolescent anxiety in staggering proportions.

Vignette 15: Jordan

In spite of the chatter from a "Critical Protector" that tormented her, Jordan was an attractive, outgoing junior in high school. However her "real Me" needed coaching to gain the still strong voice needed to face this inner tyrant:

(I = Identify; N = Narrate; Q = Question.)

a. Critical Protector: You might say something stupid. You have to get *everyone* to like you, and you're not as good as them.

b. Real Me: You're putting impossible demands on Jordan to be liked by everyone (N—type of thought).

c. Protector: You're a fake.

d. Real Me: How does it help Jordan when you make random insults (Q—purpose)?

e. Protector: I'm just trying to make her fit in and say the *right* thing.

f. Real Me: You want her to be who others want her to be, not to find people who like who she *is* (N—intent).

g. Critical Protector: Even if she finds people who like her now, they could leave later—so she has to fit in with everyone in case she gets rejected.

h. Real Me: Where did you first get the idea that Jordan would be left or abandoned (Q—origin)?

i. Protector: Her dad said awful things like, "You'll end up weighing 200 lbs and living in a trailer with your mom." Her mom expects a lot—she never makes good enough grades or does her chores right, and she'll *never* be as good as her sister.

j. Real Me: Do you think demanding the impossible from Jordan will keep her dad from saying cruel things, her mom from being dissatisfied, or others from rejecting her (Q—purpose)?

k. Critical Protector: Yes.

l. Real Me: Your demands make her feel unsure of herself (N—consequences). Does that help her be likeable or witty (Q—purpose)?

m. Critical Protector: No but . . . she needs me (almost pleading).

n. Real Me: What would happen if you weren't so strong? Is there another part of Jordan you're trying to hold back or block (Q—purpose; I—Part)?

o. Critical Protector: There's a real nonconformist inside that is just too different and way too energetic. She's quite scary.

p. Real Me: Can I talk to her? . . . (to new Part) What's it like being so restricted (Q—feelings)? Does the critic need to be afraid of you (Q—purpose).

q. Exuberance: I am different. It seems like others could judge Jordan more when she acts like a clone. If I had a little room to show Jordan's unique side, people would have nothing with which to compare her. I just add a little flair when it's warranted.

r. Real Me (to Critical Protector): What is it like to hear from "Exuberance" (Q—feelings)?

s. Critical Protector (calmer): I'm still not sure if others can handle her . . . but maybe she's not as scary as I thought.

t. Real Me (to Critical Protector): Jordan will always need you to give her guidelines. You've been trying to help all these years (N—intent) but with information that was too harsh. You can help her avoid unnecessary rejection and fit in with people with whom she fits (truth statement).

Typical of many teens, Jordan's Critical Protector is tenacious. Adolescents look at themselves and others with microscopic vision. It may seem that the "Real Me" made little progress in connecting with this contentious Critic, but Higher Selves do not have agendas of any kind, even beneficial ones like communion. They simply witness, narrate, and ask questions to understand all personality parts. In the process, the still *small* voice can become a still *strong* voice, helping Jordan find guidance at odd moments. During inner dialogue, her Critic remained prominent, but she began feeling less driven to seek universal acceptance on a day-to-day basis.

Polarization

Jordan's "Real Me" did ask her Critic one of the essential purpose-clarifying questions—(n) "Is there another personality part you are trying to block?" Personality parts often become polarized into opposite positions. This Critic is in league with a people pleaser that is enforcing conformity. All people have universal qualities that they share with other humans and unique characteristics that are precious to themselves. The fully present person is engaged in a balancing act between *universal* and *unique* facets that vie for expression appropriate to the moment. If one quality is suppressed, the chemistry for a needed response is askew.

When the Real Me questioned Exuberance (p), the Critic was able to hear it for the first time; and, perhaps, devote less energy to squelching it—allowing a natural ebb and flow to emerge. The parade of polarized personality parts is infinite: intellectual/emotional, caution/courage, active/ passive, accepting/rejecting. . . . Jordan's Critic teaches a valuable lesson: When a personality part is unyielding, it may be intent on repressing its (opposite) complement in the continuum that makes a person whole.

CONSOLING HURT, WOUNDED ENERGIES

A parent's worst nightmare is that his or her child might fall prey to sexual abuse. Perceptions of these experiences can become recorded by inner voices that harp on such misinformation as—"It's your fault," "You'll never be safe," "You're trapped" (Shapiro, 2001). Even the physical sensations of the abuse itself can be encapsulated in *emotional buttons*. Yet, these experiences can also be opportunities for children to understand the role personality parts play and how to find comfort from within.

Vignette 16: Jesse

Twelve-year-old Jesse had been molested by her live-in brother-in-law when she was nine. Her sister told her it was not abuse because she had not protested. Jesse never spoke up to her bossy older sister, and she certainly did not know how to say "No" to her brother-in-law when he had always been so kind to her. Four years later, when her sister's family finally moved out, Jesse told her mother. Together, Jesse's mother and counselor helped her discover a "Punisher" that kept her pain in place. They dug deeper to find a "Consoler," and coached it to address any personality parts that were stuck in the past: (N = Narrate; Q = Question.)

   a. Punisher: There must have been something you could have done to stop the abuse. You could have said *No*, told someone, or gone to live with your grandparents.
   b. Consoler: Why do you keep throwing up to Jesse that it was her fault (Q—purpose)?
   c. Punisher: (Quiet but not calm.)
   d. Consoler: Are you trying to make Jesse think she can control or fix everything (Q—purpose)?
   e. Punisher: Spontaneous head nod (tearful).
   f. Consoler: I know you wish Jesse could have stopped her abuse, and I totally understand the reasons why a 9-year-old girl would not know how to handle such a complicated situation (N—intentions, hidden question to provoke inner searching).
   g. Younger part of Jesse: (Feels relieved, but still a little tense.)
   h. Consoler: I'd like to give little Jesse a hug. Cross your arms so opposite hands touch your shoulders and give them alternating taps . . . about ten . . . (narrates butterfly hug).
   i. Young Jesse: I'm afraid that Punisher will come back and blame me some more.
   j. Consoler: It did that for a long time . . . . It kept you from knowing it is not Jesse's fault (N—consequences, makes a statement of truth, continues butterfly hug).
   k. Young Jesse (Feels fine.)

By questioning the purpose of the Punisher, the Consoler finally connected with it—(e) "Are you trying to make Jesse think she can . . . fix everything?" Addresses from the true Self stop subvocal directors from battering *wounded inner children*. The Consoler is coached to help young Jesse discover the *mysterious* truth that the consoler knows—(f) "I understand the reason why . . ." The butterfly hug is started (h) to focus on the little bit of tension that is left. (g). In the process, a new worry surfaced—(g) "I'm afraid the Punisher will come back. . . ." The brain stimulation of the butterfly hug (see Vignette 8) aids insight as well as relaxation. Jesse's fear of the Punisher returning ("It blamed you for a long time . . .") is narrated and a statement of truth to test for change is made—(j) ". . . *it is not Jesse's fault*."

REVIEW AND PRACTICE EXERCISES

The Self's ability to observe enhances the art of dialogue. The goal is *not* to encourage or reassure disheartened personality parts, but (a) to recognize inner voices, (b) to seek the meaning of their messages through narrating and asking questions, (c) to listen for emerging responses, and (d) to remain fully engaged. Personality facets that have been feared, denied, and suppressed are all worthy *opponents* with whom to converse, allowing a person to grow in awareness and flexibility. The first goal (a) cannot be realized without using the language of parts in daily diction. Instead of saying, "I'm worried," "confused," or "annoyed," become comfortable with the phrasing: "A part of me is worried," "confused," or "annoyed."

REVIEW

Steps to Dialogue

A. Preparing distressing thoughts for dialogue.
1. **Notice any distressing thoughts** about yourself or other people.
2. **Rephrase first-person "I" statements** ("I should . . ." "I'll never . . .") into second-person "You" statements ("You should . . ." "You'll never . . .") to dis-identify with the message. Third-person statements ("They better . . ." "She always . . .") are correct grammar for distracting parts that focus on people or objects in the world.
3. **Identify the personality part** that is *voicing* concerns. It helps to first focus on verbal (controlling) subpersonalities, rather than vulnerable energies that are recognized by body tension and emotional release.
    a. Is it an **inner director** that is trying to make emotional energies stay in control, be safe, work harder, please others, or reach perfection?
    b. Is it a **fixed personality** that is trying to distract vulnerable energies by blaming, boasting, avoiding, isolating, or clinging to people or objects in the world?
    c. (Optional) **Represent the subvocal message** with an image, picture, object, name, or symbol. Chapter 4 suggests ideas for emoticons, tarot cards, drawings, dramatic exaggerations, and symbols to represent personality parts.
4. **Write the subvocal message** preceded by the part's identity or name—"Pusher: You better . . ." "Clinger: He has to . . ."

B. Responding to misguided voices.
1. **Identify a name for the deepest part of your Self**. It may simply be "Real Self," a symbol of your will, a spirit guide (from Chapter 2), or a tarot card image (from Chapter 4).
2. **Find words to narrate** what the personality part that has spoken is trying to do.
    a. **Are its intentions** to predict, warn, doubt, scold, order, remind, convince condemn, speculate, order, wish, advise, and so on?
    b. **Is it causing feelings** of pressure, frustration, fear, timidness, hopelessness, regret, helplessness, guilt, sadness, insecurity, jealousy, righteousness?
    c. **What are the consequences** of its line of reasoning? ("When you . . . Jane feels . . ." "Doing . . . could result in . . .")
3. **Formulate questions** when it is not clear what the part is doing, or when you need to go further than narrating intentions, feelings, and consequences:
    a. **Clarify the meaning** of vague messages—"What is bad about . . .?" "What would it mean to . . .?"
    b. **Clarify the origin** of misinformation—"When did . . . first get that idea?" "Where do you think that worry comes from?"
    c. **Clarify the motive** of thoughts—"Why are you bringing this up now?" "How do you think it helps . . . to . . .?" "What is the reason for . . .?" "Why . . . instead of . . .?" "What would happen if . . . did not . . .?" "Is there another part you're

holding back?" "Do you want the last word because you think you are being asked to give up your power or disappear?"

4. **Silently speak** the words you've formulated to narrate (intentions, feelings, or consequences) or question (the meaning, origins, or purpose of) a subpersonality's message.
   a. "**Go inside**" and address the personality part you previously identified.
   b. **Use second-person "You" statements**—"You are reminding . . . to . . ."
   c. **Refer to yourself or others in the third person** by using your name or the pronouns he or she—"You're scolding Joyce and telling her she is lousy" (Vignette 10, b).
   d. **If you journal** narrated observations and questions in writing, also speak silently inside, without reading, when you address a personality part.

5. **Listen for responses** from subpersonalities. They can speak more words or become quiet. You may notice a sense of connection or agreement, or a part may seem to withdraw.
   a. If the subpersonality continues to speak or if a new part offers a different message, **repeat steps A2 through B4d.**
   b. If a nonverbal, emotional part emerges, and you feel fear, sadness, or the desire to cry, **narrate the release of feelings**—"It is fine to cry" or "make noise" "Breathe" "Don't hold back."
   c. Help yourself process sad, tearful, tense feelings and reinforce peaceful sensations with the **butterfly hug** as though it came from your core Self—Cross your arms so opposite hands touch your shoulders and give them alternating taps (about 10 for children and 20 for adults).
   d. After responding to a personality part and listening, you may notice a sense of inner calm. To test if real change has taken place, make a **statement of truth** and notice if any part wants to react or if the feeling of calm persists—". . . it is not Jesse's fault" (Vignette 16, j).

6. **Manage impasses** when a personality part seems to resist making a connection or releasing tension.
   a. Focus on the questions—"Do you think you are being asked to disappear?" or "Is there another (opposite) personality part you are trying to hold back? . . . Can I talk to that part?"
   b. **Ask suppressed parts questions** like—"Do you understand the other part's concerns?" "Do you think its concerns are realistic—why or why not?" "If you were allowed more freedom, how would you express yourself?"
   c. After hearing from a suppressed part, **ask controlling directors** if they have fewer or greater concerns and narrate or question their ideas.
   d. **Visual aids and props** can be helpful during dialogues. In Chapter 3, Sasha (Vignette 11) comforted a crying doll that represented a hurt part. When talking to suppressed energy, tarot cards or emoticons (Chapter 4) representing vocal parts can be placed in a chair to *listen* while the true Self talks to vulnerable energies.
   e. **It is not necessary to break an impasse**. The Higher Self can always end a dialogue by complimenting an inner director on its strength.
   f. **Personality parts do not need to change, integrate, or disappear**. Core Being is strengthened any time it identifies, narrates, or questions individual facets.

7. Be aware of the emergence of a new part.
   a. A suspicious protector that predicts that an irritable wife might be plotting to end a marriage is very different from an angry distracter that ruminates on all of a spouse's flaws to avoid feeling fears of abandonment.
   b. **Notice negative reactions you have toward a part**. This indicates the presence of another subpersonality. Narrating its messages and asking it questions can make its identity clearer—"You seem annoyed with the predictions this protector is making

about . . . 's wife. Are you afraid that the Blamer is going to strike out and make . . . 's wife leave you? Is it hard to trust me (your core Self) to stay connected to the Blamer and help it through its bitterness?" When your real Self is in charge, it will always feel compassionate, caring, or curious toward even the most hostile subpersonalities (Schwartz, 1995).

c. **As you become familiar with a part through dialogue, give it an identity**. This increases awareness of what is happening internally. Any unnamed part that is ignored can turn against you.

PRACTICE

The best way to learn dialogue is to journal mental chatter in a similar fashion to many of the vignettes in this chapter. People can write thoughts as they occur and later review them to ensure that the central Self is identifying parts, narrating types of ideas and feelings, and questioning purposes and meaning.

Research shows that individuals assigned to write about an emotional topic on consecutive days had improved physical health. Varied use of personal pronouns was a major contributing factor to a positive outcome (Campbell & Pennebaker, 2003). For this reason, the art of dialogue that unfolds during journaling is an important activity. Elizabeth Gilbert, in her wonderful book, *Eat Pray Love* (2006), describes her most private notebook that she reaches for when she is spiraling in panic where she writes conversations with an infinitely wise voice that is always available any time day or night. As people become familiar internal dialogue, it flows freely without attention to the details of identifying personality parts or narrating and questioning them.

Vignette 17: Kate

Kate was well practiced in the art of dialogue. Sleep deprivation was her nemesis. After a couple of hours of restful sleep, she would awake to a clamor of voices chatting about her greatest agonies or ecstasies. Her private notebook was filled with odes to her insomnia where she would write herself to sleep:

Small me: I'm scared . . . throat, chest tight. . . . Wise one within will you help me tonight?
Wise One: Name the fear.
Small me: I'm overwhelmed. There's too much on my plate.
Wise One: What tightens Kate's throat?
Small me: I feel all alone. I cannot feel you.
Wise One: I'm here.
Small me: It's hard to believe (that you're here). Have I gotten in over my head?
Wise One: It's not for you to decide. Just allow things to happen and do *only* your best.
Small me: Ah . . . the lullaby from my childhood my mother sang to me . . . *Just do your best*.
Wise One: Stay in (a place of) love. . . . Work from love. . . . Love is all that matters.

Kate fell asleep repeating the last line as a mantra, thinking she had somehow channeled the Beatles.

On another night, she was tackled by the sirens of ecstasy. With her IQ pumped up a few billion points, the following unfolded:

Me: Why am I having an orgy of thoughts, I'd like to know!
  Will they stay or will they go?
  But go they must!
  Divine within, come back to the home you never left.

(Continued)

Are you smiling as you watch ego feasting on itself?
What say you now to this cannibalistic sight?

Divine: I'm perched on high. You leave me little room.
    I watch amazed at synaptic booms.
    I never appear an unbidden guest.
    My powers are great, so ask within,
    "Are you sure I'm wanted to still this din?
    . . . Has everyone had its say—
    Overexcited from too much day?"

Me: I still hear some thoughts:
    "I could show this poem to. . . . It might help him. . . ."
    Is that Show-off Suzy flashing her wares, or . . .
    Helpful Hanna who *really* cares, or. . . .
    Sammie the Slave Driver saying, "Do more, Do more, Do more. . . ."

Divine: So do you want my full presence, my beloved?
    I will bring rest. I know the day is done. Not a thing is left to do.
    I know your secrets . . . your desire to impress.
    But magic happens when you rest.
    Riches come from rest well received.
    Rest in my love and rejoice in whatever you receive.

Kate was awed into a peaceful sleep. Sometimes writing comes more easily to her than the meditation exercises in Chapter 25. For those who are just beginning to learn that talking to your Self is the very opposite of insanity, the following exercise is offered. It addresses the details of dialogue until it unfolds naturally.

Exercise 1

Connecting with Misguided Personality Parts

A 26-year-old woman named Camille had given birth to a baby 8 months previously. She identified a "Size Critic" and an "Inner Comforter" during therapy. However, as she began to dialogue, a new part emerged. Such techniques as the butterfly hug (Vignette 8) and the truth test (Vignette 11) were used to ensure that her real Self thoroughly connected with misguided personality parts. Uncover *suggested* answers in the right column as you move through the dialogue.
(I = Identify; N = Narrate; Q = Question.)

Camille's Dialogue	Suggested Answers
Size Critic: I'm fat; my belly is so big? (Change "I" statement to a "You" message to show that it came from a personality part, not Camille's true self)	Size Critic: You're fat; your belly is so big!
Comforter (N—feelings the Critic is causing): *You are making Camille feel*———	Comforter: You're making Camille feel unattractive and hopeless. How is calling *her* names going to help? (Note that the Comforter refers to Camille in the third person.)
Critic: She's lazy and won't exercise.	

Camille's Dialogue	Suggested Answers
Comforter (Q—reasons for laziness):————	Comforter: Why doesn't she want to exercise?
Critic: She can't spend money on the gym. It would be wasteful to spend money on herself.	
Comforter (N—contradiction in Critic's thinking): ————	Comforter: You're telling her she is too lazy to exercise, but you don't want her to spend money on herself. It seems like you have her in a bind.
Critic (feels calm and quiet for a moment . . .) New voice: She cannot spend time away from her husband. She has to keep him happy.	
(I—new part. Is it a Controller, Protector, Pusher, Pleaser, or Critic)? ————	New part: Pleaser
Pleaser: She cannot spend time away from her husband. She has to keep him happy.	
Comforter (N—type of thought and resulting feeling): ————	Comforter: When you give Camille an order to keep her husband happy, she feels resentful.
Pleaser: But her husband expects her to keep him happy and not to run around.	
Comforter (Q—origin of misinformation): ————	Comforter: Where did you get the idea that Camille has to keep people happy?
Pleaser: Her parents got divorced when she was 10 because her dad cheated. But he said it was Camille's fault. He hated being alone and made Camille feel bad for him. He even asked her to do things that might make her mother want to come back to him. He still does that!	
Comforter (notices anger and tension in arms; N—release of feelings verbally and nonverbally. Use such props as a pillow and feed Camille lines): ————	Comforter: Young Camille had every right to feel angry. You can give a pillow a few punches and pretend you're 10. Tell him it wasn't right. He was an adult; he could have gone on with his life and not involved you.
Comforter (notices a little tension remains and sets up the butterfly hug to process remaining emotion): ————	Comforter: Let me give you a hug while you silently repeat what you just told your father and add any words or actions you like. (Crosses arms so that opposite hands touch shoulders and gives them alternating taps, about 20).
Comforter (notices inner calm; gives Camille a statement of truth to test if she fully understands that it is fine to have time for herself): ————	Comforter: It's okay for Camille to be away from her husband to go to the gym
(Younger part confirms truth test with an additional statement): Your husband's not like your dad. He can take care of himself, and he won't leave (feels calm and connected).	

Seasoned professionals will recognize that the butterfly hug, hitting pillows, and talking to imaginary people are imports from other treatment orientations. *Empowering Dialogues* is a marriage of many therapies that brings a trousseau of something old, something new, something borrowed, and something true to the clinical setting. The stage is set to breathe new life into therapy. The last two chapters will clarify the delivery of protocols and sources from which they have emerged.

Chapter 6

Therapists' Guide to Empowering Dialogues

"Why are you wandering foolishly in the forest?" a son asked his elderly mother.
"I am looking for God," she smiled slyly.
"Isn't God everywhere and always the same?" the young man queried.
"Indeed, the Holy One is, but I am not," countered the matron in delight. (Shulem, n.d.)

Clinicians often feel they are wandering foolishly in their efforts to help people out of wooded thickets that entrap them. But wise therapists know that the way out is to go deeper in. Entering their consulting rooms to be fully engaged with others, counselors become extraordinary, leaving their everyday selves behind. Neophytes, barely out of graduate school, may be transformed by their compassion and literally love their clients through problems. The excitement of learning a new approach can infuse sessions with a healing energy. Journeymen, who have acquired skills and techniques, come to the therapy hour armed with a structure. As long as they do not try to mold people to match their theories, their sense of *expertise* induces enough confidence to just be with

---

The landscape mandala shows the division of polar opposites (earth mother/sky father) producing a new synthesis. The 13-year-old artist placed a tree with an expansive canopy in the foreground expressing her desire to interact with friends who seem to appear on the horizon. The focal point draws the eye endlessly inward—suggesting spirituality that surpasses the artist's years. Designed by Lela Posey and graphically interpreted by Gavin Posey.

those who seek help and allows needed ideas to emerge. Master healers are reborn into the love that brought them to the profession. They have learned that their best teachers are those who come to them in need. After thoroughly analyzing one or many therapeutic strategies, they synthesize the essence of how to use their personhood to reach others.

Empowering Dialogues Within offers new paths to lead clients into the heart of their darkness—to hunt the voices that haunt interiors of the mind and illuminate them. Each person is uncharted territory. There is no "yellow brick road" leading to the center of the Self, but therapists who are acquainted with personality parts and Selves can be guides to help people track trails to true Being. Innovative ideas and a well-defined processes bring excitement and confidence to helpers in their clinical encounters. The method requires practice, but its simplicity can lead counselors to meet others with the most effective part of their own selves. The conception of this uncomplicated approach was born of powerful influences.

THERAPY THROUGH DIALOGUE

The author was dedicated to *eye movement desensitization and reprocessing therapy* (*EMDR*—to be described later) before finding her own way to guide clients. Treatment orientations that are also used to treat severe trauma are included at its conferences. In the early 2000s, she had attended workshops on *ego state therapy* (see Chapter 7). EMDR begins by identifying a person's negative, self-referencing beliefs, while ego state therapy assumes that thoughts, behavior, and experiences organize into *states* that behave like personalities. When the author returned to her own clients, their misguided beliefs started to morph into critical, controlling, three-dimensional subpersonalities.

Over the years, the author developed a fondness for bullies when teaching children and adults how to use a *verbal aikidō* (described in her book *Making Hostile Words Harmless*) to reflect intimidating words without absorbing them. This type of language can create a sort of self- (or part) hypnosis when used in the inner realm. Self-hypnosis is qualified because verbal patterns are not employed to induce a trance, per se, but to evoke involuntary (desired) responses.

Vignette 1: Janette

Janette had an inner critic that bullied her in social situations. But she was also aware of a "Spiritual Self" that brought quiet calmness. She had recently started attending an adult Bible class at her church: (N = Narrate; Q = Question.)

a. Critic: You're not as spiritual as others.
b. Spiritual Self: You're comparing Janette to others (N—intentions to compare).
c. Critic: Yea—you need to become better.
d. Spiritual Self: Can she ever be good enough for you (Q—purpose)?
e. Critic: When you reach that point, you will know it.
f. Spiritual Self: So, until Janette reaches that point, are you going to point out flaw after flaw and make her miserable (Q—purpose, N—feelings)?
g. Critic: (Quiet; feels calm.)

Janette's counselor helped her "Spiritual Self" follow a basic tenant of hypnosis—using video talk to narrate her critic's thought process. By pointing out that the inner bully was comparing, a core Self arrested these unwanted patterns. Questions that asked whether the critic was going to continue to point out flaws, subtly *suggested* it had a choice. Suggestion is the heart of hypnosis.

ROLE OF THE COUNSELOR-COACH

The therapist coaches clients to access their Higher Selves by feeding them lines to dialogue with misguided personality parts. Counselors must first recognize dictatorial, distracting voices and emotional energies that surround core Being and materialize or reify them into objects that can be addressed.

The review of steps to dialogue outlined in Chapter 5 begins with recognizing inner voices. The therapist in Vignette 1 noticed a statement Janette made that identified a personality part. She complained, "I'm not as spiritual as others." Introducing the language of parts in a nondidactic way, her counselor replied, "A part of you doesn't think you are spiritual. It sounds pretty critical of you." A clear distinction is made between the part (it) and Janette (you). This facet has also been given an identity—it is a critic. Janette readily agreed that she is always giving *herself* a hard time. Once a subpersonality has been named, it can more easily be used to raise awareness of internal dynamics.

Begin Dialogue: Parts Talk

Capitalizing on Janette's acknowledgment of the critic, the therapist began to set up dialogue through linguistic maneuvers. The first-person "I" statement ("I'm not as spiritual . . .") was rephrased as a second-person "You" statement. The counselor-coach suggested, "Perhaps this critic is saying, 'You're not as spiritual as others.'"

Then she probed to identify the true Self. The idea was presented that somewhere deep within Jeanette something did not want this critic to compare her to others. There was a barely detectible head nod in agreement, so the counselor continued, "I wonder what you call the part of you that sees through the critic's comparisons, that gives you peace of mind or even an instant of comfort." Without hesitating, Jeanette, who is obviously interested in religion responded, "The *Holy Spirit* gives me all of that." Her counselor changed the name slightly to establish it as an internal resource—"So it is your "Spiritual Self" that knows this sort of nagging, in a Bible class, of all places, isn't right!" Again, Jeanette's head spontaneously nodded in agreement.

Some psychologists can be dismissive of religious language, not recognizing empowering resources these clients bring into the counseling setting. In Chapter 5, the dialogues evolved through client-counselor discussions. Or people brought in scripts they had journaled on their own. Obviously, many people were not of a spiritual ilk, but had other nomenclatures to suggest unifying forces within—"At Ease," "Logical Self," "Giggles," "Knower." However, it may be difficult for some people to identify titles for the true Self until they are experienced in dialogue; therefore, the search for a reference is never belabored. Just plain "Self" is entirely suitable until a more descriptive term is discovered.

THE SELF OBSERVES AND QUERIES

With inner voices and core Being named, peoples' identities begin to shift from personality fragments to their true Selves. Coaching can begin in earnest. The Self is directed to narrate or describe thinking patterns, resulting feelings, or consequences of a line of reasoning. Jeanette was told, "Have your 'Spiritual Self' *go inside* and tell the critic it's comparing Jeanette to others and listen to how it responds" (b). It helps therapists to be familiar with labels for a variety of thought processes—*warning, predicting, doubting, scolding, condemning, degrading, ordering, reminding, convincing, guessing, wishing, advising, comparing,* and so on.

If Jeanette had talked to the critic aloud, she would have been asked to speak silently to the part. Brain mapping studies show that counting aloud activates motor areas of the cortex used in normal, wakeful states, while subvocal counting energizes the frontal lobes, which become dominate during meditation. A focused inward journey is encouraged through silent speaking. This feels natural, evokes responses from parts and Selves, and helps people distinguish argumentative messages from true guidance.

Jeanette's core Self was also guided to ask questions about the meaning, origin, and purpose of disturbing comments—(d) "Can she ever be good enough?" and (f) "Are you going to point out flaw after flaw and make her miserable?" At first, clients are given the exact words to use. As dialogue becomes more familiar, they are taught that Higher Selves only make two responses—(1) they either narrate or point out what a personality part is thinking, or (2) they ask questions to clarify a comment. Jeanette might have been given a choice—"Does your 'Spiritual Self' want to tell the critic it's adding more pressure (N—feelings) or ask if she can ever be good enough (d)?" Gradually, the counselor-coach simply asks, "What could your real Self point out to or ask this personality part now?"

The list of helpful questions for Higher Selves to ask personality parts are repeated here from Chapter 5. They will become obvious and natural as clinicians engage their clients in dialogue:

6.4

- *Origin questions:* Where do you think . . . (Jeanette) first got that idea?
- *Meaning questions:* What is bad about . . . ? What would it mean to . . . ?
- *Motive questions:* What is the reason for . . . ? Why . . . instead of . . . ? What would happen if you did not tell Jeanette . . . ? What do you really want for Jeanette? . . . What role would you like for yourself if you did not have to control (protect or push) Jeanette? Is there a less extreme position you could take ? Do you want the last word because you think you are being asked to disappear?
- *Polarity questions (to dominant parts):* Is there another, opposite part you're trying to hold back? What are your concerns about it? (To suppressed parts): If you were allowed more freedom, how would you express yourself? Do you understand the other part's concerns? Do you think its concerns are realistic?
- *Questions to identify new parts:* When your critic tells Jeanette she's worthless, it sounds like another part wants to make the critic disappear. Can you ask that part if it is angry at the critic? Is it worried that your true Self won't be able to take charge? How do you see this part? What would you call it? "Superhero" parts that do not like negative verbiage can easily be mistaken for the true Self, but the core Being is always compassionate, caring, or curious toward even the most hostile subpersonalities (Schwartz, 1995).

Listening Within

Clients report responses they hear to statements or questions posed by the Self. Counselors become eavesdroppers and continue to encourage narration or inquiry—"What could your spiritual Self point out now?" "What could the knower ask here?" If clients step outside the boundaries of narrating and querying, counselors need to become active and identify debates. Jeanette might have said to the critic, "She will catch up to the others in her class" (b). Then the therapist would have explained that this is a reassurance that fuels the critic. She might have experimented with how narrating ("You're comparing Jeanette to others") feels different from reassurance.

Eventually, clients will notice a lack of response from personality parts. They may say, "I don't hear anything." The counselor points out engagement of a part by the Self: "The critic has become quiet. . . . How does that feel?" Although some people experience the sound of silence as strange, most notice relief or even a sense of connection (g). An inner bully has been befriended, and the Self empowered. Even though another misguided part will surely rise again, the decibel level of the *still small voice* has been strengthened. It will gradually become a more audible still *strong* voice.

Therapists remain watchful of clients' tones and demeanors to notice if their next statement suggests the reactivation of the personality part or the emergence of a new one. As clients become more familiar with multitudinous facets through dialogue, it is important to give them identities. This increases awareness of what is happening in the community of Self. Any unnamed, ignored parts can sabotage progress. However, laughter and pearls of wisdom suggests that clients are allied with their true Selves. The process can start anew with the therapist pointing out statements that suggest a subpersonality's emergence or the presence of reasonable, intuitive, transcendent Selves.

COACHING AIDS

Counselors and clients can simultaneously journal dialogue. Jeanette, (Vignette 1) a college student, often brought a notepad to sessions to jot down important points. Together, she and her therapist wrote her dialogue line by line as it unfolded. In previous sessions, she had learned that her true Self simply needed to narrate and question subpersonalities, and she had experienced the benefits of using her counselor's words to speak silently to inner parts. After journaling the dialogue in Vignette 1 verbatim she remarked, "Now I see what you've been telling me all along!"

WRITTEN WORDS

Writing slows down the process. This helps clinicians and clients consider the best response to verbiage from powerful bullies within and teaches dialogical patterns. In Chapter 5 (Vignette 11), Theresa's "Fixer" told her that she must help her ex-husband if *he* thought she was obligated. Together, she and her counselor looked at the Fixer's words on paper and pondered its intent. Taking time to think engaged Theresa's intuitive Self and she announced, "It's holding me hostage to my ex-husband's impossible demands!" This was easily transposed into a narrative response—"You hold Theresa hostage to her ex-husband's impossible demands." Normally, Theresa talked so quickly and with so much detail that her therapist could barely follow her line of thought. Journaling gave her relief from fruitless rambling and focusing on others' behavior.

Not every session needs to be journaled, but in the beginning having a verbatim account of dialogue to study helps clients see the process of (a) narrating intentions, feelings, and consequences related to a thought; and (b) questioning a message's meaning, origin, and purpose.
Even when clients do not want to journal, it can be helpful for therapists to write a script of the interplay between parts and the Self.

The line that finally calms an agitated facet can be written on a three-by-five card as a reminder that clients can take home to repeat silently to a disturbing subpersonality. One young man with a powerful people pleaser found he regained his composure by looking at a cue card that read, "Do you believe you can control what others think of you?"

Clients vary greatly in their ability to write dialogues. Some just need to be given a question to write that begins an internal exchange—"How can we find peace since our (adult) son left home two nights ago and may be lying dead in a ditch somewhere overdosed on drugs?" The dialogue just flowed: "Forgive yourself for all of your past mistakes . . . focus on the grace that *is* in your life . . ."

Other people are so cut off from their core Self that they draw a total blank with the first question or observation—"I'm tired of being a nervous wreck." "What does Marcus need to do to let go of his worries?"

When no answer is forthcoming, the therapist steps in forcefully—"Let's talk to the part that's making things difficult" (they journal together). Self: "I know it's hard for Marcus to have faith. What thoughts make it hard?"

Marcus quickly wrote: "I'm afraid."

His counselor made the written query: "Of what is Marcus afraid?"

He pondered and then wrote: "Dying."

His counselor knew he was haunted by Vietnam flashbacks and more recent memories of surviving "C" (he will not even say the word cancer). She put down the words: "How soon is your end coming?"

He spoke and then wrote: "I don't know. It's not up to me."

His therapist wrote as his core Self: "Ah, we finally know who is giving Marcus so much trouble—you're his Controller, and you've just admitted there is something over which you have no power. Do you have any other questions?"

Marcus smiled and then wrote: "Am I going to suffer when I die?"

The answer came from within. He had connected to his Core, "You are already suffering with your incessant worrying, only your thoughts bring about pain."

Marcus now had something tangible that he could take home and study when his formerly unnamed fears came over him and a guide to help him practice the art of dialogue.

The work of R. Sherlock Campbell and James W. Pennebaker (2003) underscores this vital process of writing. They reviewed numerous studies in which college students and prisoners were asked to write about emotional issues on consecutive days. Campbell and Pennebaker compared those essays with essays written by control subjects who were asked to write on superficial topics. Persons who wrote about upsetting instances had fewer physician visits for a period of time following the exercise. Campbell and Pennebaker used a semantic instrument to analyze the use of pronouns in particular. They found the more individuals varied their use of pronouns, the more their health improved. They theorized that pronouns offer a different lens through which individuals see the world.

Teaching clients the language of parts and having them practice in writing not only addresses emotional issues but teaches flexibility in pronoun use. Therefore, it is important to encourage writing both in and out of sessions. Chapter 2, Exercises 1 and 2, also create written experiences that offer easy ways of connecting with the Self by tickling the memory to recall powers within that help clients survive adversity and by fueling passion toward future goals.

VISUAL AIDS

Once clients have experienced the process of dialogue, the "Community of Self" (Figure 5.1) from Chapter 5 provides a clear portrayal of the subdivided nature of the mind. It was used to explain to Janette (Vignette 1) that her Spiritual Self is a "Central Self" that dialogues with all personality parts. Her (triangle-shaped) critic is pointed at an (exploding-shaped) emotional entity, telling it— "You're not as spiritual as others." "You need to become better." "When you're finally good enough, you'll know it." By narrating and questioning ("You're comparing . . ." "Can she ever be good enough?" "Are you going to keep on making her miserable?") her Spiritual Self draws the critic's attention to her core Being, away from vulnerable energies.

Jeanette's critic could have been a judger, complaining—"Others are not spiritual enough; they are hypocrites who are too involved in worldly matters." First, her Spiritual Self would have been coached to say—"You like to focus on flaws in others." "Does it help Jeanette feel better to think about others' spiritual shortcomings?" On the "Community of Self" (Figure 5.1), she would be shown the boldface triangles that face outward trying to manage or control the world. It would be easy to ask—"Which triangle parts (in Figure 5.1)) try to *direct* emotions?" and "Which ones try to *distract* emotions?" The directing, distracting, and emotional components of the triune personality and the Central Self are clearly illustrated.

PROPS

Chapter 4 has several visual aids for identifying inner facets. Exercise 6 shows how to use smiley or frowny faces made with keyboard strokes to represent various personality facets and true Selves. These **emoticon images** can be drawn on three-by-five cards that are folded in half so that they stand up. They are particularly helpful when clients hear a cacophony of inner voices. Each misguided message can be written as a caption below the emoticon, and an image for the true Self can face them one at a time to narrate and question them.

Exercise 8 explained how to sort **tarot card pictures** so they can also be used to identify personality parts and Higher Selves. The images in the standard Rider-Waite deck can add amazing depth to therapy. Often people have difficulty gaining any sense of their true Self. After looking at a stack of cards that symbolize positive forces or sources for guidance and support, people can choose pictures that *touch* them and discover that they have a compassionate, caring, supportive Self. Other cards personify critical or demanding parts. People can enjoy arranging the tarot cards they have chosen on a table to show the positions subpersonalities or Selves currently play in their inner lives.

Tarot card arrangements are easy to photocopy. They can be kept in client charts and taken home as reminders of inner dynamics. One young woman commented that seeing the charging knight and graceful page with a sword on her refrigerator every morning reminded her that she could be gentle with her anger and not storm at everyone.

Therapists who explore the subdivided mind are advised to be well supplied with **stuffed animals, dolls, or figurines** that can symbolize controlling, protective, pushy, pleasing, critical, vulnerable, distracting parts, and Higher Selves. Exercise 9 in Chapter 4 gives additional ideas on how to scavenge for objects to represent inner facets and Selves. A gloomy Eeyore, fretful Piglet, pushy Rabbit, disapproving Owl, and curious, observant Pooh are especially helpful props to portray parts and core Being. They work equally well with adults and children.

Experiment to find out if clients relate best to emoticons, tarot cards, objects, or their own drawings. Any image makes inner voices or cognitions three-dimensional and helps people dis-identify from them—"That is not you, it is only a part of you." Paradoxically, symbols that portray sources of inner strength help people connect to them and aide in reflecting and questioning misguided messages.

When dealing with a polarity, props for the dominant end of the duo can be set aside, and the representation of the suppressed part placed nearby where the therapist can coach the Higher Self to ask it questions.

The emoticon cards provide a visual reflection of Celia's internal dynamics. She is a concrete person who drives heavy equipment. Deep symbolism found in tarot cards and childish stuffed animals hold little interest for her.

Vignette 2: Celia

Celia was no longer afraid of a phantom ghost of her ex-husband charging through the walls to do violence to her (see Chapter 4, Vignette 4). Her son could even phone his father on a calling card from her house. She came to her session ready to discuss her son's next step toward increased contact with his father, but when she wrote her name on the waiting room sign-in sheet, she made a tiny error and innocently asked for whiteout.

Celia's counselor said the mistake had to stay. Once in therapy chambers, Celia could not concentrate on visitation issues. Her "Fixer" (that previously complained that she should have been able to prevent her husband from perpetrating domestic violence) was shouting, "If you can't fix that scribble, you're going to have to straighten your house from top to bottom." Her therapist asked why she looked amused as she reported the Fixer's orders, and she replied that her "Ms. Whatever" part was laughing hysterically in the background.

Emoticon cards for the Fixer and Ms. Whatever were put on a chair. Her therapist suggested that the Fixer be placed in a remote area of the room so that her true Self could talk to Ms. Whatever and find out what was so amusing. The answer was a firm "No!" Celia preferred to get rid of Ms. Whatever and move *her* to a different chair. Rephrasing in the language of parts, her counselor said, "The Fixer is saying, 'Ms. Whatever should be banished. It is too dangerous to have her around.'"

"But it wasn't always that way," Celia mused. "I used to do my laundry when I ran out of clothes. Now the Fixer makes me run a load every day, even if there is hardly anything to wash. I can hear Ms. Whatever laughing, but I'm not connected to her anymore. It's like there is a window separating us."

"Does the *real you* know when you were last connected?" coached her counselor.

"When I got married, my husband controlled every move I made, and the Fixer took over. Maybe neatness and order was a way of covering up the terror I constantly felt."

"Now, can you find out why Ms. Whatever laughs?" encouraged her therapist.

"She's telling me, 'It's over. There's no need to be a fanatic.'" Celia placed Ms. Whatever side by side with the Fixer.

6.8

IMAGERY AIDS

In addition to visual aids, the counselor-coach helps people develop private images that can only be viewed in the mind of the beholder. Clients who refer to their **true Self** as "just me," my "real Self" or my "Reason" may enjoy experiencing a more powerful image provided by the exercises in Chapter 2—"Tunneling Inward" (Exercise 3), "Mountain Spirit" (Exercise 5), and "Flowing Water" (Exercise 10) offer a means to connect people to powerful resources within. Therapists do not simply talk clients through the narratives given, but set up the scene and ask clients about the images that come to them.

From Exercise 3, Chapter 2:

Counselor: Imagine a meadow. . . . Describe it to me. . . . Are there any trees, flowers, or animal life?
Rita: The meadow has bright green grass with little flowers popping up everywhere. . . .
Counselor: In the distance there is a mountain . . . find out how to reach it. . . .
Rita: I'm following a path that leads to a beautiful mountain in the distance. Although it is far away, time collapses, and suddenly, I'm there. . . .
Counselor: Notice that there is a path going up the mountain or a hidden opening that leads to a tunnel that cuts through to the heart of the mountain. Both routes hold promise . . . you will know which one to take. . . .
Rita: I see some bushes and notice an opening behind them. I'm intrigued because from somewhere far away, deep inside there is a glow lighting the way. . . .

Clients who have personality traits that make interpersonal encounters problematic can find revealing truths about their characters with the dwelling imagery in Exercise 2. This is also an excellent exercise to use with couples. It helps identify character traits that may be contributing to conflicts and avoids diverting content. Therapists may want to explore the "Interactive Guided Imagery" techniques of Martin Rossman and David Bresler (2000) to further their understanding of this method of co-creating images with clients. Although not a mental image, the designs produced while creating mandalas (Chapter 2, Exercise 4) offer symbolic dialogue between Selves and parts and may simply be enjoyable and calming for the artistically inclined.

FOSTERING MINDFULNESS AND MEDITATIVE STATES

Developing powers of observation is fundamental to strengthening the witness Self. Therapists can use mindfulness, Exercises 6 through 9 in Chapter 2, to help clients experience their observant Self. Initially, it will help clients to lead them through these experiences. Noticing thoughts and sensations is a warm-up for internal dialogues with subpersonalities. When thoughts are racing too quickly for dialogue or when people are overwhelmed with anxiety, simply concentrating on a focal point and practicing "Aware Breathing" (Exercise 7) along with "Mindful Meditation" (Exercise 8) can restore a sense of calm. The disturbing issue should not be abandoned, but revisited when some degree of stillness is attained. Troubling personality parts are invited to resurface, but a serene Center has been engaged to describe and question their misguided messages.

Tarot cards can also be used for a meditative activity, to instill a sense of calm, or to identify a safe place. Have clients choose a card from the *inner Self* stack (Chapter 4, Exercise 8) that portrays a sense of peace or calm. Ask them to imagine themselves inside the card and interactively explore the scene with them. Do not be surprised at the object of a person's focus or the tiny details they include.

Vignette 3: Kate

Kate chose to focus on the Ace of Pentacles card. She began describing what she saw in first person: "I am a star enclosed in a circle. I'm nestled in a hand that reaches out from a cloud, and I feel totally secure. It is as though I'm lying in the hand of God—nothing can touch me. I know below me is a green garden with a topiary gate where people (thoughts) can enter. But I need total solitude, so the hand lifts me higher into a dark sky past the stars until I am in the still void of space, and here I find the peace I need."

Kate did not know that the pentacle suit in a tarot deck represents coins or security. Other clients who are attracted to this particular card see the upheld star as a symbol of independence. Each person projects what they need to see in the card of their liking. Tarot cards offer a repertoire of safe-place scenarios for people that extends beyond the usual beach and bedroom backdrops and opens a door to the imagination.

COUNSELING EMOTIONAL ENTITIES AND ABREACTION

Contacting encapsulated emotions can move beyond coaching the Self. Sometimes the therapist must directly address a difficult personality part. In Chapter 4 (Vignette 4) Celia first identified emoticon images for the subvocal messages that marched through her mind. Before she was able to do this, her therapist had to help her release an outpouring of affect that an emotional entity had been storing.

Vignette 4: Celia

Celia heard a personality part say, "Your ex-husband is coming into the room. . . . You're not safe!" It was this inner protector that caused her to bolt from the room where her son was having a conference call with his father. Her therapist coached her reasonable Self to silently point out the Protector's intentions— "You're trying to shield Celia from something that cannot happen now." Describing its verbiage silenced the incessant Protector, but she could still sense a fearful part lurking within.

Going deeper, her counselor coached Celia's core Self to silently mirror the emotional entity's feelings: "Tell the frightened part it has every right to finally feel terror. . . . You went through a lot."

As her eyes brimmed full of tears, a strong voice spoke up, "I don't like that! Celia has to stay in *control*. She will be useless if she feels the horror of it all over again!"

Recognizing the importance of helping the emotional part release trapped tension, her therapist addressed this inner Controller directly—"Of course you don't want Celia to reexperience past terror, but it's safe now. She had to be in control when she was constantly on guard with her husband. Now he lives 1,500 miles away; it's safe to feel how awful it was."

Cecelia was sobbing. Her counselor spoke to the emotional entity—"Don't hold back; cry; your real Self can cross your arms across your chest so the tips of your hands alternately tap just above your shoulder bones" (demonstrating while she talked).

As Celia cried, the Controller pleaded, "I don't want her to feel it."

Her counselor kept focusing on the emotional part—"You can let out all the old fear and allow your true Self to comfort with the shoulder taps. Your Self was inside the whole time your ex was terrifying you with his threats; it was holding you up, helping you survive."

Cecelia tapped her shoulders for a little longer and then stopped. Her therapist asked, "Is the frightened part still there?" She appeared to listen for a moment and said "No." Have your real Self tell the Protector, "Celia is safe now," and find out what it says. Again Celia appeared to listen intently and, after a moment, she reported that the Protector was quiet and seemed more connected to her.

Any time people have angry, sad, or fearful emotions, these vulnerable (or forceful) energies were activated by misguided messages of dominant subpersonalities. Coaching people to question a line of thinking (much in the manner of cognitive therapy) will totally or partially relieve the pressure on emotional entities. Celia in the previous vignette enjoyed telling her protector, "You're trying to shield her from something that cannot happen now," but fearful affect lingered. When people have endured traumas like domestic violence, often tensions from the experience are stored in *emotional buttons* that become parts of the personality. Outdated information from the experience is also recorded in inner voices ("You're not safe"; "stay in control") but questioning these misguided messages will not relieve a deposit of long-held tension.

Freud and his mentor Josef Breuer (1893, translated 2004) found that recalling an event and releasing related affect permanently resolved symptoms related to the event. They called this process **abreaction**. After Celia's protective subpersonality was quieted, her core Self was coached to contact the emotional entity with the words, "You have every right to finally feel your fear. . . . You went through a lot." Simply validating her feelings and encouraging her to notice them was enough to start abreaction. As Celia's eyes were brimming full of tears, the voice of the "Director of Control" jumped in saying Celia would be useless if she reexperienced former emotions. Now the therapist stepped outside of the role of a coach and addressed this controller directly, both validating the past ("Of course you don't want Celia to reexperience those emotions . . ."), while staying in the safety of the present ("It's safe to feel how awful it was . . . now.") This *dual focus of attention* further assists emotional release.

Therapists who recognize the importance of releasing emotions are keenly aware of affect and **encourage discharge**—"It's fine to cry"; "Don't hold back"; "You can make noise"; "Breathe"; and so on. Simple reminders to cry and make noise are important because a favorite censoring mechanism to choke back tears is to hold the breath and stifle sound. Celia's therapist added a new tool in the processing of emotion: the butterfly hug.

PROCESSING EMOTIONS WITH BRAIN STIMULATION

The butterfly hug is an innovation of *eye movement desensitization and reprocessing therapy (EMDR)*, which encourages clients to follow clinicians' horizontal (or diagonal) hand movements with their eyes. This causes *dual attention (brain) stimulation (DAS)* to unlock frozen information and stored tension.[1] The brain cortex, with its repositories of helpful information and capacities for reason, is engaged to reevaluate early experiences.

Francine Shapiro developed EMDR in the early 1980s when she researched the mystifying therapeutic effects of rapid eye movements that helped veterans resolve flashbacks from wars. Eye movements were employed in Vignette 6, Chapter 4 when Dulci's eyes darted back and forth between tarot cards representing "Eternal Pressure" that she had to make things right and a "Sun Seer" telling her that she only had limited control. As Shapiro gained a better understanding of her method, alternating body taps and auditory tones were found to be effective DAS in expediting the reevaluation of disturbing material. In teaching workshops, Shapiro has stated that EMDR could have more simply been named "reprocessing therapy."

In 1997, a practioner of EMDR was inspired to use alternating hand taps that simulated the flapping of a butterfly's wings with a large group of children who had survived hurricane Paula in Acapulco Mexico.[2] The positive results from using these self-induced DAS opened new vistas for reprocessing traumatic events. In Vignette 3, Celia's therapist instructed her to execute the **butterfly hug** as though it came from her real Self—"You can . . . cross your arms over your chest . . . allow your true Self to comfort you."

Several examples in Chapter 5 employed this butterfly hug once feelings started flowing. In Vignette 8, Emily's real Self silently said, "You still have a voice inside that makes you feel guilty for your dad yelling at your sister. . . . Cross your arms and tap your shoulders so I can give you a hug (that will help your People Pleaser reprocess maladaptive information)." In Vignette 16, 12-year-old Jesse's Consoler was coached to give her a butterfly hug after suggestions that there were reasons

---

[1] Based on observation and research, alternating, bilateral (left-right) visual, audio, or tactile stimulation appears to reprocess unhelpful information stored in the brain during trauma or repeated abuse to a level of current accuracy. During the procedure, a state of balanced or dual attention is achieved by focusing on an internal experience (image, thought, sensation) and external stimulation (eye movement, auditory tones, taps). Simultaneous attention to a disturbing memory and present context results in decreased disturbance and new associations between memory networks (Shapiro, 2001).

[2] Lucina Artigas gave the children 8.5 by 11 inch sheets of paper folded into four sections. In the upper left corner, the children drew an image of the worst part of the hurricane. Focusing on the image, the children crossed their arms over their chests and alternately tapped the area between their clavicle and shoulder approximately fifteen times. Then they drew the next image that came to their mind in the upper right corner of the paper and repeated the butterfly hug. A third and forth image were drawn, each following the butterfly hug. By the third image, most of the children were drawing less horrific images or future-oriented pictures. Those whose sketches remained disquieting were instructed to think about what they wanted in the future during the last butterfly hug and to draw that image. At the end of the exercise the children had bright smiles on their faces and thanked the "doctors" for helping them. This is the report remembered by the author when Artigas received the Creative Innovation Award at the 2000 EMDRIA Conference.

why a 9-year-old girl could not stop sexual abuse. This helped place attention on truths that Higher Selves hold. Gradually, Jesse felt calmer. Although shoulder taps are used in limited ways in these examples, therapists who have been trained in EMDR might want to employ them or eye movements more extensively every time the core Self speaks silently to a personality part.

ABREACTING ANGRY AFFECT

Crying and sobbing are not the only form of emotional release or abreaction. Breuer, Freud's mentor, believed that strong affect, such as anger, must be discharged with **motor activity** along with verbal expression. A little less than 100 years later, the originator of EMDR also concluded that the release of body tensions, indicating suppression of certain body reactions during an experience of trauma, "should be encouraged (by) act(ing) out the associated movement, such as striking out. This allows stored (muscular) information to be adequately processed" (Shapiro, 2001, p. 184). Therapists can firmly hold a seat cushion on their hip and tell clients to alternately poke or punch the pillow while speaking in a role-play. The alternate pokes or punches encourages DAS to reprocess and release anger more efficiently.

In Chapter 5, Exercise 1, Camille noticed feeling tension in her arms while remembering that her father tried to use her to lure his wife back to him after his infidelities. Even as an adult, Camille became his ploy for contact with his ex-wife. Feeling tension in arms and curled fists are common indicators of suppressed anger. Camille's therapist coached her Comforter to validate this feeling— "You had every right to feel angry"—and encouraged discharge—"You can give a pillow a few punches just to find out how much anger is inside." Feeding the **unspoken words** she was not able to say in the past, Camille repeated, "What you did was not right. . . . You were the adult. . . . You didn't need to involve me in your messed up life."

Expressing anger physically and verbally with the therapist aids a dual focus of attention by bringing past suppressed words and movements into a safe present. When clients' energies seem spent, the newly engaged Will can be encouraged to **silently rehearse** empowering words and movements with brain stimulation (butterfly hug, eye movements, etc.). In Exercise 1, Camille's Comforter continued, "Let me give you a (butterfly) hug while you silently repeat what you just told your father and add any words or actions you like." Mentally rehearsing unspoken words and movements with brain stimulation helps focus attention on the adaptive information core Selves hold. Indeed, Camille felt more connected to her "Self" after the butterfly hug.

It is important that counselors neither evade nor push clients to discharge forceful energies they *should* feel. Like a surfer, they need to catch anger indicators and ride the wave until it is spent. Because EMDR therapists move their hands back and forth in front of clients' faces to facilitate making eye movements, occasionally fear can be triggered in a person who has experienced physical abuse. One young woman grabbed her counselor's wrist and barely whispered, "Don't touch me." At that point, the therapist could have offered her slight resistance as she clutched his wrist and encouraged release of anger—"Push on my wrist. . . . Say it louder, 'Don't touch me.'" Both the discharge of body tension and expression of *unvoiced* words would have been served.

TESTING FOR CHANGE WITH STATEMENTS OF TRUTH

Whether therapy has remained at a cognitive level by narrating and clarifying a line of thinking or focused on discharge of emotions, it is wise to determine if a portion of work is complete by coaching the core Self to make a statement of truth about the original issue. At the end of Vignette 3, Celia's counselor asked her real Self to tell her Protector subpersonality, "Celia is safe now." She then listened to find out if further warnings were triggered. This is similar to the last part of the treatment protocol in EMDR in which the client is asked to rate the truth of a *positive cognition*.

An EMDR therapist would have Celia rate the truth of the statement, "I'm safe now," on a scale of one to seven.

In Chapter 5, Camille punched a pillow while telling her father in a role-play it wasn't right for him to make her responsible for his happiness. Later, her therapist tested her newfound calm by having her make a statement of truth to a younger part of herself—"It's okay for Camille to take time away from her husband . . . (because he can take care of himself)." Her original issue in that session had been feeling responsible for the happiness of her loved ones (especially her husband) because she had been a slave to her father's emotional needs as a child.

COMPARISON TO RELATED APPROACHES

Two other approaches to the subdivided mind warrant close examination. Their similarities to and differences from this text lead to a deeper understanding of empowering dialogue.

INTERNAL FAMILY SYSTEMS THERAPY

Richard Schwartz was a devotee of structural/strategic family therapy with its taboo against inquiring about an individual's inner life. However, in the early 1980s, he was stymied by a case in which the functioning of a family was markedly improved, while their adult daughter continued to have bouts of bulimia. Out of frustration with the limitations of his theoretical model, Schwartz crossed into forbidden territory and asked the young woman what she experienced before she went on a binge-and-vomit spree. She began describing a confusing commotion of inner *voices*. Through working with her and many more of his clients, the inner quarrels they described gradually separated into a group of entities he called *parts* and Schwartz's *internal family systems* (IFS) *therapy* was born.

Personality Parts and the True Self

Because of Schwartz's background, he imagined personality parts and the true Self to operate like a family system that is vulnerable to the same forces that cause external domestic dysfunction. A personality part is a discrete mental unit with emotions, expression, abilities, desires, interests, talents, temperaments, and worldviews. Parts may even have different ages (Schwartz, 1995, p. 34). They *almost* sound like "alter personalities" that are formed to cope with a specific life struggle and remain intent on maintaining their identities. However, personality parts want to play a constructive role and will relinquish their extreme position once they are assured that the core Self can safely lead the system.

The core or true Self is both a compassionate inner leader and an expansive, limitless state of mind that has been and is always present in an individual. When young people do not receive proper support from caretakers, a chain reaction is triggered inside. Some parts become self-critical, controlling, and watchful to prevent and "manage" further difficulties, while other facets rebel and distract with tantrums, over- or undereating, poor bowel and bladder control, and the like. Frightened, hurt parts have crying spells, repeat scary thoughts, or have nightmares. They become "exiles."

Internal Family Systems Protocol

The steps in IFS therapy have some commonalities with empowering dialogues. The counselor begins by feeding back a clients' problem using the language of parts. A client might comment, "I think . . . ," and the therapist translates, "So a part of you thinks. . . ." The person is asked to use **insight** to focus on the feeling, thought pattern, inner voice, or sensation associated with a particular part and to allow an image to come to mind that represents it. If an image does not appear, clients note where they sense the part is located. Clients are asked how they feel toward the identified part. Emotions other than compassion, curiosity, or acceptance suggest other personality facets are contaminating the true Self. Resentful or fearful parts may need to be identified and asked to move to an imaginary room until the real Self is finished talking to the part.

The ultimate goal is for the Self to ask the part a series of questions (a) to determine what factors keep it playing its extreme role (of protecting, pushing, pleasing, distracting, and so on) and (b) to explore what kind of function it would prefer. The process is similar to coaching the Self described in this text. The counselor might suggest the real Self ask the Critic: "Can Janette ever be good enough for you?" "Where did you first get the idea that Jordan would be left out?" "If you didn't have to protect her from getting hurt, what else would you like to do?"

Direct access is a second IFS method for doing inner work. As with insight, the client is asked to focus internally on a part and to find out if it is willing to speak directly to the therapist. Instead of coaching the Self, the therapist speaks to the facet. Sometimes this requires a slight change of grammar—"Can Janette ever be good enough?" The goal remains the same: to increase awareness of extreme messages a part is voicing and so it can ultimately trust the Self to assume leadership of the internal community. For various advantages and disadvantages of direct access, see Schwartz, 1995, pp. 123–126.

In this book, the therapist only steps in to directly address a part when it is interfering with the natural progression of the work. This happened in Vignette 4 earlier when Celia's controlling subpersonality said it did not want her to reexperience the horror of her terror. Clients with personality disorders have great difficulty with insight and may need to become familiar with their subpersonalities by counselors directly addressing them.

Theory

Schwartz takes cautions to ensure that emotional parts do not overwhelm the Self with **feelings**. When possible the Self may help a part by entering a scene from the past through imagery and help it obtain what it needed but was not available at the time of the event. Schwartz supports other means of comforting exiled parts by empathizing with their stories, holding their bodies (through imagery), accepting their flaws, playing with them, and setting up other parts as caretakers. Dialogue therapy finds that discharge is often unnecessary because narrating and questioning the types of thoughts used by controlling, critical voices is, in itself, calming. But when pockets of affective tension persist, or abreaction has already begun, the Self is taught to expedite release with the comforting (dual attention) butterfly hug and with words that foster emotional expression.

Both IFS and Dialogue Therapy engage in a mutual **teaching process**. As clients reveal their inner worlds, they are told either about their internal system or helped to identify emerging parts. After finding out what parts clients are aware of, Schwartz asks which one they would like to focus on first. Dialogue therapists listen for clues that suggest the voice of a subpersonality—"I never get anything right." Using the language of parts, the therapist might say, "It sounds like you have an inner critic that tells you, "You never get anything right." Parts are addressed as they reveal themselves. Both approaches helps clients realize the presence of a Self that can observe parts and teach non-argumentative means of asking them questions.

Structural/strategic therapists hope to restore leadership, balance, and harmony, in families. They look at polarization (extreme positions), enmeshment (smothering closeness), and triangulation (forming alliances). Schwartz attempts to do the same with the internal system and is cautious of external systems that may activate personality parts. *Empowering Dialogues Within* models itself on a **family system** that (a) has strong, flexible leaders, (b) fosters interconnection without individuals being fused or cut off, (c) allows expression of individual differences, (d) and maintains balance between members (Bowen, 1978). The internal equivalent of this is (a) a core Self that observes inner parts, (b) maintains contact with them through dialogue, and (c) recognizes any part that gets triggered by an event or person, (d) without allowing that part to monopolize through critical monologues or out-of-control behavior.

Both Schwartz and this book import **systems theory** into the internal realm. However, dialogue therapy is based on Murray Bowen's work with families—only allowing people to talk to the therapist. This central figure, with his or her probing questions, becomes the model for the neutral, curiously compassionate leadership of the Self, addressing each part in turn. When external systems (families, friends, coworkers, etc.) become too volatile, readers are encouraged to use methods described in *Making Hostile Words Harmless* (Cohen-Posey, 2008). These are Bowen-based strategies that defuse expected verbal fire when people take a stand with their family.

6.16

VOICE DIALOGUE PROCESS

Prior to the work of Richard Schwartz, Hal and Sidra Stone accidentally stumbled on the subdivided nature of the mind in the late 1970s. Dr. Stone was Jungian trained; however, his background may have merely made him receptive to a hearsay report from a colleague who had talked to a whole series of *voices* in a client. Fascinated, he began experimenting with his children and later with Sidra. Although her background was behavioral, she was a fan of Herman Hesse and had yearned to step through the looking glass and explore her own magic theater since reading *Steppenwolf* 15 years earlier (see Chapter 3). Drs. Hal and Sidra Stone may be unique in exploring a treatment approach in their relationship and then bringing it into the clinical setting.

Selves and the Aware Ego

The Stones' *voice dialogue process* enables people to enter an interior world made up of **energy patterns** that vary from barely discernible sensations to a fully developed subpersonality with its own specific agenda. They are called *selves, subpersonalities,* or *vulnerable energies* and the *aware ego.* Selves are equivalent to a personality part, not a core Self. The primary selves are the protector/controller, pusher, critic, perfectionist, and pleaser. Disowned energies may be demonic and sensual, or playful, magical, or vulnerable childlike entities.

In contrast, the **aware ego** makes decisions based on information received from pure awareness and the intention of an energy pattern, without being identified with any goal. When the ego is aware of the pusher and do-nothing energies, the tension between them is eased and personal freedom is born. This makes it difficult to ally with either polar opposite; each position can be considered without pressure to comply.

Voice Dialogue Protocol

The first step in their process is to **activate selves**, subpersonalities, or energies by having people physically move to various locations in a room and assume a posture appropriate for a subpersonality. Facilitators talk to various selves to discover their agendas, how they came to be, the services they perform, and their beliefs about the person or other energy patterns. Counselors may ask, "How do you want (Kate) to appear to others?" "What would you not want Kate to do?" "How do you feel about trying new ventures?" "What worries you the most about Kate?" "Which subpersonality is the opposite of you?" "How old are you?" "What do you look like?"

The hierarchy needs to be respected by first **discerning agendas** of dominate personalities. If people are timid, they might be asked if they have a part that wants to rule the world. If they are chronically cranky, a self could be summoned that wishes the person would be nicer. Both a self-destructive part and the subpersonality that wants to repress it will be addressed in succession to understand the reasons why they must both be respected. In a manner that might be similar to Schwartz's direct access, each self is spoken to as an individual entity and as a part of the total personality.

Facilitators use energy patterns in themselves to mirror (**resonate with**) whatever is emerging in the client. Child parts will know if facilitators are feeling aloof or rational and will not emerge. When inviting suppressed energies, the counselor should be somewhat submissive but strong enough to evoke the entity.

The session ends by having the person return to his or her original location in the room, presumably where the aware ego has be observing the discussions with various selves. The **facilitator collaborates** with the aware ego about what has happened during the experience to discover a new perspective on the problem, rather than trying to resolve conflicts. The ego is asked to *feel* the different selves as well as be aware of them.

6.17

Talking to various subpersonalities induces a nonordinary state of consciousness. Therefore, it is always important to address a major subpersonality and ask how it feels before returning to the aware ego space. **The goal** is never to banish any energy pattern, but to transform extremists into more moderate counterparts. A ruthless taskmaster can become sensitive. Not all selves need to be contacted in a session, but there is a commitment to eventually discover and honor all of them. Reclaiming parts feeds people with new energy and makes life's journey more meaningful and joyous (Stone, 1989).

This author strongly recommends that any therapists who want to explore the subdivided nature of the mind to read the Stones' book and practice the voice dialogue process with their clients. Subpersonalities taking positions and postures around the room gives a graphic representation of the interior of the mind and helps people, who are overly focused on people (objects) in their lives, turn inward. However, people who are capable of insight can easily be coached to silently speak to inner voices and may find the voice dialogue process cumbersome and even embarrassing.

SIMILARITIES AND DIFFERENCES

These theories of the subdivided mind treat personality parts on behalf of or in collaboration with the core Self. Both IFS therapy and *Empowering Dialogues Within* offer a model of personality parts and Selves and make a distinction between the two types of entities. Although the Stones do not clearly identify a Self, they are mindful of *awareness* or the aware ego. The Stones call their approach the *psychology of selves* and their method the *voice dialogue process*. However, they deny that voice dialogue is a therapy. For the sake of comparison, the empowering dialogues used in this text will be called *dialogue therapy*.

Dialogue and Subpersonalities

The "**dialogue**" that the Stones refer to is a way to psychodramatically address subpersonalities when therapists talk to various energies on behalf of clients. The aware ego is an observer and not taught to contact these parts. Dialogue therapy promotes semi-hypnotic, silent observations, and questions that are initiated by the Self to calm inner parts. This book follows Buber's model of dialogue that avoids agendas of any kind. This process is spirit filled; in dialogue therapy it is empowering to change the texture of internal monologues with responses from the Self that observe (reflect) or inquire. Buber was well acquainted with the Taoist principle of the mirror mind that "reflects without intent" (Lao Tzu, 1972, Chapter 10). In the process, none of the misguided ideas of personality parts will be absorbed. Similarly, IFS therapy teaches subvocal exchanges between the core Self and parts. It assumes that in doing so, subpersonalities will become less extreme in their messages.

Personality Structure

While the seeds of this author's approach were planted in conferences and grew to fruition in sessions with clients, she gratefully acknowledges the contribution of Schwartz and the Stones whose theories clarify internal dynamics of the subdivided mind. The Stones' classification of **major subpersonalities** (protector/controller, perfectionist, pusher, critic, and pleaser) led her to notice how similar they were to Erik Erikson's developmental crises: self control (*autonomy versus shame and doubt*), preventing guilt (*initiative versus guilt*), pushing (*industry versus inferiority*), pleasing others (*identity versus role diffusion* and *intimacy versus isolation*). Erikson's last two crises, *integrity versus despair* and *generativity versus stagnation* are seen in the rise of the integrated (connected), transcendent Selves.

This book holds that major subpersonalities evolve during **developmental crises**, not from a need to protect vulnerability (the Stones) or a lack of trust in the real Self (Schwartz). Although the core Self is inborn, it will not be able to fully guide until verbal skills and intellect are matured.

6.18

Directors of control, protection, task completion, and pleasing will emerge as trustees until the person has acquired skills for their rational, intuitive, transcendent Selves to guide. The Stones propose that the infant's unique "psychic fingerprint" is defenseless and needs various "energy patterns" to armor it by internalizing rules that control behavior, secure safety, and ensure acceptance. Schwartz has faith that people are born with a compassionate, confident inner Core, but is concerned that it can be compromised by overzealous parts. These facets stop trusting true leadership due to poor support from caretakers.

Schwartz identifies **three categories of roles** in which parts often find themselves: "managers," "firefighters," and "exiles." The author of *Empowering Dialogues Within* is grateful to Schwartz's clear vision, but renamed the three personality functions: directors, distracters, and emotional entities.

- **Directors**, "primary subpersonalities" (Stone & Stone, 1989), and "managers" (Schwartz, 1995) all perform similar superego tasks that help people conform to social demands and family rules.
- **Distracters** and firefighters (Schwartz, 1995) have no counterpart in the Stones' model. This text appreciates Schwartz's identification of personality traits and coping strategies gone awry (firefighters) as a subpersonality. His explanation of their role (to calm and distract emotional entities when pressure from directors is too great) makes the dynamics of the internal community clear.
- **Emotional entities**, "disowned subpersonalities" (Stone & Stone, 1989), and "exiles" (Schwartz, 1995), like child ego states, carry unresolved experiences from early life or raw instinctual (id) energy.

Schwartz names emotional parts "exiles" because he believes the internal system attempts to push pain, fear, and shame out of awareness. However, they can be easily triggered and explode with emotion and sensation. The Stones date the suppression of "vulnerable energies" to age five. However, these energies may surface in nightmares, flashbacks, fleeting twinges, and attractions to persons with characteristics similar to those who caused the original hurt. This book holds that **emotional entities** are sparked by the controlling critical messages of directors or external persons and experienced as localized bodily sensations and the release of feelings. The fact that they express themselves somatically, rather than subvocally does not mean they have been suppressed.

In IFS therapy, teaching the **relationships between parts** helps subpersonalities learn to trust the Self. The interplay between parts can be dramatically seen in voice dialogue as facilitators help peoples' subpersonalities assume various positions and postures around the room. The association between parts is not discussed in dialogue therapy. However, with an economy of effort, visual displays of the dynamics between parts and the Self are shown by using props or arranging tarot cards on a table. Space can be used in a three-dimensional way when a ratlike critical part squats on a crying doll (emotional entity) until an angelic form helps it loosen its grip through dialogue.

The Self

Schwartz believes using an angelic figure as a prop to represent the true Self creates a "self-surrogate." The Self is the **seat of consciousness** and is invisible. "It is the place from which a person views and interacts with his or her parts" (Schwartz, 1995, p. 220). This text heartily agrees that the Self is the ultimate Witness that compassionately observes. However, dialogue therapy holds that it is useful to create self-surrogates through imagery exercises (in Chapter 2) or with the wonderful symbolism in some of the tarot cards. These give people labels that capture qualities of their true Selves—confidence, compassion, independence, comfort, peace, and even divinity.

Schwartz **definition** of the true or core Self holds that it is both an empathetic inner leader and an expansive, limitless state of mind that is always present in an individual. The Stones' aware ego hovers above the fray but is not as elevated and eternal as in the previous description. This book avoids theoretical speculation on the nature of either parts or Selves. They are defined by what they do: parts are divisive facets of the personality; the Self is a process of forming meta-cognitions (thoughts about thoughts) that observe, question, and dialogue with distressing inner voices.

Technical Jargon

This text *prefers* clear, descriptive language for inner entities and core Being. Technical jargon that is not immediately understandable (*ego states, complexes, firefighters, schemas, exiles,* and *energies pattern*) is avoided. The terms *voices, subpersonalities, directors, distracters, emotional entities,* and *parts,* offer graphic references for inner facets, while the term *Selves* is reserved for mental processes that produce clarity, calmness, and empowerment.

When people connect with Self, they often refer to it as their "true," "real," "core," "inner," "higher," or "rational" Self. Whatever term they use is important, even if the connotation seems wrong to the counselor. Amiee at the end of Chapter 1 remembered a "stoic Self" that held her head high and her back straight. To many people, stoic might imply a part that suppresses emotions, but for Amiee it was a Self that drew strength from within and beyond.

SEARCH FOR SOURCE IDEAS

Although the voice dialogue process and IFS therapy have striking similarities, neither originator had any knowledge of the others' ideas. Both were captivated by the voices that are so prominent in peoples' minds, waiting to be centerpiece of a theory. Like her predecessors, this author was dedicated to other methods when her clients' personality parts discovered her. Once they made their presence known in the holy ground of counseling sessions, she was more deliberate than Schwartz and the Stones in searching for theories that would illuminate her work. The ideas of an internal system, three categories of personality roles, and major subpersonalities were a wonderful framework on which to build an understanding of the subdivided mind. Had these therapists made independent, fortuitous breakthroughs?

There is an ancient Persian fairy tale about three princes of Serendip. In their travels, they experienced many accidental (serendipitous) revelations. Close examination shows that their unexpected fortunes were the result of intelligence, wisdom, and reasoning. In science and psychotherapy, in particular, there may be no such thing as independent unsought discovery, only careful observation, plentiful experience, and well-prepared minds immersed in a culture ready to foster an idea whose time has come. Chapter 7 delves into earlier sources of the study of mind and current scientific advances to add meat and flesh to the bare bones of evolving theories of parts and Selves.

Chapter 7

Historical Context and Possible Proofs

[2]Vanity of vanities, says the Teacher,
vanity of vanities! All is vanity . . .
[8]the eye is not satisfied with seeing,
or the ear filled with hearing.
[9]What has been is what will be,
and what has been done is what will be done;
there is nothing new under the sun.
[10]Is there a thing of which it is said,
"See, this is new"?
It has already been,
in the ages before us . . .
      —(*New Revised Standard Version of the Bible*, 1989, Ecclesiastes 1:2–8)

Is it possible that *Empowering Dialogues Within* offers nothing new? Do the ancient studies of mind and spirit wedded to the new science of psychology merely reinvent themselves over and over? This subject matter is best approached with proper portions of humility and conceit. Every student of the mind has stood on the shoulders of giants, yet they tweak information with enough nuance to help it move spiralwise round a kernel of truth or shift outward toward the fulfillment of some elusive knowledge.

The spiral mandala on this chapter opening can suggest a longing for growth toward wholeness or the need to translate knowledge into useful forms.

FORERUNNERS TO THERAPIES OF PARTS AND SELVES

In its infancy, psychology recognized mental components. Freud identified his famous *id, ego*, and *superego* in the 1920s. Even earlier (in 1908), Carl Jung named complexes or emotionally charged clusters of ideas and experiences (like abandonment, inferiority, etc.) that can take hold of an individual. However, both forms of analysis approached the person as a unitary whole in treatment. Only Roberto Assagioli spoke of true subpersonalities in 1927 and dealt with them as separate entities. People were asked to describe themselves by the various roles and characteristics that dominated them.

Depicting different roles and traits requires the use of the observing Self and empowers it. Paradoxically, the less people identify with a particular part, the more adeptly they play it (Assagioli, 1965/2000). The goal of Assagioli's *Psychosynthesis* is to reconstruct subpersonalities around a higher inner Center and to assimilate energies inflowing from the Self or superconscious. But his work was far outside the mainstream. It took 30 years before other therapies began encouraging interaction with personality parts.

GESTALT THERAPY

During the decade of conformity in the 1950s, a group of therapists took a radical tangent to psychoanalysis. Their Gestalt Institute in New York and its most charismatic founder, Fritz Perls, must have understood the modern expression *living on the edge*. He believed the Self exists "at the boundary of interaction and contact." Partial constructions of the Self emerge during different phases of figure/ground (gestalt) formation. Originally, these phases were called *id* and *ego* functions, but bore little resemblance to their Freudian namesakes.

In the id phase (like Taoist *yin* energy), the Self is passive, diffuse, and acted on. In the ego (*yang*) phase, there is active doing and decisiveness to form figures. Interpersonal problems surface when dominant **ego functions** alternate with responsive **id functions** and become internalized as the top dog and underdog. The top dog is a righteous, demanding authority that knows what is best and threatens catastrophes; the underdog is a defensive, apologetic, wheedling crybaby. They engage in constant battle in or out of a person's awareness.

If this theory seems complex and abstract, the method is lively and engaging. An empty chair is employed on which people can place their top dog or underdog: an upsetting (imaginary) object, a difficult person, an urge to binge eat, their headaches, society, memories of a deceased parent, and so on. Any image, emotion, or recollection that people place in the chair is a mental construction, even if it is based on external reality. People are often only aware of one side of an internal conflict. By switching back and forth between chairs with dialogue, they become more aware, creating choice and the opportunity for change.

The goal of Gestalt therapy is not to recreate a *Steppenwolf* world (see Chapter 3) of dueling counterparts, but to find the *middle mode* by exploring many polarities. This third function is *not* the sum of passive id and active ego functions, but is a new gestalt that is greater than the totality of its parts—thoroughly present, powerful, engaged, and free. The following vignette, still a fresh memory after 30 years, is a testimony to the power of Gestalt therapy.

Vignette 1: Kate

Kate's "underdog" was playing the damsel in distress, not knowing what to do about a problem that was plaguing her. Her therapist said, "Sit in that chair and be the 'Kate Who Knows.'" A new being (middle mode) came forth and glibly gave her the answers she was seeking.

In an even more striking example, a different therapist in a different time asked Kate to put her ex-husband in the empty chair and tell him, "Don't ignore me." In that chair, she placed not only her ex-husband, but also, the doting mother who once said her problems were boring, the father who talked endlessly about his fascinating legal cases but ignored Kate, and her "top dog" with its lofty expectations. As directed, her underdog weakly pleaded, "Don't ignore me." Her therapist gently pushed, "Say it again. . . ." The phrase was repeated several more times until it came out with such force that the walls of the room reverberated, and all present were awed into silence.

Without switching chairs, the uncertain underdog had been replaced by a formidable voice that tapped into a source of strength deep within Kate's belly. Now fused to power from within, it became difficult for Kate to play the victim in the future.

The term *Gestalt therapy* was first used as the title of a book written by Perls, Hefferline, and Goodman in 1951. After its founder's death in 1970, Gestalt therapy lost the limelight of public attention, but it spawned many ideas that found their way into other methods. The excitement of direct contact between therapists and clients, emphasis on experience in the here and now, and the use of active experimentation inspired others to uncover many alternative approaches to therapy.

EGO-STATE THERAPIES

The term *ego state* first became popularized by Eric Berne when he baptized the parent, child, and adult ego states in 1961. Later these flowered into nurturing, spoiling, structuring, and critical-parent ego states and cooperative, resistant, spontaneous, and immature-child ego states. John and Helen Watkins developed a different type of *ego-state therapy* in the early 1970s. Both Berne and the Watkinses came across the concept of ego states in the work of Paul Federn.

Paul Federn

Federn was one of Freud's earliest and most faithful disciples, but his ideas differed from those of other psychoanalysts. Freud defined *ego* from the German *Das Ich*—the I. Ego is the identifying and alienating aspect of the Self—*This is me* and *That is not me*. For Federn, the *ego* was an energy that united thoughts and feelings into a new entity.

An ego state (first defined in 1952) is a system of behavior and experiences, separated from other such states by a boundary that is more or less permeable. The elements in an ego state would only contain ego energy. The ego (self sense) remains constant, but different states could pass in and out of it when invested with ego energy. When a system was not invested with ego energy, it continued as a unit but was represented as an object. Although Federn was the first to define an ego state, he never realized the significance of his concept or how to use it in treatment (Watkins & Watkins, 1997, p. 25).

Eric Berne's Transactional Analysis

All analysts must undergo treatment, and Eric Berne's doctor was none other than Paul Federn. Berne recognized the merits of an ego state and made use of it in his popular transactional analysis (TA) to describe systems of feelings and behavior patterns (Berne, 1964). They can organize external stimuli as **parent ego states**, internal experiences from early life as **child ego states**, and current awareness as **adult ego states**.

A particular ego state can switch in with such power that a person relates to a current experience with the facilities of a child. While Freudian analysts were focused on working through the feelings of what Berne referred to as the child ego states, he recognized the importance of *object energy* in parent ego states. Unlike Freud's superego, which acted as a conscience carrying cultural values, parent ego states were very personal, internalized images of early caretakers. However, Berne did not describe a course of treatment for parent ego states. Therapy focused on keeping the adult ego state from being contaminated by recognizing when child or parent ego states were intruding (Erskine, 1997).

Inner Children and Erskine's Integrative Transactional Analysis

The idea of personality facets became popularized by the quest for the *inner child* that was encouraged by twelve-step self-help groups and the abuse survivors' movements. Books abound on nurturing, recovering, liberating, rescuing, freeing, affirming, forgiving, and finding your inner child. There is an *inner child therapy* that stresses learning about toxic shame, family dysfunction, and personality development; disclosing abuse and neglect; embracing feelings; identifying inner dialogues; reparenting the inner child; and empowering the inner adult (Potter, 1992). These themes echo many of John Bradshaw's in his best-selling book, *Homecoming: Reclaiming and Championing Your Inner Child* (1990).

While inner child advocates and other therapies were focusing on child ego states by encouraging dramatic expressions of sadness and anger, Richard Erskine began stressing the importance of eliciting emotional statements from parent ego states. His ideas evolved from Eric Berne's TA to *integrative transactional analysis*. Therapists direct clients to get into the skin, feelings, and experience of the parent ego state, talk to this state directly to understand its struggles, and gently confront it on what it needs to understand or do on behalf of the child ego state. Compared to the Stones' voice dialogue process, Schwartz's IFS therapy, or this book, which talks to a variety of directing or distracting subpersonalities and emotional entities all in one session, integrative TA favors working with dominant subpersonalities. However, all these approaches to the subdivided mind would agree that it is best to address *internalized parents*, that block the path to emotional entities or true Selves, first.

Watkins and Watkins Work with a Family of Self

John and Helen Watkins were accomplished hypnotherapists. They developed ***ego state therapy*** in the early 1970s and began working with different personality parts in people who were considered normal (not multiple personalities). The Watkinses' definition of an ego state remains true to Federn's original description, except that either object or ego energy could be contained in a unit. Otherwise, they agree with Federn that ego states are organized patterns of behavior and experience enclosed by variable boundaries. These patterns may include beliefs and behaviors triggered by particular situations, fairly fixed traits that compromise coping strategies, or memories and feelings from an earlier age. There is a *core ego* that is fairly constant in the way it presents itself to the individual and to the world. Its boundaries are not rigid, and it can expand or contract. When it expands to include various ego states, these are experienced as self (ego) energy or foreign (object) energy (Watkins & Watkins, 1997, pp. 25–36). For instance, a man might say, "I just cannot be myself around my boss," not realizing that he has been restrained by an (foreign) ego state telling him that he better not say anything stupid.

The Watkinses typically used hypnosis to do ego state therapy that involved the use of a variety of techniques to resolve conflicts between parts that constitute a "family of self" (Watkins & Watkins, 1997, p. 96). The goal is integration or cooperation between parts and a mutual meeting of needs, not fusion where ego states disappear.[1] Some states are defined by a time dimension (an old man, teen, or infant) or by their function, trait, or role (nurturer, critic, executive, daredevil, curiosity, and so on).

Communication between states is facilitated by therapists asking a part what it needs or what it wants the person to do. Every ego state involved in a problem might be invited to a conference table,

---

[1] Integration is defined in dialogue therapy as the process of the Self engaging and making contact with personality parts.

told to find a place to sit, and asked to discuss an issue. An adult part may decide to carry a young one's pain. At times, facets are encouraged to talk to each other, but therapists often work with destructive ego states.

A therapist uses **resonance** to take on an ego state's feelings and sensations or *alter egos* for a part to speak on behalf of a subpersonality. This is beyond empathy, which merely reflects feelings. The Watkinses emphasized that ego states only surface while a person is under hypnosis. In contrast, the Stones, Schwartz, and this author have no difficulty accessing various subpersonalities without formal inductions.

John Watkins was renowned for his pioneering work with dissociation and multiple personalities. The comprehensive theory of plurality of parts in *normal* personalities that he and Helen developed owes a debt to their clients who struggled with what is now called **Dissociative Identity Disorder** (DID). These clients have *alter personalities* that originally dissociate (detach) during trauma by forming separate identities, developing solid boundaries, and becoming infused with (Federn's) foreign object energy. They do not require hypnosis to emerge and will take charge when the *host personality* does not want to deal with a life event. The person is left with a sense of lost time and amnesia for what occurred while the alter was *out*. These fragmented identities think of themselves as separate from their host, yet live inside of him or her. They are frozen in time and have a clear image of their age, and the reason they came to be. They view their host and other alters as objects, may fight for control of the body, and keep their presence concealed through the use of amnesia.

Ego states do not have identities—just patterns of thoughts, emotions, and behavior. Vignettes in Chapter 3 show a clear distinction between an **ego state versus an alter**. Alice's "Mr. Nasty" (Vignette 2) told her she enjoyed her abuse. This critical ego state took root from her mother's misguided thinking. Donna (Vignette 3) had an alter that screeched that if her father had not started molesting her when she was a baby, it would never have come to exist to help her weak, miserable, juvenile self through countless hours of pain.

Although Watkins and Watkins did not identify different types of ego states (parent, child, directors, distractors, and so on) or distinguish them from a core Self, they did discover a "**hidden observer ego state**" that they believed is less emotional and has greater wisdom than other inner parts. Conducting experiments involving hypnotic suppression of pain, they gave subjects suggestions not to feel hurt when their hands were immersed in iced water. Typically, people would deny any sensation. Then the Watkinses would ask, "If there is any part that feels the pain, lift your finger and signal that you are ready to come out and talk." A voice would speak, admitting to feeling the ache of coldness. Other hypnotists had observed this phenomena and called the underlying *cognitive structure* that felt the pain a "hidden observer" (Watkins & Watkins, 1997, pp. 87–95).

Ralph Allison, another psychiatrist who treated Multiple Personality Disorder, found entities, which he calls "**self-helpers**," that differed from disturbed alters. The self-helpers had no identifiable time and reason for existence and no defensive function, but had such accurate perception that they were able to advise therapists of their mistakes, mend broken pieces of personality, and understand the mysteries of a person's life (Allison & Schwarz, 1999).

OBJECT RELATIONS THEORIES

The psychotherapy pot had been stirred by Perls. Federn wrought rumblings even in the heart of psychoanalysis. Several others began to look more closely at the inner images of the Self and others (objects) that the very young develop and how these images affect interpersonal relationships. They used their own nomenclature for divisions of the Self:

- *True Self*: A Self that feels creative, spontaneous, and real; that emerges with *good enough* parenting; that is opposed to a "false Self," which is typically perfectionistic, self-centered, controlling, avoidant, or the like, and that is formed by complying and rejecting parts of oneself (Winnicott, 1965).

- *Grandiose Self*: A Self that becomes unhealthy when the ego is overwhelmed by demands for external success due to early unmet needs for nurturing or valuing (Kohut, 1971).
- *Internal object*: An object that is loving/rejecting, rewarding/punitive, or protective/attacking and that represents a primary caretaker and his or her way of relating to the child.
- *Internal Self*: A Self or a mental image that is good/bad, superior/inferior, or obedient/nothing (Manfield, 1992). Because young children cannot tolerate having contradictory feelings about themselves or caretakers, they develop split images that relate to an inner "cold mommy," which protects the "caring mommy" from juvenile wrath. Attitudes can flip in an instant, just as moods can change from euphoric to despairing, depending on which side of the Self is being represented.

Object-relations therapists (1950s–1970s) discovered that some patients could not tolerate interpretations of their inner life; and instead, were constantly focused on objects (people) in the world. They examined personality parts originating from early development, prior to Freud's "genital stage" when feelings of guilt emerge. Characteristics of blaming, avoiding, and clinging to the very people whom they needed for safety, self-worth, and life force produced outer turmoil, but reduced intolerable anxiety. Such patients may not have difficulties with inner adversaries, but instead, they burden loved ones and coworkers with helplessness, aloofness, arrogance, or impossible expectations. These theories are helpful to therapies of the subdivided mind that identify distracting parts that help people avoid emotions.

COGNITIVE THERAPIES AND SCHEMAS

Aaron Beck and Albert Ellis are considered the founders of *cognitive therapy* (1960s). It took 20 years for this approach to become interested in the subdivided mind. Initially, cognitive therapy held that maladaptive behaviors and disturbed moods are the result of irrational thinking patterns called **automatic thoughts**. Instead of reacting to the reality of a situation, an individual is triggered by his or her own distorted viewpoint.

Gradually, cognitive therapists began talking about internal dialogues that are generated by "cognitive structures" or "systems of concepts and judgments." There was more talk about subsystems of thoughts. Then Aaron Beck himself made a distinction between automatic thoughts on one level and "**schemas**" on another. Schemas are subsystems within the personality that result from previous experience and are used to classify, interpret, evaluate, and give meaning to an event. A follower of Albert Ellis further stated that specific beliefs may be generated from *underlying* schemas (Rowan, 1990, pp. 108–109).

Another cognitive theorist in the 1980s proposed the idea of a "**subself**" or a cognitive unit that receives input from current events, one's self-concept, and emotional states, and sends output to other subselves for organization and action. These multiple subselves are connected to a deeper "unitary self."

The term **self-schema** was employed to define packets of information about the self that guide the processing of information. It contains data from repeated experiences categorized according to themes (I'm helpless, I'm worthless, I'm inferior) that seek matching facts. The more often a self-schema is used to process information, the more dominant it will become (Rowan, 1990, pp. 155–160).

Schemas can also serve as the foundation for future images of one's self called "**possible selves**." They are more than a goal or an intention and contain a blueprint for future action. Most people have multiple possible selves representing a range of desires, dreams, and feared phantoms to avoid (Markus & Nurius, 1987). Clearly, cognitive therapists were coming to terms with the multifaceted personality that could not be captured by simply referring to irrational, automatic thoughts.

7.6

PHILOSOPHICAL CONTEXT
AND CONTRIBUTIONS

Even though the founding fathers of psychology recognized interior parts like ids, egos, complexes, and archetypes, they dealt with people as whole beings. It seems an interesting coincidence that Berne, the Watkinses, the Stones, and Schwartz (1960s–1980s), who all came from very different theoretical orientations, began to identify ego states, inner selves, and personality parts as the units for treatment. The truth may be that they were caught up in a sweeping *postmodern* movement.

IMPACT OF THE POSTMODERN ERA

Some academics divide history into three major epochs—premodern, modern, and postmodern. In the premodern era, body, mind, and spirit were all considered worthy of contemplation, but science, art, and government were fused under the rule of the church. Some date the advent of the modern era to the invention of the printing press. Science, art, and government began to separate, evolve, and thrive, giving rise to social values of equality, freedom, justice, and individual rights; scientific advancements in biology, chemistry, and physics; and artistic experimentation. But then science began to dominate. Matter became the only thing that mattered. The value of social *science*, mind, and spirit was questioned. Complaints about the *loss of meaning* and quantity versus quality grew (Wilber, 2000).

In 1926, one scientist knew enough to know what he did not know. In his "Uncertainty Principle," Werner Heisenberg proposed that it is impossible to measure the location, speed, and direction of subatomic particles all at the same time. Worse yet, the very act of observing a particle can change its course! This stood Isaac Newton's assumption (the real world exists, regardless of whether it is observed) on its head. Despite Einstein's constant argument that "God does not play dice with the universe," Heisenberg's theory of uncertainty and unpredictability prevailed and laid the groundwork for quantum mechanics (1930s–1940s). This is the science of subatomic particles behaving badly.

Riding close on Heisenberg's heels in 1931, the mathematician-logician, Kurt Gödel, stated that questions exist that are neither provable nor disprovable. Gödel's "Undecidability Theorem" was seized by philosophers to point out that there are true statements that cannot be proved, making the invisible mind and spirit again worthy of study. A mathematician working at IBM supported Gödel's theorem by stressing the fundamental limits of mathematical proofs (Chaitlin, 1987). Science was now fraught with unpredictability, undecidability, incompleteness, randomness, and unknowables. The arts and social studies were revalued and reconciled with their prodigal sibling—science.

Whether it is due to Heisenberg and Gödel putting science in its place, the mass media of television shrinking the world in the 1950s, or an explosion of worldwide communication through the Internet in the 1990s, the **postmodern era** has arrived. Catchwords like *inclusiveness, diversity*, and *multiculturalism* abound. Science, the arts, and social values are integrated, rather than fused, as they were in the premodern era. Heisenberg's theory that subatomic particles *must* be understood as probabilities, opened the door for subpersonalities to be possible components of the mind. A climate that embraces external cultural diversity might welcome internal multiplicity as well. With reality on shaky ground, psychology was released from the stranglehold of cause-and-effect science.

A DIALOGICAL PHILOSOPHY

In the same country (Germany) and time (late 1920s) that Heisenberg was probing the misbehavior of subatomic particles, a philosopher was intent on pointing out "mis-meetings" that happen between individuals. Dialogue therapy owes a debt to A *Philosophy of Dialogue*, originated by Martin Buber (see Preface). He identified "I-it personality parts" that ensure survival through controlling their environment and others for personal gain. Although able to impose their will, they create the pain of isolation with preconceived notions. Fortunately, people have an "inborn Thou" that yearns for genuine encounter and emerges in spontaneous moments to make contact with people and the world around them. Such I-Thou meetings are without agendas, keep people fully human, and make connections through dialogue without lessening opposition. Buber's ideas of community, the central Thou, and cherishing opposing parts have been transported to the internal realm. His theories polish and give brilliance to **dialogue therapy**.

PSYCHONEUROLOGICAL EVIDENCE

Although the postmodern mood does not demand proof of personality parts and Selves, questions linger. Are subpersonalities and core Being made up constructs (albeit useful), or is there some evidence of their existence? Strangely, there is more research pertaining to barely detectible Higher Selves than to the more *vocal* subpersonalities.

HARD EVIDENCE OF HIGHER SELVES

Where in the brain could one possibly expect to find the intuitive, transcendent Self that is the locus of pure awareness and will? Andrew Newberg, director of nuclear medicine at the University of Pennsylvania identified the "neurological seat of attention and will" in the thalmus.

Newberg studied Tibetan mediators and nuns with a camera that observed activity in different brain structures. During focused, calm states, neurological changes occurred that disrupted normal brain processes. The **thalamus**, deep in the brain, became very active and *communicated* a lucid sense of reality to the **prefrontal cortex**. This pleasant experience was interpreted according to any related beliefs held in memory. The back and top of the cortex (associated with senses, movement, and spatial orientation—knowing who and where you are) showed decreased activity (Newberg, 2006, p. 179). A young woman described this exact phenomena when she said, "The overanxious part of me (in her outer cortex) thinks I can prevent accidents by folding my laundry the right number of times, but deep within (in her thalamus) I know the truth."

Dean Hamer is a neurobiologist who focused on the chemical correlates of Higher Selves. He wanted to prove that spirituality or self-transcendence (embodying the Higher Self's "at-one-ness") can be inherited. He extracted DNA from 1,000 subjects and administered each person a personality inventory with a scale that scored "self-transcendence."[2] Then he began a daunting search for the one gene that all subjects with high self-transcendent scores had in common. Other researchers pursuing such mystical DNA pointed him toward emotion-regulating neurotransmitters. Forty-seven percent of people with one type of gene for controlling emotional flow had high self-transcendent scores, and 53% of the people with another kind of gene had low scores (Hamer, 2004, p. 74).

Voila! Dr. Hamer reduced the Higher Self to an inherited gene that controls neurotransmitters regulating emotion to and fro between nerve synapses. He proposed that such a gene would offer an evolutionary advantage by encouraging people to persevere through hardships in spite of the inevitability of death. Indeed, the Higher Self's wisdom, compassion, determination, and spirit is prosurvival for us as individuals and as a species. However, the news is not all good. If the "**self-transcendence gene**" is a hardwired trait, a little less than 50% of people have it. Does this mean that only *some* people will be able to use "energy inflowing from the Higher Self" to help them muddle through the demands of their subvocal critics and the whims and wounds of their emotional energies.

Controlled Hallucinogen Experiment

Fortunately, Hamer cites other research that suggests life experience plays a role in revealing the Higher Self. In 1962, twenty divinity students participated in an experiment testing the limits of environmental influences. It involved a hallucinogenic drug, a 100-item questionnaire that measures lingering mystical experiences, and a moving Good Friday sermon given by Reverend Howard Thurman (the mentor of Dr. Martin Luther King Jr.). The researcher using strict experimental design was Walter Pahnke, a physician and theologian, supervised by his Harvard advisor, Timothy Leary.

---

[2] The Temperament and Character Inventory (TCI) was developed by Robert Cloninger, professor of psychiatry at Washington University in 1987. It measures cultural influences, character and underlying biological dimensions, and temperament (Hamer, 2004, pp. 21–30). Especially unique is a 33-item self-transcendence scale that measures: (a) self-forgetfulness—becoming easily lost in thought, nature, and art; (b) transpersonal identification—having blurry distinctions between self and others; and (c) mysticism—being fascinated with the inexplicable. People have varying degrees of self-transcendence, but there is not an overall difference in the trait between ages, races, religions, or church attendance. However, women score 18% higher than men. In twin studies, close to half of identical twins and a little more than 20% of fraternal twins had similar scores on the self-transcendent scales. This is what would be expected since the DNA of identical twins is twice as similar as the DNA of fraternal twins (p. 47).

It is no surprise that the 10 young men who took a hallucinogen before the sermon had an average score of 61% on the mystical experience questionnaire *6 months after* the experiment, while the control group (who took a nicotine placebo) scored 12% (Doblin, 1991).

What is amazing is that a follow-up study conducted 25 years later revealed that the positive effects persisted and continued to improve on the experimental group. Pahnke died in a scuba accident in 1971. Rick Doblin, a psychology student at New College in Florida, took up where Pahnke left off. From 1986–1989 he located, interviewed, and administered Pahnke's 100-item questionnaire to nine people from the control group and seven from the experimental group.[3] Those who had taken the hallucinogen now had an average score of 67% compared to unchanged scores of those who took the nicotine placebo. The experimental group recalled the Reverend Thurman's service in detail, reported subsequent (nondrug induced) spiritual experiences, resolved career decisions easily, believed in eternal life, and described a heightened sense of joy. Even more significant, the control group barely remembered the experiment and reported no positive persisting changes (Doblin, 1991).

The Good Friday Experiment and follow-up poses the question: Can certain experiences arouse the Higher Self to a more prominent role, even in people without a self-transcendent gene? Although *all* participants in the experiment were divinity students, the control group had low scores for mystical experiences even though they had been matched to the experimental group in personality and religious background. Is this research an advertisement for a fast track to exposing the Higher Self through drugs? Two of the controls later experimented with psychedelics but the overall average of the group did not increase.

Although a hallucinogen can rightly be considered a jarring environmental influence, perhaps it created a chemistry that sealed camaraderie, comfort of being with fellow students, and inspirational oratory into memory. During some forms of meditation, there is a 65% increase in dopamine—the neurotransmitter that increases a sense of well-being (Newberg, 2006, p. 180). The lucid sense of reality offered by the thalamus during focused, calm states has its own built-in alchemy to increase the validity of new, positive insights and hold them in place.

Meditation Study

An experiment conducted by a psychology student at the University of London may show that "our genes are more like a family recipe handed down by word of mouth than a precise set of instructions" (Hamer, 2004, p. 212). Spiritual enlightenment takes practice. C. J. Hammerl gave a questionnaire that measures self-directedness, cooperativeness, and self-transcendence to 159 participants recruited from Buddhist meditation centers in the London area. Those with 2 or more years of meditation practice had notably higher scores in self-transcendence than those interested in meditation or than those just starting meditation exercises. Scores on self-directedness and cooperativeness scales did not vary between the three groups (Hamer, 2004).

DNA research, long-term effects of a hallucinogen experiment, and controlled studies on the impact of meditation on a "self-transcendent trait," strongly suggest that something lies in the core of our Being that gives life meaning and purpose. Some people may need to discover or learn to trust an inborn trait, while others can cultivate inner knowing.

PROOF OF PARTS

Even if a certain gene offers a chemical basis for the transcendent Self and the thalamus explains the locus of its operation, how could personality parts have analogous brain structures? In the 1960s, research began to document separate functions of the right and left brain hemispheres.[4]

---

[3] One subject who took the hallucinogen needed an injection of Thorazine and refused to participate.
[4] Roger Sperry pioneered research on right/left brain hemisphere functions. He was assisted by Michael Gazzaniga whose continued work with brain-damaged subjects led him to believe that each hemisphere is capable of assuming many tasks for the other, except for language, which is located in the dominant hemisphere.

7.10

Twenty years later, one of the initial investigators, Michael Gazzaniga (1985), found evidence that the original findings were oversimplified. In his book, *The Social Brain*, he stated that the brain is made up of independent "**modules**," each with its own location, instincts, emotions, and abilities to initiate action. Our experiences have multiple aspects that are processed and stored in various modules as images and sensations. Fortunately, there is a "speech module" in the left brain that can *watch* impressions and impulses generated by other **processing centers** and interpret reality. The task of this verbal, narrative self is to prioritize information coming from various brain units, make meaning out of discordant images, and cover-up disagreements. During growth, the verbal system becomes the *overseer* of the others and creates the illusion of a "centric self" operating independently. But it is really nothing more than a brain device that unifies independent modules by producing explanations and rationalizations to harmonize their impressions.

Exactly how independent modules and the speech module correspond to director, distracting, and emotional personality parts is unclear, but it does suggest some physical basis for their existence. It is no wonder that Richard Schwartz boldly stated that "(personality) parts exist from birth either as potentials or in actuality" and that he was aware of Gazzaniga's research (Schwartz, 1995, p. 57, p. 15.).

Although it is heartening to know that psychoneurologists and other researchers are finding biological correlates and other measures of such elusive concepts as personality parts and the core Self, laboratories and experimental designs recede as clinicians step into their consulting rooms with people battered by subvocal messages. Such counselors light the way into uncharted territories, being privileged to witness discoveries that parallel those of scientists.

Vignette 2: Pam

Pam, a 60-year-old recovering alcoholic with several years of sobriety, has her share of troubles: major job stress, financial woes, serious physical problems, and a fair-weather relationship with her adult daughter that depends on her daughter's need for help.

Two years previously, Pam almost lost her life to a home invader who held her hostage and sexually battered her. In spite of it all, Pam does well for months at a time and only comes to therapy when she's in crisis. She returned to treatment due to debilitating anxiety episodes she thought were caused by demanding protocols at work. However, she quickly made the connection that the onset of apprehension coincided with her assailant having his prison sentence reduced to 15 years on appeal when kidnapping charges were dropped. This made the possibility of parole, while she was alive, a reality. Her logical Self quickly dispelled fears of him finding her, and the session focused on practicing mindful meditation (Chapter 2, Exercises 9–11) to *cleanse* Pam's body of tension.

Pam came to her next session complaining of an awful week. Her deceased uncle's attorney informed her that she would have no part of the uncle's inheritance, which was bequeathed to Pam's already well-to-do children. She said this pronouncement made her feel utterly worthless. Her therapist showed her several cards from a tarot deck and asked which picture gave her a good feeling. She chose a hand reaching out from the clouds to hold an encircled star and an angel blowing a horn. To Pam, one represented ultimate security ("Secure Hand") and the other was the Divine calling out to the innocent.

From another stack, Pam chose any cards that suggested the part of her that tells her she is worthless. Pam first picked a crippled man and a beggar plodding their way along a street. Her therapist suggested that this card might represent the part of her that is made to feel worthless and asked her to look again for a picture that would carry a disparaging message. A high-and-mighty emperor was chosen, and the cards were randomly laid on the table.

Looking at the card that suggested security, Pam was asked to silently speak to "Mr. High-and-Mighty" and tell him he was inside adding insult to all the injurious, worthless messages she received from people on the outside.

(Continued)

Pam looked up with a puzzled expression and said, "I don't know what this is, maybe a thought or a feeling, but I heard, 'all is well and you are whole and worthy.'" She was transformed from the angry, bitter person who had come to the session into a glowing being.

Pam arranged the cards on the table with the secure-hand card above the trumpeting-angel card. The cripple and beggar were placed next to the secure hand where they could receive some support, and Mr. High-and-Mighty was turned on his side so he could look up and see who was in charge. Pam's therapist photocopied this montage for a home reminder.

As she left, Pam said, "By the way, in spite of my awful week, I had no anxious episodes and those mindful exercises kept me focused at work."

Pam is a person with mystical and spiritual inclinations. She would likely score high on any personality test that measured self-transcendence. It was not necessary for her secure Self to patiently narrate and question the critical voice telling her she was worthless until it was arrested into silence. Her spark of divinity deep within, which often gave her uncanny visions, was ready to speak words of freeing truth. Pam had journeyed far enough inward to find her way out.

Terminologies for Parts and Selves

Personality Parts	Selves
Id: Unconscious part of the mind that is made up of both genetic instincts and acquired impulses (sex, hunger, aggression). These are suppressed from awareness. *(Freud)* **Superego:** The part of the personality structure associated with ethics, standards, and self-criticism. It is formed by identification with important and valued persons in early life, particularly parents. The supposed or actual wishes of these significant others are taken over as part of the child's own standards. *(Freudian Analysis, 1900s, id, ego, and superego)*	**Ego:** A mediator between basic drives (sex, hunger, and aggression) and internalized rules from society. It prevents people from acting on every (id) urge and being so morally driven that they cannot function *(formulated in the 1920s)*. The identifying and alienating self-sense—"This is me" and "That is not me."
Complex: An emotionally charged cluster of ideas or experiences. At the center of a complex is a core issue (like abandonment), which attracts similar life experiences. They can take charge of an individual in turns and each one has a separate sense of I-ness." **Persona:** The masks or personalities we wear for the world. Social roles formed as people grow up, which incorporate expectations of family, church, school, and society. **Ego:** Conscious identity of the individual that can be hurt or wounded and needs protection. *(Jungian Analysis, 1908)*	**Self:** Archetype derived from the collective unconscious that provides energy to create patterns, meaning, orientation, and individuality, and to fulfill potential. It is at the center and the circumference of the psyche and is the organizing principle of the mind. *(Concepts of archetypes and complexes predate Jung's break with Freud in 1912.)*
Subpersonalities: The nuclei of various parts of the Self containing fragments of what we believe we are, what we want to be, how we think we should appear to others, values that others project on to us, internalizations of significant others, and images of what we can become that exist at various levels of organization, complexity, and refinement. *(Assagioli—Psychosynthesis, 1927)*	**Higher Self:** "A center of pure awareness and pure will capable of mastering, directing, and using the mind and body." It feels both individual and universal and has a sense of freedom, expansion, and communion with others. *(Assagioli)*
Functions: Partial constructs of the Self that emerge during different phases of figure/ground (gestalt) formation. Dominant *ego* functions ("top dog") alternate with responsive *id* functions ("underdog") at the boundary of interpersonal contact. *(Gestalt Therapy, 1950s)*	**Middle Mode:** A new formation that is greater than the sum of passive *id* and active *ego* functions—thoroughly present, powerful, spontaneous, engaged, pervasive, and free. *(Gestalt)*

Personality Parts	Selves
Apparently Normal Personality: Avoids traumatic memories by detaching, numbing, and causing amnesia. **Emotional Personality:** Reexperiences overwhelming events as though they were currently happening with related visual images, sensations, and motor activity. *(Traumatology, 1940s)* **Alter:** Personality part that dissociates during trauma, develops solidified boundaries, and forms separate identities in people with *Dissociative Identity Disorder.*	**Self-Helpers:** Alters that have no identifiable time and reason for their existence, no defensive function, and have such accurate perception that they are able to offer guidance on therapy and understand the mysteries of peoples' lives. *(Allison's work with MPD, 1980s)*
Ego State: Organization of behavior and experience into a pattern that is separated from other states by a permeable boundary. The *core ego* is fairly constant in its presentation of the individual to the world. *(Ego State Therapy, 1970s)*	**Hidden Observer:** An ego state that tends to be less emotional and wiser than other ego states and may give guidance regarding therapy. *(Watkinses and others)*
Ego State: A coherent system of feelings and behavior that organize external stimuli (parent ego states), internal experiences from early life (child ego states), and current awareness (adult ego states). *(Transactional Analysis [TA], 1960s)*	**Adult Ego:** Full current mental abilities (not a state) without input from a parent or child ego state. *(Erskine—Integrative TA, 1970s)*
False Self: Created by denying parts of oneself to create characteristics that are rigidly compliant, perfectionistic, self-centered, controlling, avoidant, etc. *(Object-relations, 1950s)* **Internal Object:** Mental representations of a primary caretaker and his or her way of relating to the child that is loving/rejecting, rewarding/punitive, or protective/attacking. **Internal Self:** Mental representations of the Self that are good/bad, superior/inferior, or obedient/nothing. **Grandiose Self:** Unhealthy when the ego is overwhelmed by demands for external success due to early unmet needs for nurturing or valuing *(Kohut, Self Psychology, 1970s).*	**True Self:** The part of the Self that feels creative, spontaneous, and real; that can emerge with "good enough" parenting (Winnicot, 1960s). *(Object Relations Theory evolved from 1950s–1970s: Klein, Fairbairn, Winnicot, Guntrip.)*
Schema: A subsystem within the personality that results from previous experience and is used to classify, interpret, evaluate, and give meaning to an event. **Self-Schemata:** Packets of information about the Self that guide the processing of information. **Subself:** A cognitive unit that receives input from current events, one's self-concept, and one's emotional state and sends output to other cognitive units for organization and action. Multiple subselves are connected to or integrated with a deeper-level unitary Self. *(Cognitive Therapy, 1980s)*	**Possible Selves:** Future-oriented self-conceptions that are more than an intention and contain a blueprint for goal achievement. Multiple possible Selves in one person can represent a range of desires, dreams, and feared phantoms to avoid for the future (Marcus, 1980s). *(Cognitive Therapy developed by Ellis [1950s] and Beck [1960s] began thinking about schemas in the 1980s.)*

Personality Parts	Selves
Subpersonality: Subvocal voices in one's inner dialogue which vie for attention and dominance. They vary in degree of detachment and need to control. Healthy subpersonalities are representations that navigate social situations. *(Wilber—Transpersonal Psychology, 1980s)*	**Transpersonal Self:** Emerges from a universal dimension that uses the personality to witness mental, emotional, and physical experiences and provides guidance for growth. **I-I:** "Inner Self that is the Witness of the ordinary 'I.' " *(Wilber)*
Selves: Energy patterns that may vary from vague feelings or sensations to a fully developed subpersonality with its own specific agenda. *(Stone—Psychology of Selves, 1970s)* **Operating Ego:** Driven by its own agenda to protect, control, accomplish, affiliate, or to meet repressed needs. Makes decisions based on this agenda. "Primary selves" form operating egos until aware egos can function separately.	**Aware Ego:** Makes decisions based on awareness and appropriateness of a subpersonality's agenda (to protect, control, accomplish, or affiliate) without being identified with that agenda. *(Stones—Psychology of Selves, 1970s)*
Part: A discrete and autonomous mental system with emotions, expression, abilities, desires, interests, talents, temperaments, worldviews, and possible associated ages. *(Schwartz—Internal Family Systems [IFS] Therapy, 1980s)*	**Core/true Self:** Both an inner compassionate, confident leader and an expansive, boundary-less state of mind, which has been and is always present in an individual. *(IFS)*
Part: Any subvocal message that tends to be devisive and cause distress in its attempts to manage the details of life. *(Cohen-Posey—Dialogue Therapy, 2008)*	**Selves:** Mental processes of forming meta-cognitions (thoughts about thoughts) that observe, question, and dialogue with distressing inner voices to produce clarity, calmness, and empowerment. *(Dialogue Therapy, 2008)*
I-it Parts: Ensure survival through using and controlling their environment and others for personal gain. Although able to impose their will, they create the pain of self-inflicted isolation. *(Buber—Philosophy of Dialogue, 1928)*	**Inborn Thou:** Yearns for genuine contact with people and the environment. Transcends the Self through I-Thou encounters. **Central Thou:** Dialogues with personality parts by relating to and radiating outward to all facets. *(Buber)*
Mental Modules: Independent locations in the brain where experiences are processed and stored as sensations and images. Each one has its own instincts, emotions, and ability to take action. *(Gazzaniga—Neuropsychology, 1980s)* **Verbal Self:** Located in the left brain. "Watches" images, sensations, and impulses generated by other modules to makes meaning out of conflicting impressions by spinning a narrative *(Gazzaniga)*. May be more controlling than guiding.	**Self-transcendence gene:** Tendency to be absorbed in nature, thought, or art; to identify with others, and to be fascinated with the inexplicable. **Thalamus:** Regulates incoming sensory information and communicates a lucid sense of reality to the cortex during focused, calm states. *(Newberg, 2006)*

Development of Higher Faculties

Chapter 1 focused on the involution, or peeling away of layers, of Self to reveal it in its most transcendent form. However, the evolution of our ability to reason may be both a prerequisite and a partner to the transition from a personal Self to a Higher Self (Wilber, 2000). Likewise, spirituality advances through stages of development that are dependent on the Self's expanding ability to incorporate viewpoints of others, scientific rules, opposing hypotheses, and transcendent unity.[1]

---

[1] Stages of the elevation of spirit are a combination of ideas from Wilber (2000) pp. 47–53, Rowan's thoughts on intuition and meditation, and the author's background in the development of monotheism.

EVOLUTION OF REASON

Jean Piaget's (1896–1980) four cognitive structures are presented in the chart on pages B.3 and B.4. These are ways of experiencing and operating on the environment. In the **sensory-motor** stage, objects only exist that can be seen or touched. After making the **preoperational** shift, a child will have a concept of water even when it is not present; but a pint of water in a tall glass will seem greater than a pint in a flat bowl. In the **concrete operational** stage, a concept remains the same even if it is shown differently—two square feet can take different shapes. Mental operations can be performed and reversed (2 + 4 = 4 + 2). Although in the **formal operational** stage, the ability to form hypotheses and tackle ideological problems becomes interesting, many high school graduates and adults do not think formally (Atherton, 2005).

As valuable as Piaget's four developmental stages are, researchers and philosophers now identify postformal stages of thinking. Formal operations are used to relate one concept to another, while **vision-logic** establishes networks of those relationships. When using **transrational thought**, people can tap into the hard drive of a universal intelligence to gain any understanding they need. This is because knowledge is an intrinsic part of the mind and not something to be acquired (Arnold, 2003).

ELEVATION OF THE SPIRIT

As the Self unfolds and becomes more independent, intuitive, flexible, and free; spirituality elevates. The *belief systems* of religion should not be confused with the *spiritual process* of connecting to a source that validates, defines, and directs life. The beginning of spiritual life is controversial. Are young people too egocentric to relate to something beyond themselves? Or, does the same inability to repress impulses allow access to **innate spiritual instincts**? A young couple was asked by their 4-year-old if she could talk to their newborn baby alone. The couple was amazed to hear her say over the nursery intercom, "Please baby, tell me about God because I'm beginning to forget" (story from Ekankar spiritual movement).

The same stages of spirituality seen in the history of mankind are found in the development of individuals. **Animism** held the belief that everything was spirit filled—rocks, ancestors, and the elements. The superstitious and fear-filled lives of these cultures are similar to the world of preschoolers who ritualize a bedtime and watch for monsters. Adults can fall under the spell of this magical thinking when they say a good word three times to ensure their salvation or feel called to do vengeance.

The spirits in animism might have human qualities but no material form. Agricultural societies (8000 BCE) made objects to represent divine power and engaged in **idol worship**. These new gods had special abilities to control fertility and protect cities. This is the spirituality of school-age children trying to master new technologies. Hero worship is their way of finding safety and power through others. Adults, ready to bargain with the Almighty for divine favor or gain cult followings with spellbinding speeches, pop music, and ads, all make use of idolatry.

Development of Higher Faculties

Evolution of Reason	Involution of the Self	Elevation of Spirit
1. **Sensory-motor stage (infancy):** Learn through senses and motor movements.	1. **Symbiotic, survival Self:** Self-object fusion. Survival, instinctual, viewpoint. *Trust bond* with nurturer. No Ego	1. **Innate spirituality:** Pure being. Access to innate spiritual instincts.
2. **Preoperational stage (early childhood):** Formulation of symbols to represent objects.	2. **Counterdependent Parts:** Egocentric, first-person magical view. **Emotional parts** learn *autonomous* control of body functions and take *initiative* to exercise the Will. Id (versus ego) impulsively *acts out* desires and demands.	2. **Animism:** All is animated with spirit. Use Voodoo curses, good luck charms, rituals, and superstitions. Intuition: natural, perceptive knowingness.
3. **Concrete operational stage (elementary school→ preteen child):** Formation of concepts, generalizations, ability to sequence size, weight, etc.	3. **Other-powered Parts:** Other-centric, second-person viewpoint. **Distracting parts** *avoid* emotions. Primitive ego accommodates to others' beliefs for validation. Uses *industry* to acquire skills largely through imitation.	3. **Idol worship:** Sacrifice to appease and placate the gods. Bargaining for safety and power. Intuition used to tune into (fit in with) the group—pop music, ads, rabble rousing.

(Continued)

(Continued)

Evolution of Reason	Involution of the Self	Elevation of Spirit
4. **Formal operational stage (adolescence through adulthood):** Logical abstract thinking. Analysis is used to separate, classify and relate one concept to another.	4. **Role-dependent Parts:** Sociocentric, third-person viewpoint. **Director parts** or superegos internalize rules and *act in* unwanted emotions and impulses causing anxiety and depression. Mythic membership seeks *identity* and roles.	4. **Traditional religions:** Codes of laws, right beliefs, good versus evil, right versus wrong. Reward the faithful; punish the dammed. Intuition used for social reward.
$\Downarrow$ **CONTINUED DEVELOPMENT**	5. **Independent Self:** Worldcentric, scientific viewpoint. Individual, **rational Self** solidifies *identity.* Can be judgmental. Adult ego balances values and needs with introspection and expression.	5. **Skepticism and deism:** Doubting of traditional beliefs. Rule of natural and moral law. Intuition used for scientific discovery and righting social wrongs.
	6. **Interdependent Self:** Pluralistic world viewpoint. **Intuitive Self** is less judgmental. Seeks *intimacy.* Mature ego finds consensus between values and desires.	6. **Ecumenical liberation:** Heal divisions, seek justice, and take social action. Intuition used for social healing and brotherhood.
Post Formal Thinking	**Post Conventional Second Tier Viewpoints**	**Postdenominational Mysticism**
1. **Vision logic:** Taking multiperspectives and reconciling opposites. Relating networks of concepts to each other.	1. **Integrated Self:** Holistic, process viewpoint. *Centaur (centered) Self*— Counterforces (reason/emotions, activity/passivity) become balanced—aiding flexibility, spontaneity, increased awareness, and actualized potentials.	1. **Pantheistic, theist:** Nature mysticism—God is in all; all is in God. New-age thought—God-mind expressed through all people. Intuition becomes regular. Wake up to the mindful witness.
2. **Transrational thought:** Pure thinking in pursuit of knowing *(gnosis).* Underlying truths are grasped through synthesizing data.	2. **Transcendent Self:** Cosmic viewpoint. Self is transcended by relating to what is similar and different in others and finding unity with all. *Generative* Self shows the Way to the next generation.	2. **Formless, nondual:** Union with underlying Oneness. Witness becomes one with the witnessed—"I am the sunset." Intuition approaches a problem as though it is not a problem.

After years of struggle with polytheistic gods that ruled all human actions and abodes, the great leaders of the Axial Age (800–600 BCE), in a worldwide religious awakening, planted the seeds of modern day **traditional religions**. In the West, monotheism took root with codes of laws, right beliefs, and otherworldly consequences. This is the spiritual comfort zone of rule/role directors where the ego bows to the internalized good and right. Wrongdoing is suppressed without need of sacrificial offerings. Religions with fundamental doctrines might be appealing to modern-day traditionalists.

In the age of reason and rule of science (1600–1700), traditional values came under fire. The death of God was rumored. The American deists (Thomas Jefferson and Benjamin Franklin) saw reason as the guide to truth and God as the first cause of physical and moral laws. Earlier, John Locke and Jean-Jacques Rousseau formulated ideas on which modern-day democracy is based— breaking the stranglehold of traditional monarchies. The independent Self, capable of balancing carnal impulses with higher values, has less need for eternal condemnation. **Skeptics and modern deists** might find themselves in Unitarian Fellowships comprised of agnostics, humanists, liberal Christians, Jews, and even neo-pagans where ethics and social action take priority over belief.

The skepticism of traditional religions served as a spiritual house cleaning that made way for a new religious flowering and a wonderful habitat for the sensitive, interdependent Self that celebrates diversity and working in harmony. The beliefs of liberal Quakers express an **ecumenical liberation** with their idea that all people are sons and daughters of God, their focus on finding the Light of God within, and their desire to take social action. Most traditional religions have evolved branches that welcome diversity and activism. Motivation is strong to heal society's wounds and create a brotherhood of faiths.

POSTDENOMINATION ELEVATIONS OF SPIRIT

At some point, the awakening of spirit moves beyond the confines of a particular denomination. Nametags and dogmas attached to major religions are dissolved by the similar methods that the Muslim, Jewish, Christian, and Hindu mystics practice. The very word *mysticism* suggests mystery and the unknown. Rather than attempting to believe *in* God, mystics adopt spiritual practices to help manifest or connect *with* the Divine. This takes precedence over the particular rituals or jargon each tradition uses.

Nature mystics, like some Native Americans and Wiccans, are **pantheists** who experience God in everything. New-age **theists** identify an impersonal force or cosmic order that manifests itself personally, perfectly, and equally in all people. The integrated Self, ready to notice the unity that underlies diversity, finds such ideas in concert with its holistic worldview. Meditation may focus on what would normally distract (in a sweat lodge), a thought (mantra), symbolic design (mandala), or the flow of breath and thoughts (mindfulness). During such practices, people detach from mental processes by witnessing them.

By uniting with the absolute oneness of the cosmos or the Way (*Tao*) a **formless, "nondual" mysticism** is achieved. Symbols of nature and the divine—the earth goddess, the Great Spirit, Buddha, and Christ are abandoned to experience Oneness. Supreme Reality is timeless, formless, beyond opposites, and, therefore, *nondual*. Seasoned mediators who have been able to witness the ebb and flow of thoughts now detach from their observant Self into the empty mind of "not this, not that." It is a matter of perceiving without a perceiver (Wilber, 2004). Instead of looking at the sunset, you become the sunset. Only the transcendent Self whose separation from others is becoming illusionary is capable of this in fleeting moments or for brief periods of time.

Appendix C

Psychotherapy Approaches Referenced in the Text

Analysis, Freudian: Disorders of the mind are considered the result of the rejection by the conscious mind of factors, which then persist in the subconscious as repressed instinctual forces, causing conflicts that may be resolved or diminished by discovering and analyzing repressions and bringing them into consciousness through the use of such techniques as free association, dream analysis, and so on. *Sigmund Freud began developing his ideas in the early 1900s.*

Analysis, Jungian: Explores a client's psychic reality through symbols in dreams, sand play, painting, fairy tales, myth, and so on. Deeply ingrained and destructive life patterns are made conscious. This exploration is more concerned with maturation and individuation of the personality, finding underlying meaning in suffering, and discovering life's purpose, than with diagnosing psychopathology. *Carl Jung broke from Freud in 1912.*

Cognitive Therapy: Maladaptive behaviors and disturbed moods are the result of inappropriate or irrational thinking patterns called *automatic thoughts*. Instead of reacting to the reality of a situation, an individual reacts to his or her own distorted viewpoint, which can be restructured through therapy. *Albert Ellis and Aaron Beck, 1950s and 1960s.*

Dialogue Therapy: Different facets of the personalities are identified by narrating and questioning their agendas. The core Self is coached to "go inside" and dialogue with demanding parts in a nondefensive, nonattacking (I-thou) manner to validate them without yielding. This empowers the Self and "hypnotizes" dominating parts to relinquish control. The use of images, symbols, objects, and literary characters that add dimension to dialogues and clarify the dynamics of the internal landscape is encouraged. *Cohen-Posey, 2008.*

Ego-State Therapy: Ego states are hypnotically activated and made accessible for contact and communication with the therapist who can then use a variety of behavioral, cognitive, analytic, family therapy, or humanistic techniques to resolve conflicts between them. *Jack and Helen Watkins developed this treatment approach in the early 1970s.*

Eye Movement Desensitization and Reprocessing Therapy (EMDR): A person's distress is heightened by targeting negative beliefs, images, and body sensations. Eye movements or other forms of "duel attention (brain) stimuli" are applied to reprocess trauma until a positive belief related to that trauma can be endorsed. *Shapiro, 1980s.*

Family Systems Therapy: The family is viewed as an emotional unit with opposing forces driving individuals to act as one and pushing them to express their different thoughts and feelings (**differentiation**). When tension occurs between two people in the family, especially the parents, they may project (**triangulate**) it on to a third member. Individuals may attempt to reduce anxiety with parents and other family members by *emotionally cutting themselves off* (moving far away, rarely visiting, avoiding sensitive issues, and so on). During treatment, the therapist talks to all family members in turn, asking many questions to elaborate the thinking of each person in the presence of others. Everyone is included, balance maintained, and differentiation encouraged through the therapist's leadership. *Bowen, 1960s.*

Gestalt Therapy: *Gestalt* is a German word that suggests that structures or patterns make up the whole of an experience. In therapy, a person is helped to "complete gestalts" by resolving conflicts between competing parts of the self that interfere with having needs met. The therapy involves increasing awareness of one's dominant need in the (gestalt) field through exercises that heighten awareness of *what* people are doing and *how* they are doing it. *Perls, 1950.*

Hypnotherapy: A hypnotic state is induced through suggestion, confirmation, and prediction in which clients may experience some of the following: (a) increasingly narrowed focus of attention, (b) calmness and stillness, (c) age regression, (d) heightened recall, (e) receptivity to acceptable ideas, (f) visualization, (g) identification of conflicting ego states, (h) pain suppression, and so on. *In the 1970s, John and Helen Watkins discovered ego states while using hypnotherapy.*

Interactive Guided Imagery: Employs simple visualization of a safe place, metaphorical solutions, inner advisor, and so on. Images are developed and embellished through dialogues between client and counselor. Techniques are used for relaxation, relief of physical symptoms, and to kindle inner resources for supposedly "insolvable" problems. *Rossman, and Bresler, 1980s.*

Internal Family Systems (IFS) Therapy: The relationship between internal parts is clarified and restructured in order to restore leadership, balance, and harmony to the system within. Personality parts are asked questions through *direct access* by the counselor or through insight (imagination) by the client's "true Self." Under the true Self's supervision, various parts may talk to each other and work out conflicts. *Schwartz, 1980s.*

Object Relations Therapy: Works with "disorders of the self" or personality disorders in which people focus on objects (people) in their environment rather on internal processes. The defenses people use to avoid painful emotions (instead of struggling to control or express them) are illuminated. Such defenses include blaming, splitting conflicting feelings about others into all good or all bad, wholeheartedly endorsing or rejecting others' standards, and acting out feelings instead of experiencing them (bragging, clinging). These are brought to light by gentle mirroring—"For a moment you touched on fears of failure which seemed to bring up bad feelings about yourself, so you quickly shifted to remembering an achievement." *Klein, Fairbairn, and Guntrip, 1950s–1970s.*

Psychology of Selves or Voice Dialogue Process: Various selves, subpersonalities, or energy patterns are activated by having a person physically move to different locations in the room and assume postures that seem appropriate for each subpersonality. A facilitator talks with *energy patterns* to discover their agendas, how they came into being, if their strategies are effective, and so on. Inner parts never talk to each other, only to the facilitator. Finally, the person returns to their original location in a "position of awareness" where the facilitator and the person's *aware ego* collaborate on what has occurred during the session. *Developed in the 1970s by Hal and Sidra Stone.*

Psychosynthesis: Investigates and treats disorders of the mind and spirit, and assists the natural inner drive to evolve and become the fullest realization of the Self. The underlying assumption is that self-actualization can be blocked both by a lack of access to the subconscious and to the superconscious with its "spiritual instincts." It leads to the door of theology, but stops there. Treatment includes (a) recognition and emergence of subpersonalities through conflict, dreams, and fantasy; (b) coordination and working through relationships between parts; (c) reconstruct of subpersonalities around a higher inner center; (d) recognizing and assimilating energies inflowing (synthesized) from the Self and *superconscious*; and (e) using those energies in altruistic services. *Assagioli, 1920s.*

Transactional Analysis (TA): Helps people recognize what *ego state* they are operating from to follow the transactional sequences they engaged in as they interact to regain their inner childs' innate sense of "okay-ness" so that it will be able to obtain the recognition or "strokes" it needs to function in a positive manner and as a whole person. *Berne, 1960s.*

Transpersonal Psychology: Extends self-actualization to self-transcendence, employs standard psychotherapy techniques or meditative practices appropriate to a person's level of psychospiritual development, and assumes that all people have an impulse toward spiritual growth. *Walsch, Vaughan, Grof, Deikman, Wilber, and Tart, 1970s.*

GLOSSARY

Note: Terms preceded with an asterisk (∗) are unique to this text.

Abreaction: Recalling an event and releasing or discharging related emotions, which immediately and permanently resolve symptoms related to the event (Freud & Breuer).

Archetype: Psychic imprints, inborn patterns of experience. First used by Plato to refer to ideal forms. Symbols, expressing common human needs and potentials, act as an organizing principle. Archetypes include the maternal instinct, spiritual force, the shadow, persona (public self), **anima/ animus** (image of our opposite gender), father, child, hero, maiden, wise old man, trickster, God (need for meaning), and self (need for unity) (Jung).

Bodhisattva: A human who has been liberated from the world of illusion that voluntary accepts rebirth to help others achieve the same state.

Chakras: Sanskrit word for disk. Signifies one of seven basic energy centers in the body that correlate to major nerve ganglia branching from the spine and to levels of consciousness (1) Base level—security, survival instincts; (2) Abdomen center—taste/sexual appetites, wants, needs, pleasure; (3) Solar plexus—personal power, control, freedom; (4) Heart—integration, love; (5) Throat—expression, communication; (6) Third eye—vision, intuition, images; (7) Crown—empathy, unity, connection to transcendental spirit.

Collective unconscious: The reservoir of our experiences as a species including myths, religious images, and archetypes that influences all our experiences and can be accessed through dreams and symbols (Jung).

Consciousness: Direct awareness of all thinking, sensing, perceiving, desiring, willing, and acting, which we can observe, analyze, and judge. Varies by state—waking, dreaming, deep sleep, or altered (Wilber/Assagioli).

∗**Controller**: A director subpersonality concerned with following rules/roles of society that can become consumed with controlling emotions, following conventions, and appearing "normal."

Cosmic worldview: Recognizes the relatedness of all things and their union with world process.

∗**Counterdependent parts**: Formed when toddlers separate from their source of nurture. Personalities fragment into impulses, wishes, and demands that are acted out with a first-person, egocentric viewpoint. Corresponds with Erikson's psychosocial crises of *autonomy versus shame and doubt* and *initiative versus guilt* when toddlers and preschoolers are learning to control body functions and exert their wills. See **Emotional entities**.

∗**Critic**: A director subpersonality concerned with feedback and self-correction that can become consumed with constant comparing and monitoring to preempt negative comments from others.

Desensitize: To make emotionally insensitive by long exposure or repeated shocks.

Dialogue: Open, direct communication (spoken or silent) between (or within) persons who converse spontaneously without withholding or promoting an agenda (Buber). Communication that involves asking questions and showing understanding (Cohen-Posey).

∗**Directors**: Hidden personality parts that record verbal messages and impressions of valued persons and cultural dictates organized around developmental tasks (see **Controller, Protector,**

Pusher, Pleaser) and preempting oppression (see **Critic**). Commonly known as *superegos, parent ego states, major subpersonalities,* or *managers.* See **Role-dependent parts.**

*Dis-identify: Identifying subpersonalities with names, images, character types, or dramatic exaggerations to make them more recognizable. This reinstates them as inner objects (resulting from introjection) that can be faced, questioned, "seen through," and redirected.

Dissociate: Cutting ties with the Self and other inner voices by an ego state that forms *solidified boundaries,* resulting in a sense of *not-me-ness.* Disruptions in consciousness, memory, identity, or perceptions of the environment.

Dissociative Identity Disorder (DID): The existence in a single individual of two or more distinct identities or personalities that alternate in controlling behavior. Believed to be caused by early, extreme trauma. Formerly called Multiple Personality Disorder.

*Distracters: Fixed personality parts that encapsulate traits or biological tendencies, which tend to cause problems in social and work settings and help avoid anxiety. Controlling, clinging, blaming, arrogance, isolation, and addictions are typical distracting tactics. Commonly known as character and temperament. Formed from **Other-powered parts** (see entry).

Dual focus of attention: Maintaining awareness of a disturbing past event while staying in the safety of the present.

Ego: See Appendix A, **Ego, Adult ego, Aware ego, Ego state, Core ego, Superego.**

Empowerment: Actions that strengthen the Self, rather than trying to control others.

*Emotional entities: Instinctual personality parts that encapsulate sensations and energy in motion or emotion. Includes fight/flight, attraction/repulsion, and sexual instincts. Commonly known as the id, child ego state, vulnerable selves, or exiles. See **Counterdependent parts.**

Evolution: Process of development from simple to complex forms, or a gradual process of change resulting from the need to *adapt* to environmental changes versus *a desire* to improve.

Holistic worldview: Identifies the underlying process that connects interdependent models.

I-I: Expansive Self that is the Witness of the ordinary "I" (Wilber).

I-It Stand: A one-sided, self-conscious way of facing nature, persons, art forms, or God with preconceived notions for the purpose of imposing one's will (Buber).

*Independent Self: Rational Self that solidifies the myriad roles that have been internalized. Late adolescents or young adults can take a scientific, rational, worldcentric viewpoint. Erikson's psychosocial crisis of *identity versus role confusion.*

*Integrated Self: Joins polarities (body/mind, activity/passivity) without diminishing opposition. Connection replaces deciding ego. Process-oriented viewpoint values all parts. Corresponds with Erikson's psychosocial crisis of *integrity versus despair.*

Integration: The process of the Self making contact with various personality parts, especially ones that have been feared, hated, or denied to increase awareness, versatility, and self-trust *rather than* to make compromises (Rowan, 1993, p. 188). Harmonious working together of subpersonalities (Assagioli), which results from parts having a one-on-one relationship with the central Self (Cohen-Posey).

*Interdependent Self: Intuitive Self becomes less judgmental than the independent Self. It is softer, sensitive, and open to diversity in this adult stage of development that can take a pluralistic viewpoint. Corresponds with Erikson's psychosocial crisis of *intimacy versus isolation.*

Introjection: Internalization of parental and cultural messages with related feelings that keep young ones connected to significant others when separated from them. From the Latin, *iectio,* which means *to throw in.* First used in 1912 by a colleague of Freud's as a synonym for "incorporation."

Involute: Process of rolling away outer edges to reveal an inner core Self. Opposite of evolve.

I-Thou stand: A two-sided, multiconscious stance toward nature, persons, art forms, or God with complete openness, spontaneity, and acceptance without an agenda, purpose, or need to agree for the purpose of dialogue (Buber).

Lower unconscious: Container of fundamental drives, urges, intense emotions, sources of phobias, obsessions, and delusions (Assagioli).

Mammalian brain: The reptilian brain plus the **limbic system**, which contains the hippocampus, thalamus, and amygdala. Considered responsible for emotions related to survival—appetite, sex, competition, and avoiding pain and repeating pleasure. Capable of learning.

Mandala: Sanskrit word meaning container of essence or magic circle (*manda* means essence; *la* means container). Circular designs that organize perception, thought, and physical responses in beneficial ways.

Magical worldview: First-person viewpoint in which the ego is all-powerful.

Middle unconscious: Inner region of experience, imaginative activities, and mental processes that can easily be brought into awareness or consciousness (Assagioli).

Mindfulness: Developing awareness by "paying attention in a particular way, on purpose, in the present moment, nonjudgmentally" (Kabat-Zinn).

Modernity: Historic epoch between the 1600s and the 1950s to the 1970s in which art, social values, and science became differentiated and evolved in their own right. Ultimately science became dominant (Wilber). See **Premodernity** and **Postmodernity**.

Mysticism: The art and science of establishing a conscious relationship with the mystery of life: (a) **Eastern, metaphysical**—the I-I (expansive Self that witnesses the ordinary I) moves from realms of *physical* perceptions and sensations, to *emotional* tensions, to fleeting *thoughts*, and falls into an opening where it becomes what it observes—all are in it and it is in all (Wilber); (b) **Earthy, social**—melting boundaries between the (I-Thou) Self and others by cherishing differences and embracing more of the world (persons, nature, art, and all that is eternal) and creating a cosmos of pure spirit in the midst (Buber).

Mythic worldview: Second-person viewpoint. Omnipotence of the ego is transferred to the gods.

Neocortex: The main brain of the primates who are the latest mammals to appear in the last two million years. It sits on top and to the front of the brain. All animals have a neocortex, but only in primates is it highly developed. It is responsible for higher cognitive functions such as language, reasoning, planning, and solving complex problems.

*Other-powered parts**: Tendencies to be dependent, demanding, oppositional, and withdrawn. Formed by copying and coping with valued persons and culture. Seeing through the eyes of others gives a second-person, mythic viewpoint. Corresponds to Erikson's psychosocial crisis of *industry versus inferiority*. See **Distracters**.

Persona: The masks or personalities that help people adapt to various social settings. How others see and know us.

Personal unconscious: Area of the mind that includes anything that is not presently conscious but can be (Jung).

Personality: Enduring patterns of perception, behavior, and thought (Standard). Fixed traits, inner voices, and emotional tensions that respond to and cope with everyday details (Cohen-Posey).

Personality Parts: See Appendix A—**Subpersonality** . . . inner voices.

*Pleaser**: A director subpersonality concerned with affiliating and belonging that can become consumed with putting others' needs first and winning approval.

Pluralistic worldview: Interdependent parts working in harmony; acknowledgement and appreciation of diversity.

Postmodernity: Current epoch (beginning in the 1950s or 1970s) that integrates art, science, and social values. Subjective experience and pluralistic views may be valued over objective science and worldcentric views. See **Modernity** and **Premodernity**.

Preconscious: Thoughts that are not in immediate awareness but that can be recalled with effort.

Premodernity: Historic epoch prior to 1600 that was dominated by religion, which oppressed the individual and science but valued body, mind, and spirit. See **Modernity** and **Postmodernity**.

***Protector**: A director subpersonality concerned with preventing unnecessary risks that can become consumed with avoiding mistakes, flaws, or catastrophes of any kind.

Psychology: The study and science of mental (but not spiritual) processes and behavior.

Psychotherapy: Treatment of mental disorders by various means involving communication between a trained person and the patient.

***Pusher**: A director subpersonality concerned with task completion to succeed in life that can become consumed with compulsive achievement and advancement.

***Role-dependent parts**: Internalized rules and roles from valued persons and culture. *Acts in* acquired traits and innate impulses. Internal roles gives a third-person, sociocentric viewpoint. Corresponds with Erikson's psychosocial crisis of *identity versus role confusion*. Become **Directors**.

Schema and Self-schemata: See Appendix A.

Self: See Appendix A—Self, **Higher Self, Real Self, Aware ego, Core/true Self**.

Sensory Integration Disorder (SID): A neurological disorder that results from the brain's inability to integrate certain information received from the body's five basic sensory systems resulting in over- or undersensitivity, unusually high or low activity levels, clumsiness and carelessness, difficulty making transitions, and difficulty with self-soothing.

Shadow: Aspects of the personality (positive and negative) that have been relegated to the unconscious because conscious life will not permit their expression. They appear in dreams as a person of the same sex (Jung).

Sociocentric worldview: Third-person view places power in social units versus deified others (Wilber).

Spirit: A source that validates, defines, and directs one's life.

Subconscious: A term, obsolete in psychiatry, that now includes the **unconscious** and **preconscious**.

Superconscious: Region from which we receive higher intuitions and inspirations—the source of states of contemplation, illumination, and ecstasy (Assagioli).

***Symbiotic Self**: Stage of self-development that enjoys a symbiotic (mutually interdependent) bond with caretakers in which boundaries between the wishes and needs of each party are unclear. Correlates with Erikson's psychosocial crisis of *trust versus mistrust*.

Symbol: The best possible expression for something that is unknown. Symbols are the language of the unconscious (Jung).

***Transcendent Self**: Universal Self moves from realms of *physical* perceptions and sensations, to *emotional* tensions, to fleeting *thoughts* into an opening where it becomes what it observes—all are in it and it is in all (Wilber). Boundaries between Self and others (I-Thou) are melted by cherishing differences—creating a cosmos of pure spirit in the midst. Has a cosmic viewpoint that realizes the interrelatedness of all things. Corresponds to Erikson's psychosocial crisis of *generativity versus stagnation*.

Transpersonal: Experiences involving an expansion or extension of consciousness beyond the usual boundaries and limitations of time or space.

Unconscious: The place where unknown wishes and needs are kept and play a significant role in conscious behavior.

Will: Dynamic inner power capable of directing, focusing, challenging, concentrating, involving, and controlling the mind and body.

Worldcentric view: Transfers power from the group to the rule of scientific, universal beliefs (Wilber).

Yoga: Yoking the powers of the mind by special disciplines of concentration developed in India thousands of years ago. Traditional yoga is a method of joining the individual self with the Divine, Universal Spirit or Cosmos. Yogin practice yoga.

REFERENCES

Allison, R., & Schwarz, T. (1999). *Minds in Many Pieces: Revealing the Spiritual Side of Multiple Personality Disorder*. Portland, OR: New Books.

Arnold, T. (2003). *Nature and Development of Paranoesis (Transrational Thinking)*. Available from www.hyponoesis.org.

Assagioli, R. (2000). *Psychosynthesis: A Collection of Basic Writings*. Amherst, MA: Synthesis Center. (Original work published 1965)

Atherton, J. S. (2005). *Learning and Teaching: Piaget's Developmental Theory*. Retrieved January 2008, from http://209.85.165.104/search?q=cache:2sR-/.

Berg, Y. (2003). *The 72 Names of God: Technology for the Soul*. New York: Kabbalah Center International.

Berne, E. (1964). *Games People Play: The Basic Handbook of Transactional Analysis*. New York: Ballantine Books.

Bowen, M. (1978). *Family Therapy in Clinical Practice*. Northvale, NJ: Jason Aronson.

Bradshaw, J. (1990). *Homecoming: Reclaiming and Championing Your Inner Child*. New York: Bantam Books.

Buber, M. (1970). *I and Thou*. New York: Touchtone. (Original work published 1923)

Campbell, R. S., & Pennebaker, J. W. (2003). The Secret Life of Pronouns: Flexibility in Writing Style and Physical Health. *American Psychological Society, 14*(1), 60–65.

Chaitin, G. (1987). *Information, Randomness, and Incompleteness: Papers on Algorithmic Information Theory*. New York: Barnes & Noble.

Cohen-Posey, K. (2000). *Brief Therapy Client Handouts*. Hoboken, NJ: John Wiley & Sons.

Cohen-Posey, K. (2008). *Making Hostile Words Harmless: A Guide to the Power of Positive Speaking for Helping Professionals and Their Clients*. Hoboken, NJ: John Wiley & Sons.

Cunningham, B. (2002). *Mandala: Journey to the Center*. New York: DK Publishing.

Doblin, R. (1991). Pahnke's "Good Friday Experiment:" A Long-Term Follow-Up and Methodological Critique. *Journal of Transpersonal Psychology, 23*(1). Retrieved January 2008, from http://druglibrary.org/schaffer/lsd/doblin.htm.

Eckankar Spiritual Movement. (n.d.). Available from http://www.eckankar.org.

Erikson, E. H. (1964). *Childhood and Society*. New York: W. W. Norton.

Erskine, R. G. (1997). *Theories and Methods of an Integrative Transactional Analysis*. San Francisco: TA Press.

Fincher, S. F. (1991). *Creating Mandalas: For Insight, Healing, and Self-Expression*. Boston: Shambhala.

Fincher, S. F. (2000). *Coloring Mandalas: For Insight, Healing, and Self-Expression* (2nd ed.). Boston: Shambhala.

Freud, S., & Breuer, J. (2004). *Studies in Hysteria*. New York: Penguin Group. (Original work published 1893)

Frankl, V. (1963). *Man's Search for Meaning: An Introduction to Logotherapy*. New York: Washington Square Press.

Gazzaniga, M. (1985). *The Social Brain: Discovering Networks of the Mind*. New York: Basic Books.

Gilbert, E. (2006). *Eat Pray Love: One Woman's Search for Everything across Italy, India, and Indonesia*. New York: Penguin Books.

References

Gottlieb, A., & Pešié, S. (1995). *The Cube*. San Francisco: HarperSanFrancisco.

Gray, J. (1992). *Men are from Mars, Women are from Venus*. New York: HarperCollins.

Hamer, D. (2004). *The God Gene: How Faith Is Hardwired into Our Genes*. New York: Doubleday.

Hesse, H. (1963). *Steppenwolf* (Rev. ed.). New York: Henry Holt. (Original work published 1927)

Hoff, B. (1982). *The Tao of Pooh*. New York: Penguin Books.

James, W. (1890). *The Principles of Psychology*. Mineola, NY: Dover Publications.

Kabat-Zinn, J. (1994). *Wherever You Go, There You Are: Mindfulness Meditation in Everyday Life*. New York: Hyperion.

Kohut, H. (1971). *The Analysis of the Self*. New York: International Universities Press.

Kramer, K. P. (2003). *Martin Buber's I and Thou*. New York: Paulist Press.

Labyrinth. (n.d.). *Wikipedia*. Retrieved September 2007, from http://en.wikipedia.org/wiki/Labyrinth/.

Lennon, J., & McCartney, P. (1967). *I Am the Walrus. Magical Mystery Tour*. Hollywood, CA: Capitol Records.

Leuner, H. (1969). Guided Affective Imagery (GAI): A Method of Intensive Psychotherapy. *American Journal of Psychotherapy*, 23, 4–22.

Manfield, P. (1992). *Split Self/Split Object*. Northvale, NJ: Jason Aronson.

Markus, H., & Nurius, P. (1987). Possible Selves: The Interface between Motivation and the Self-Concept. In K. Yardley & T. Honess (Eds.), *Self and Identity: Psychosocial Perspectives*. Chichester, West Sussex, England: John Wiley & Sons.

Maslow, A. (1970). *Motivation and Personality* (2nd ed). New York: Harper & Row.

May, R (1977). *The Meaning of Anxiety*. New York: W. W. Norton.

McNamara, C. (2003). *Field Guide to Developing and Operating Your Nonprofit Board of Directors*. Minneapolis, MN: Authenticity Consulting, LLC.

Moody, H. R., & Carrol, D. (1997). *The Five Stages of the Soul*. New York: Anchor Books.

New Revised Standard Version of the Bible. (1989). Oxford: Oxford University Press.

Newberg, A., & Waldman, M. (2006). *Why We Believe What We Believe: Uncovering Our Biological Need for Meaning, Spirituality and Truth*. New York: Simon & Schuster.

Nijenhuis, E., Van der Hart, O., & Steele, K. (2004). *Trauma-Related Structural Dissociation of the Personality*. Available from Trauma Information Pages web site: www.trauma-pages.com/nijenhuis-2004.htm.

Noss, J. B. (1967). *Man's Religions*. New York: Macmillan.

Ouroboros. (n.d.). *Wikipedia*. Retrieved September 2007, from http://en.wikipedia.org/wiki/Uroboros/.

Paisley, B. (2003). *Whisky Lullaby. On Mud on the Tires* [CD]. Nashville, TN: Arista Nashville.

Perls, F., Hefferline, R. F., & Goodman, P. (1951). *Gestalt Therapy*. New York: Julian Press.

Potter, A., (1992). *Inside Out: Rebuilding Self and Personality through Inner Child Therapy*. Muncie, IN: Accelerated Development.

Rossman, M., & Bressler, D. (2000). *Guided Imagery for Self Healing*. Novato, CA: New World Library.

Rowan, J. (1990). *Subpersonalities: The People Inside*. New York: Brunner-Routledge.

Rowan, J. (1993). *The Transpersonal: Psychotherapy and Counseling*. New York: Routledge.

Schwartz, R. (1995). *Internal Family Systems Therapy*. New York: Guilford Press.

Shapiro, F. (2001). *Eye Movement Desensitization and Reprocessing: Basic Principles, Protocols, and Procedures*. New York: Guilford Press.

Shulem, B. (n.d.). *Torah Psychology: Solution Oriented Conversations that Help People Change*. Retrieved May 2006, from www.shemayisrael.co.il/orgs/torahpsychology/.

Stone, H., & Stone, S. (1989). *Embracing Our Selves: The Voice Dialogue Manual*. Novato, CA: New World Library.

Truss, L. (2003). *Eats, Shoots, & Leaves: The Zero Tolerance Approach to Punctuation*. New York: Gotham Books.

Tzu, L. (1972). *Tao Te Ching* (Vintage Books ed.). New York: Random House.

References

Watkins, J. G., & Watkins, H. (1997). *Ego States Theory and Therapy*. New York: W. W. Norton.

Wilber, K. (2000). *Integral Psychology*. Boston: Shambhala.

Wilber, K. (2004). *The Simple Feeling of Being*. Boston: Shambhala.

Winnicott, D. W. (1965). *The Maturational Process and the Facilitating Environment*. New York: International Universities Press.

Yalom, I. (1980). *Existential Psychotherapy*. New York: Basic Books.

ABOUT THE AUTHOR

 Kate Cohen-Posey has been practicing psychotherapy in Central Florida since 1973. She is currently the director of Psychiatric and Psychological Services in Lakeland, Florida. Her interest in producing informational booklets for her clients led to the publication of *Brief Therapy Client Handouts* (Hoboken, NJ: John Wiley & Sons, 2000). Always seeking more direct, elegant ways of approaching treatment, her current work is an outgrowth of years of training in humanistic, hypnotic, and brief therapies, independent study of Martin Buber's philosophy, and inspiration from within. A dynamic presenter, she has a passion for teaching professionals a method that helps people find their way out of mental anguish by going deeper inside.

AUTHOR INDEX

Abbot, B., 4.1, 4.2
Allison, R., 7.5
Arnold, T., B.2
Assagioli, R., 1.3, 1.4, 1.5,
    1.7, 2.4, 2.11, 2.15, 3.3,
    4.11, 7.2
Atherton, J. S., B.2

Beck, A., 7.6
Berg, Y., 5.2
Berne, E., 3.9, 3.16, 7.3,
    7.4, 7.7, C.2
Bowen, M., 5.3, C.1
Bradshaw, J., 7.4
Bresler, D., 6.9, C.2
Breuer, J., 6.11, 6.13
Buber, M., 1.7, 3.2, 5.3,
    6.18, 7.7, 7.8

Campbell, R. S., 5.27, 6.7
Carrol, D., 1.4, 1.8, 2.13
Chaitin, G., 7.7
Cloninger, R., 7.9
Cohen-Posey, K., 4.19,
    6.16, C.1
Costello, L., 4.1, 4.2
Cunningham, B., 2.8

Doblin, R., 7.10

Ellis, A., 7.6, A.2, C.a
Erikson, E. H., 1.9, 3.4, 3.5,
    6.18
Erskine, R. G., 7.4, A.2

Federn, P., 7.3, 7.4, 7.5
Fincher, S. F., xv, 1.5, 2.8, 2.9

Frankl, V., 1.5, 2.4
Franklin, B., B.5
Freud, S., 6.11, 1.3, 1.5, 2.8,
    3.9, 4.5, 6.11, 7.2, 7.3,
    A.1, C.1

Gandhi, 1.13
Gazzaniga, M., 7.10, 7.11,
    A.3
Gilbert, E., 1.5, 1.6, 5.27
Gödel, K., 7.7
Goodman, P., 3.9, C7.3
Gottlieb, A., 4.5
Gray, J., 3.6

Hamer, D., 5.14, 7.9, 7.10
Hefferline, R. F., 3.9, 7.3
Hesse, H., 3.1, 3.2, 3.3,
    3.18, 6.17
Hoff, B., 2.1, 2.4, 2.18, 4.21

James, W., 1.5, 4.21
Jefferson, T., B.5
Jung, C., 2.8, 3.1, 3.3, 3.5,
    7.2, G.1, G.3, G.4

Kabat-Zinn, J., 2.14, 2.15,
    5.13, G.3
King, M. L., 7.9
Kohut, H., 7.6, A.2
Kramer, K. P., xi, xii

Leaary, T., 7.9
Lennon, J., 2.17
Leuner, H., 2.7, 2.11, 2.18,
    4.4
Locke, J., B.5

Manfield, P., 7.6
Markus, H., 7.6
Maslow, A., 1.5
May, R., 2.4
McCartney, P., 2.17
McNamara, C., 1.6, 3.9
Moody, H. R., 1.4, 1.8, 2.13

Newberg, A., 7.9, 7.10, A.3
Nijenhuis, E., 3.7
Noss, J. B., 2.11
Nurius, P., 7.6

Paisley, B., 3.6
Pennebaker, J. W., 5.27, 6.7
Perls, F., 3.9, 7.2, 7.3, 7.5,
    C.2
Pešié, S., 4.5
Picasso, P., xv
Potter, A., 7.4

Rossman, M., 6.9, C.2
Rousseau, J., B.5
Rowan, J., 1.3, 1.5, 1.6,
    1.13, 2.15, 3.1, 3.3,
    7.6, G.2

Schwartz, R., 3.4, 5.27, 6.5,
    6.15, 6.16, 6.17, 6.18,
    6.19, 6.20, 7.4, 7.5, 7.11,
    A.3, C.2
Schwarz, T., 7.5
Shapiro, F., 3.7, 5.24, 6.12,
    6.13, C.1
Shulem, B., 6.1
Steele, K., 3.7
Steppenwolf, 3.1, 3.2, 6.17,
    7.2

SUBJECT INDEX

A

Abbot, Bud, 4.1–4.2, 4.23
Abreaction, 6.11–6.14, 6.16, G.1
Accommodation, 3.4
Acting, as third phase of willing, 2.4
Activism, B.4, B.5
Adaptable personalities (personae), 3.4, 4.3,
    A.1, G.3
Adaptation, 3.4
Addict voice, 4.9
Adolescent anxiety, 5.22–5.23
Adult ego, 7.3, A.2, B.4
Agitators, inside, 1.6, 3.9, 3.15–3.16.
    See also Fixed personalities; Other-
    powered parts
Agnostics, B.5
Agricultural societies, B.3
Alignment with Self, 2.9, 3.2
Allison, Ralph, 7.5
Alter, 3.8, 4.19, 6.15, 7.5, A.2
Amnesia, 3.7–3.8, 7.5
Analysis:
    Freudian, C.1
    Jungian, C.1
Anger/anger management, 4.10, 5.20–5.21
Anima/animus, 1.13, 3.2, 3.3, G.1
Animism, B.3
Anxiety, adolescent, 5.22–5.23
Apparently normal personality (ANP),
    3.7–3.8, A.2
Archetypes, 1.3, 1.7, 2.8, G.1
Artigas, Lucina, 6.12
Assagioli, Roberto, 1.3, 1.4, 1.5, 1.7, 2.8,
    3.3, 4.11, 7.2
Automatic thoughts, 7.6
Autonomy versus shame and doubt, 1.6, 3.5,
    6.18
Aware breathing, 2.13–2.14, 6.9

Aware ego, 6.17, A.3
Awareness, 7.2, 7.3, 7.9
Axial Age, B.5

B

Beck, Aaron, 7.6
Belief systems, B.3
Berne, Eric, 3.9, 7.3–7.4
Bodhisattva, 1.7, 1.13
Body sensations, 2.17, 4.10
Border crossing, 2.13–2.14
Bowen, Murray, 5.3, 6.16
Bradshaw, John (*Homecoming: Reclaiming
    and Championing Your Inner Child*),
    7.4
Brain:
    brainmapping, 5.14, 6.4
    chemicals, genetic deficiency of, 3.16
    evolution outward, 1.9
    hemispheres, left/right, 1.8, 7.10, A.3
    mammalian, 1.9, G.3
    modules/processing centers, 7.11, A.3
    neocortex, 1.9, G.3
    psychoneurological evidence, 7.9–7.12
    stimulation, processing emotions with,
        6.12–6.13
    verbal Self, A.3
Breath, witnessing, 2.13–2.14, 6.9
Bresler, David, 6.9
Breuer, Josef, 6.11, 6.13
Brief Therapy Handouts, 5.20
Brother (inner guide), 1.7
Buber, Martin, xi, xii, 1.7, 3.2, 5.3, 6.18,
    7.7–7.8
Buddha/Buddhism, 5.10, 7.10, B.5
Butterfly hug, 5.16, 5.29, 6.12, 6.13
Butterfly metamorphosis, 1.9

Introducing a creative and positive approach for dealing with difficult people...

Making Hostile Words Harmless creatively offers a unique collection of effective exercises and bully-busting responses guaranteed to defuse difficult exchanges.

Based on the martial art of Aikido—the "way of harmony" —as a model to teach the verbal arts of confirming, inquiring, understanding, and evoking, this unique book:

- Helps you and your clients learn empowering skills that will enable you to deal with negative verbiage and hurtful words

- Presents an easy-to-remember acronym, 'AAAH,' for neutralizing negativity: Acting-as-if, Asking questions, Active listening, and Hypnotic and humorous responses

- Offers sample dialogues, case vignettes, and other tools for using this approach

Infused with wisdom and a strong dose of humor, *Making Hostile Words Harmless* presents a unique combination of ancient philosophy and current psychology that offers antidotes to venomous communication with goal of ending word warfare.

ISBN 978-0-470-28194-9 • Paperback
$24.95 • 128 pp. • April 2008

WILEY
Now you know.

To order, call 1-877-762-2974 or visit us online at www.wiley.com/psychology.

Also available from amazon.com, bn.com, and other fine booksellers.